More Praise for *Trust Matters*

"It has been awhile since I read the first edition of *Trust Matters*, but I remember the influence that Megan Tschannen-Moran's skillful blend of story and analysis had upon my thinking and its subsequent contribution to my own work. This second edition is even better! Like the first, it is insightful, peppered with wisdom, born of experience, and shaped by intellectual endeavor. Much of this book focuses on the key roles of school leaders in responding to issues of betrayal, repair of broken trust, and the need to build bridges with parents and community in contexts of unprecedented levels of governmental and public scrutiny; and underpinning the messages, prompts for reflection at the end of each chapter give the same powerful message that trust and trustworthiness are key components in teachers' and schools' capacities to enhance student learning and achievement. For its humanity, closeness to practice, and evidence-based improvement messages, this book is a must-read for all educators."

—**Christopher Day, professor of education,**
University of Nottingham

For Bob, Bryn, and Evan
from whom I have learned the most important
lessons about Trust
and for Michelle, Andrés, Jennie, Erika, and Theo
who have enriched those lessons with beautiful
demonstrations of the Power of Love

Trust
Matters

Leadership for Successful Schools

SECOND EDITION

MEGAN TSCHANNEN-MORAN

JB JOSSEY-BASS™
A Wiley Brand

Published by Jossey-Bass
A Wiley Brand
One Montgomery Street, Suite 1200, San Francisco, CA 94104–4594—www.josseybass.com

Jossey-Bass books and products are available through most bookstores. To contact Jossey-Bass directly call our Customer Care Department within the U.S. at 800-956-7739, outside the U.S. at 317-572-3986, or fax 317-572-4002.

Wiley publishes in a variety of print and electronic formats and by print-on-demand. Some material included with standard print versions of this book may not be included in e-books or in print-on-demand. If this book refers to media such as a CD or DVD that is not included in the version you purchased, you may download this material at http://booksupport.wiley.com. For more information about Wiley products, visit www.wiley.com.

Library of Congress Cataloging-in-Publication Data

Tschannen-Moran, Megan, date
    Trust matters: leadership for successful schools/Megan Tschannen-Moran.—Second edition.
        pages   cm
    Includes bibliographical references and index.
    ISBN 978-1-118-83437-4 (pbk.); ISBN 978-1-118-83798-6 (pdf); ISBN 978-1-118-83795-5 (epub)
        1. School supervision—United States—Case studies.   2. Teacher-principal relationships—United States—Case studies.   3. Educational leadership—United States—Case studies.   I. Title.
    LB2806.4.T77   2014
    371.203—dc23

                                                                    2013043616

Printed in the United States of America
SECOND EDITION

PB Printing   10 9 8

CONTENTS

Once upon a record-breaking cold Chicago morning, my husband, Bob, then a young inner-city pastor, got a call from a church member with a disability saying that she would like to go to church. Being kind-hearted, with an indomitable spirit, Bob was determined to get her to church despite the obstacles. He had to borrow a car, start it, and warm it up in subzero temperatures. With persistence, he was able to get the car started and running. Presently, however, the engine light came on and the smell of smoke ignited an alarming realization: the oil was frozen in the oil pan. Without lubrication, the engine had overheated and died—resulting in a costly repair to replace the engine.

This incident has much to teach us about trying to run a school without trust. Trust serves as a lubricant of organizational functioning; without it, schools are likely to experience the overheated friction of conflict as well as a lack of progress toward their admirable goals. There is no way to lead schools successfully without building, establishing, and maintaining trust within and across the many and varied constituencies they serve. With trust, schools are much more likely to benefit from the collaborative and productive efforts of their faculty and staff, which in turn help generate the results for students that educators yearn for.

Schools once enjoyed the implicit trust of their community and school leaders felt they could take for granted the trust of both their internal and external constituencies. School leadership was, by and large, a high-status, low-stress job. Now, too often, it is the reverse. We live in an era in which all of our social institutions and their leaders have come under unprecedented scrutiny. As a result, trust has become increasingly difficult for leaders to earn and maintain in our complex and rapidly changing world. This trend away from trust poses a special challenge for school leaders because trust is so vital for schools in fulfilling their fundamental mission of teaching students to be engaged and productive citizens. Understanding the nature and meaning of trust in schools has, therefore, taken on added urgency and importance. School leaders need to appreciate and cultivate the dynamics of trust to reap its benefits for greater student achievement as well as for improved organizational adaptability and productivity.

Without trust, schools are unlikely to be successful in their efforts to improve and to realize their core purpose. I have written this book to offer school leaders practical, hands-on advice on not only how to establish and maintain trust but also how to repair trust if and when it has been damaged. To illustrate how the dynamics of trust play out in schools, I have integrated into this book the case studies of three principals: one who succeeded in cultivating the trust of her faculty, and two who, although well intentioned, were unsuccessful in harnessing the vital resource of trust, and whose schools therefore suffered impaired effectiveness. Through these case studies, I hope to show the role school leaders play in fostering high-trust relationships among teachers, students, and parents. Although the names used in these stories are pseudonyms, the case studies themselves are based on real principals and interviews with teachers who worked in their schools. Each of the three principals led an elementary school with a population of primarily low-income and minority students; the three schools were within a few miles of one another in the same urban school district. But the similarities ended there. The approaches they took to school leadership—and, subsequently, the relationships they built with their faculty and staff members—were very different. These cases provide vivid examples of the ways in which even well-meaning school leaders can end up engendering the distrust of their faculty and the high cost that is inevitably paid when that occurs: morale plummets, productivity declines, and schools lose good people.

Chapter 1 explores why trust matters in schools. This chapter introduces the three principals. Gloria Davies was an overzealous reformer who alienated her faculty and was engaged in an intense power struggle. Fred Martin, the "keep-the-peace principal," lost the faith of his faculty by avoiding conflict. The culture of distrust that resulted had a negative impact on his school's effectiveness. Gloria's and Fred's stories evidence, respectively, the "fight" and "flight" responses to conflict. These two cases are contrasted with the story of Brenda Thompson, a "high-support, high-challenge principal" who, through caring and hard work, earned the trust of her faculty. Whereas Gloria took too much responsibility for the task of school improvement and Fred took too little, Brenda successfully balanced a concern for the task of improving school performance with the concern for cultivating positive relationships within her school. As chapter 1 illustrates, because changes in the social and political environments of schools have transformed the context for building trust in schools, school leaders need to be more attentive and exercise wisdom when it comes to issues of trust.

Although people generally have an intuitive understanding of what is meant by trust and have some basis on which they make trust judgments of others, trying to articulate a precise definition of trust is not easy. Chapter 2, in which I draw on my own experience as a school principal as well as a solid literature review, provides a comprehensive definition of trust: it is the willingness to be vulnerable to another based on the confidence that the other is *benevolent, honest, open, reliable,* and *competent.* Each of these facets is illustrated with stories of Brenda's leadership, which touch on both her leadership style and how that style played out among her faculty. Brenda demonstrated proficiency in all five facets of trust. She extended care to her faculty, was respected as a person of high integrity and commitment, avoided hidden agendas, worked hard, and distinguished herself as an educational leader. These attributes enabled Brenda to evoke an extra measure of effort from her teachers. As a result, in part, of Brenda's trustworthy leadership, the students of Brookside Elementary achieved better-than-expected performance in both tangible and intangible ways. Their achievement scores improved significantly, and the building as a whole enjoyed increased engagement and success.

Trust is a complex and dynamic process. Chapter 3 explores factors that influence the development of trust. The dynamics of initiating trust include such elements as institutional supports for fostering trust and the role that reputation plays. Personal factors such as one's disposition to trust, values and attitudes, as well as moods and emotions are also explored. Authentic trust is the goal of this development process.

Chapter 4 explores the dynamics of betrayal—including what happens to provoke betrayal in a previously trusting relationship. This is illustrated by the story of Fred, a well-meaning and affable principal. Fred's unwillingness to make hard decisions or to hold teachers accountable left his faculty feeling unprotected, vulnerable, and betrayed. This principal's steadfast avoidance of conflict allowed a pervasive climate of distrust to emerge. The costs to the school of a culture of distrust included constricted communication, limited access to faculty insights through shared decision making, and reduced organizational citizenship and commitment.

Chapter 5 examines revenge and the range of victims' responses to betrayal. This chapter tells the story of Gloria, who was determined to make positive change when she took charge of an underperforming school. Her methods, however, were seen as manipulative and unfair; they broke trust with the faculty. These tactics left teachers feeling alienated and distrustful, leading to resentment, power struggles, and sabotage. Gloria's leadership resulted in a school impaired by a culture of control. It is hard to imagine her ultimately being successful in realizing those hopes.

Chapter 6 explores the leader's role in fostering high-quality relationships among teachers in a school. This chapter also examines some of the positive outcomes of trusting school environments, such as greater collaboration and a robust sense of collective efficacy that can fuel stronger motivation and persistence. Chapter 7 examines the dynamics of building trust with students, noting how barriers to trust can be met and overcome even in a challenging and diverse urban environment. Trust hits schools' bottom line: student achievement. This chapter reports research that demonstrates this link. Alternative ways of thinking about student and teacher misbehavior that stem from attachment theory are also explored. Chapter 8 discusses the challenges and rewards in building bridges of trust with families. How the facets of trust play out in these complex and often emotion-laden relationships are investigated, as are the consequences of trust in terms of family engagement.

Chapter 9 focuses on the hard work of trust repair and gives practical advice for repairing trust when it has been damaged in schools. Contemplating the high cost of broken trust and the arduous process of rebuilding trust once it has been damaged may enhance school leaders' commitment to building and maintaining strong bonds of trust in the first place. Trust is rebuilt through the "four A's of absolution": Admit it, Apologize, Ask for forgiveness, and Amend your ways. Trust restoration is also facilitated by constructive attitudes and actions, clear boundaries, communication of promises and credible threats, and strategies for conflict resolution.

The final chapter focuses on the behaviors that make school leaders trustworthy. Trust plays an important role in principals' functions of visioning, modeling, coaching, managing, and mediating. The advice in this chapter aims to help school leaders harness the powerful resource of trust in their day-to-day work so as to make their school more productive.

In addition to the ten chapters, this book contains two useful appendixes. The first appendix presents three trust measures for school leaders and scholars interested in assessing the level of trust in a school: the Student Trust in Faculty Scale, the Parent Trust in School Scale, and the Faculty Trust in Clients Scale. These surveys are accompanied by scoring directions and norms so that practitioners can compare the level of trust in their own school with that in other schools. The first appendix concludes with suggestions for how school leaders might constructively approach the reporting of these survey results. The second appendix provides additional resources for exploring three areas of thought that may be unfamiliar to readers: attachment theory, appreciative inquiry, and nonviolent communication in education.

There is no simple recipe for fostering trust. Building trust is a complex process requiring reflection and attention to context. The section titled "Putting It into Action" at the end of chapters 2 through 10 provide practical advice for putting the chapter's ideas to work in your school. Further, the key points of each chapter are summarized in a bulleted list for easy reference. Finally, each chapter concludes with a section titled "Questions for Reflection and Discussion" that invites you to explore how the chapter's ideas might be applied to trust development in your own setting, and might prove helpful if you are using this book as part of a class, professional development series, or collaborative study group.

The positive response to the first edition of *Trust Matters* has been one of the most gratifying aspects of my professional life. The most rewarding feedback has come when people have told me that reading *Trust Matters* gave them the language and structure to have conversations that they desperately needed to have in their school but hadn't known how to have. It has also been rewarding to have my fellow professors of educational leadership share with me their graduates' feedback that *Trust Matters* was among the most impactful and memorable content in their leadership preparation program. And it has been exciting to see the dramatic growth of new research on trust in schools, by both seasoned and young scholars alike. We are certainly noticing trust in every aspect of our society, and particularly in education. I cannot take credit for this uptick in interest in research on trust, but I am pleased to be part of the conversation.

I have learned so much from the success of the first edition of *Trust Matters*—not least the power of story. I did not set out to find three prototypical school leaders who would fit into a two-dimensional theory of leadership, with leaders falling either high or low on the task and relationship dimensions. It wasn't until I was well into the analysis of the data that I realized I had in my three principal representatives of three quadrants of the model: a high-task, low-relationship principal (Gloria); a low-task, high-relationship principal (Fred); and a high-task, high-relationship principal (Brenda). The stories of these three principals provided a vivid backdrop on which to explore the multifaceted model of trust that is at the heart of this book. As exciting as that was, I still did not realize what classic leadership styles those three leaders represented until I began to travel around the country and around the world giving lectures on the content of this book. Person after person would tell me, "I recognize Fred, I worked for someone just like him!" Or, "I had the good fortune to work for a Brenda." The stories of these three principals began to take on symbolic significance and a life of their own. I remember one afternoon when one of my educational leadership interns sat weeping in my office, exclaiming, "I'm just so afraid I'm going to be a Gloria!" It is my hope that this book has helped her and will help others avoid the pitfalls of trying to reform schools without trust.

This book taps into insights from both theory and research across a variety of fields to argue that school leaders need to attend to establishing and maintaining trusting relationships in their school. It provides practical advice on how to repair damaged trust and helps school leaders learn how to overcome low trust within their school and community so as to establish effective working relationships. My hope is that this work will serve to ignite greater interest in learning more about the dimensions and dynamics of trustworthy leadership, so that school leaders acquire the knowledge and skill to better cultivate trust as a vital resource for school success.

ACKNOWLEDGMENTS

I am blessed to have been surrounded by wonderful and trust-worthy people throughout my life and during the time I have been at work on this book—people who were benevolent, honest, open, reliable, and competent. First among these is my husband, Bob. He is my oldest and dearest friend, and always a wise and helpful coach. He has sustained me with encouraging words, insightful ideas, mugs of tea, technical assistance, and a ready hug when the going got tough. It is exciting to see him using this material in his work with educators through the Center for School Transformation (www.schooltransformation.com).

I owe a special thanks to all of the contributors who shared their stories of life in school with me. I also want to thank my students at the College of William & Mary who have engaged in dialogue with me around the ideas and issues in this book and helped to clarify my thinking with their questions and comments.

In many ways, this book began thirty-five years ago in my journey as the founder and leader of an alternative elementary school in a low-income neighborhood of Chicago. I am indebted to those who joined me on that journey. Taken by the vision of a more wholesome, humane, and effective educational environment for the children of our neighborhood, we created a refreshing oasis in an all-too-tough and dangerous corner of the city. For fourteen years, the culture of trust at the school sustained us, often in the face of great adversity. Trust was crucial to the success we had in accomplishing our mission to "unleash the power of education early in the lives of disadvantaged students in order to break the cycle of poverty." The desire to share the lessons learned in that context was the impetus for writing this book.

I would not have been as fully able to articulate what made our little school so successful had it not been for the guidance of some important teachers along the way, including, Wayne K. Hoy, his wife, Anita Woolfolk Hoy, and Cynthia Uline. My colleagues at the College of William & Mary have also been wonderful examples of trustworthy leaders.

I want to thank Kate Gagnon, Tracy Gallagher, and all of the people at Jossey-Bass who have helped bring this second edition to fruition. I also benefited from a terrific team of reviewers who pushed me to make this a better book with feedback that was constructive, specific, and helpful.

Finally, my acknowledgments would not be complete without special thanks to the people who are most dear to me and who have supported me in my work on this book. In addition to my husband, my children, Bryn and Evan, and now their spouses, Andrés and Michelle, have been faithful cheerleaders and encouragers throughout the years this book has been in progress. I am also grateful for the steadfast caring and ready ear of my sister, Maura and her husband Dave Rawn. Further, I am deeply indebted to my father-in-law, Bob Tschannen, for his love and generosity, and I am sustained by the memory of both my mother, Barbara Longacre Belarde, and my mother-in-law, June Tschannen, each of whom taught me lessons of trust in her own unique way. My wish is that everyone should be as richly blessed by trustworthy companions as I have been on life's journey.

Megan Tschannen-Moran
February 2014

CHAPTER 1

A MATTER OF TRUST

I don't ask for much, I only want trust,
And you know it don't come easy.
—RINGO STARR © STARTLING MUSIC LTD

Sometimes even principals with the best of intentions don't get it right. Sometimes they are unable to lead their school into becoming the kind of productive working community that they imagined and hoped for. When these well-intentioned principals fail to earn the trust of their faculty and their larger school community, their vision is doomed to frustration and failure. Consider the stories of Gloria and Fred, two principals each leading a school in the same urban district.

MEANING WELL

When Gloria Davies learned that she had been assigned to Lincoln School, one of the lowest-performing elementary schools in her district, she was determined to turn that school around. She believed that the primarily low-income students at Lincoln, many of whom lived in a nearby housing project, deserved a better

1

education than they were getting. She wanted to implement a new, more powerful, and rigorous curriculum, especially in reading. She wanted to get teachers fired up to make the changes that were required to turn the school around. And she planned to fire any teachers who failed to get fired up on behalf of their students. This is what she believed she owed to the students. Gloria often asserted, "I don't work for the teachers, I work for the students and their families."

Midway through her third year at Lincoln, however, the school had failed to make the gains she had hoped for. Gloria was mired in an intense power struggle with the faculty at Lincoln. She had been frustrated by union rules and procedures that had limited her authority. Faculty members had filed numerous grievances against her for what they perceived as manipulative and heavy-handed tactics. Building council meetings, a mechanism for shared decision making mandated by the district, had been reduced to a war of the rule books, each side quoting chapter and verse from the district contract or the union guidelines to bolster its position. Although Gloria had been successful in removing one untenured teacher, her attempts to remove veteran teachers had been met with resistance and rebellion that went well beyond the targeted teachers. Morale was perilously low, and student achievement scores had remained stubbornly poor. To protect herself, Gloria often confined herself to her office and was rarely seen around the school, except to make unscheduled observations of teachers she was trying to remove. Sadly, Gloria's dreams of turning around this failing school had not materialized, in large part because her methods had cost her the trust of her faculty and led to resentment, power struggles, and sabotage.

Fred Martin, principal of Fremont Elementary, a few miles from Lincoln, was a friendly man with a warm smile and an easygoing disposition. He was generally well liked by the teachers, students, and parents in his community, and he was sympathetic to the difficult circumstances that many of his low-income students faced.

He was equally sympathetic to the stresses inherent in teaching in an urban context. Fred considered himself a progressive principal, and he delegated many important and controversial decisions to the building council. He viewed his low-key role with the council as one of empowering teachers as decision makers in the school. He saw himself as fair minded and could usually see both sides of a conflict. Consequently, he was reluctant to make a decision that would be perceived as favoring one side or another. He was disappointed that his students had done so poorly on the state assessments but felt that policymakers should be made to understand the challenges that he and his teachers faced.

Fred's discomfort with and avoidance of conflict had not made for an absence of strife at Fremont. On the contrary, without direct efforts to address conflict productively, discord and disagreements had escalated. Teachers felt angry and unsupported by Fred when they sent misbehaving students to him for discipline and perceived him as giving those students little more than a fatherly chat. Teachers in conflict with one another were left to their own devices to resolve their differences. When they went to Fred, he wanted to avoid taking sides and so avoided making any kind of judgment at all. Instead he referred them to the building council or told them simply that they were going to need to work things out. As a result, long-standing grudges between teachers had simmered for years. Bitterness between the teachers and the teacher's aides, many of whom were parents hired from the neighborhood, had become an entrenched part of the school culture. Teachers perceived the aides as being lazy and unwilling to do the job they were hired to do, whereas the aides found the teachers unwelcoming, demanding, and rude. In the meantime, student achievement had failed to significantly improve, despite the increasing pressure of state and district accountability measures.

Though well intentioned, neither Gloria nor Fred had been successful at shaping a constructive school environment. What was missing in both circumstances was trust. Because these

principals were not regarded as trustworthy by their teachers, neither had positive results to show for his or her efforts. On the one
hand, Gloria, the overzealous reformer, had been too impatient
for change to foster the kinds of relationships she would have
needed to enroll her faculty in the effort to make the inspiring
vision she had for the school a reality. Her heavy-handed tactics
were seen as betrayals by her teachers. Fred, on the other hand, in
trying to keep the peace by avoiding conflict, lost the trust of his
faculty through benign neglect. His attempts to keep everybody
happy resulted in general malaise and a perpetual undercurrent
of unresolved tension in the school. Although teachers liked
Fred and felt they could count on his sympathetic concern, they
could not count on him to take action on their behalf because of
his fear of making anyone angry. His teachers were left feeling
vulnerable and unprotected.

The stories of these two principals demonstrate contrasting
approaches in how principals respond to resistance to change
among their faculty—they either overly assert their authority or
they withdraw from the fray. Both responses damage trust, and
both hamper a principal's ability to lead. Gloria focused too
narrowly on the task of school improvement and neglected the
relationships that she needed for cultivating a shared vision and
fostering the collective effort required for improved outcomes.
Although she was correct in thinking that her primary responsibility was to educate her students and not to promote the comfort and ease of her teachers, she failed to grasp that principals
necessarily get their work done through other people. Fred, in
contrast, focused too much on relationships at the expense of
the task. But because the task involved protecting the well-being
of members of the school community, Fred's avoidance of conflict had damaged the very relationships he sought to enhance.
By withdrawing, Fred failed to offer the leadership, structure, and
support needed to provide the students in his care with a quality
education.

Both Fred and Gloria can been seen as having demonstrated problems of responsibility (Martin, 2002). Gloria took too much responsibility for the change initiative in her school and so prevented teachers from getting on board with and taking ownership of the process. In vigorously asserting her authority, Gloria made her point all too well that teachers were not in charge and did not have a say in the decisions that vitally affected their work life. Her actions had violated the sense of care that teachers expected from their principal, causing them to question her integrity. Their trust in her had been damaged. Fred, in contrast, took on too little responsibility, handing decisions over to teachers that they did not have the expertise to make. He did not support them adequately through mentoring and training to acquire the skills to contribute to the decision making necessary to run the school. He did not demonstrate the competence and reliability necessary to build trust. So although he was generally well liked, he was not seen as trustworthy by his faculty and the wider school community.

The problems these two principals evidence are not unusual. New principals, like Gloria, often feel the need to enter a school setting and create change. Inexperienced principals tend to be unsure of their authority; as a result, a common mistake among novice school leaders is to be overly forceful in establishing their authority within the school. Barth (1981) observed, "Most people I know who are beginning principals enter their new roles as advocates, friends, helpers, supporters, often former colleagues of teachers. By December of their first year they have become adversaries, requirers, forcers, judges, and setters of limits" (p. 148). This approach can be counterproductive when trying to develop a high-trust school. Building trust requires patience and planning, but novice principals tend to have an impatient "get it done yesterday" attitude.

Fred, however, apparently lacked important leadership skills, such as the ability to resolve conflict, and had had insufficient professional development and training to hone these skills. Perhaps he also lacked the courage and the stamina to face the sometimes uncomfortable aspects of school leadership and especially school change. In the face of resistance, he withdrew. Although empowering teachers to participate in real decision making within the school can be an effective means of reaching higher-quality decisions, Fred failed to provide the leadership and training to help his teachers be successful at shared leadership. The teachers and students in his school needed more than a sympathetic ear to help resolve their conflicts. They needed someone who could structure a process that would lead to productive solutions.

DOING WELL

Although these two scenarios are not uncommon, principals need not follow either path. Brenda Thompson was principal of Brookside Elementary, a school serving a student body similar to those at Lincoln and Fremont, in the same urban district. Through trustworthy leadership, Brenda earned the confidence of her faculty. By balancing a strong sense of care for her school's students and teachers with high performance expectations, Brenda fostered a school-wide culture of trust. Responsibility for school improvement was shared. By working hard herself, Brenda set an example and was able to command an extra measure of effort from her teachers. These efforts were rewarded with above-average performance from Brookside students on measures of student achievement.

Brenda's care for her faculty and students was evidenced in her accessibility. Brenda was rarely in her office during the school day, preferring to spend her time in the hallways, classrooms, and cafeteria. She spent lunch recess on the playground. She was available to assist teachers and students as they engaged in problem solving around the difficulties they faced. She was a trusted adviser who listened well, offering thoughtful and useful suggestions that demonstrated her expertise as an educator. She didn't blame teachers or make them feel incompetent for having a problem or not knowing what to do. Further, her caring extended beyond the walls of the school; teachers, students, and parents sought her out for help with their lives outside of school as well. Brenda's tone of caring was echoed in faculty members' care for one another and for their students. The impetus for school improvement stemmed from this caring atmosphere: caring fueled the enormous effort needed to sustain a positive school environment in this challenging context.

Brenda understood that the work of schools happens primarily through relationships, so she invested time and resources in nurturing those relationships. There were a number of annual traditions that fostered good rapport, not just among faculty members but among students and their families as well. The academic year would begin with an ice cream social at which students and their families could meet teachers and support staff in an informal and fun setting before buckling down to the serious work of school. Another important community-building tradition at the school was an annual fall sleepover called Camp Night, when students and their parents, in mixed grade-level groups, participated in enjoyable, hands-on learning experiences; had a meal provided by the Parent Teacher Association (PTA); and slept at the school. Brenda also made use of a local high-ropes course twice a year for a challenging team-building experience with the third through fifth graders and their teachers—and parents were also invited along for the fun. Brenda joined right in, wearing jeans and hiking boots—which, for the students, were an amusing contrast to her typical heels and professional dress. Brenda structured time for the faculty to work together and share ideas and resources, providing common planning time on most days. The school was not free of conflict, but the strong sense of community supported the constructive resolution of the inevitable differences.

We can learn much about the vital role of trustworthy school leadership from the stories of these three principals. They are real principals, and the voices of the teachers throughout the book are taken from actual interviews. The short vignettes scattered throughout the chapters come from encounters with teachers and parents as well as exchanges with my students over the years I have been teaching and writing on this topic.

Principals and other school leaders need to earn the trust of the stakeholders in their school community if they are to be successful. They need to understand how trust is built and how it is lost. Getting smarter about trust will help school leaders foster more successful schools.

TRUST AND SCHOOLS

When we turn a nostalgic eye toward schools in an earlier era, it seems that there was once a time when a school enjoyed the implicit trust of its communities. School leaders were highly respected and largely unquestioned members of the community. Teachers were regarded as having valuable professional knowledge about how children learn and what is best for them. When a child was punished at school, parents accepted and reinforced the judgment of school officials. If those days ever really did exist, they are not what many who work in schools are currently experiencing.

It is important that a school leader not take the general distrust of schools too personally. That distrust is part of a larger pattern in society, shaped by economic, political, and social forces. We now live in an era when all of our social institutions are under unprecedented scrutiny. We are barraged by a steady stream of media attention to scandals, revealing how business leaders, politicians, church leaders, nonprofit executives, and school leaders have acted out of self-interest rather than in the interests of the constituents whom they purport to serve. These revelations erode the trust we once had in these institutions and their leaders and undermine their basic legitimacy.

The philosopher Annette Baier (1994) observed that we tend to notice trust as we notice air, only when it becomes scarce or polluted. These days, trust in our society does indeed seem to have been damaged and is in scarce supply. As changing economic realities and changing expectations in society make life less predictable, and as new ways to disseminate information increase both the availability of and desire for negative information, we begin to *notice* trust much more. In the midst of the media blitz of bad news, trust has emerged as a favorite theme of advertisers in promoting everything from investment firms to hair salons. Many of us seem to be longing for the days when trust came more easily.

Changing Expectations

New economic realities and increasing social problems have led to mounting pressures on schools. Economically, the move toward a more global economy has increased competition and forced society's expectations of school outcomes to change. This economic shift has diminished the proportion of low-skilled jobs in developed countries. Our economy is dependent on there being a more highly skilled workforce and a larger proportion of individuals who have earned a high school diploma. Graduates must not only be proficient in basic skills but also be able to reason and solve complex problems. They must be able to work well in teams, as the problems they are likely to encounter in the workplace will be too complex for an individual working alone to solve. Schools are expected to provide a stronger workforce that will allow their nations to remain economically competitive in a global marketplace. At the same time, economic disparities are growing and the problems faced by low-income populations are growing. Although to some extent the criticism of schools in the popular media has been overblown, and our schools are doing a much better job than is frequently reported, pressure is being brought to bear on schools to adapt to a changing world (Berliner & Biddle, 1995).

Aspirations for Equity

In our society, the value of equity has taken on ever greater prominence. Citizens take seriously the expectation of equal opportunities and the right of all to achieve economic security. As people gain access to more information, they also become more conscious of growing income inequalities, as well as of the disparities in opportunities and outcomes available to people from differing social strata.

With growing awareness, those who are less powerful also wish to feel less vulnerable to the professionals whose greater power vitally affects them. Professionals of all sorts possess increasingly powerful knowledge that influences both individual and public welfare (Barber, 1983). With expanding access to information, many people are no longer content to accept the role of passive client. Doctors are finding that many of their patients have engaged in independent research about their conditions, coming with detailed questions and recommendations for their own treatment. Lawyers are encountering more clients who have read up on legal precedents and maneuvers that might be helpful to their case. Parents, too, are conducting research and feeling ever more empowered to advocate for their children's interests within the education system and to question the professional knowledge and expertise of school personnel.

Much of the responsibility for realizing our society's vision of greater equity is entrusted to our schools. Consequently, higher expectations are brought to bear on those who educate our children. The actions of school professionals influence not just our children's current welfare but also their future educational and economic potential. Previously, schools functioned largely to sort and rank students for various strata of society. Notable exceptions helped maintain the belief in our society as a meritocracy where anyone with the ability and work ethic could overcome the deficiencies of his or her origins and prosper economically or politically, but in reality, schools generally maintained the status quo in terms of social rank and prosperity. That propensity has come under attack and has largely been supplanted by the goal of fostering greater equality of opportunity and outcomes for all students, even those with disabilities and those from lower socio-economic strata (Goodlad, 1984).

However, schools—especially those that serve high-poverty populations—struggle to realize these new aspirations. More than half a century after the *Brown v. Board of Education* decision to desegregate public schools, the dream of schools' eliminating race and class distinctions and providing equal opportunities to learn seems far from becoming a reality. As educators are charged with reducing the effects of economic disparities in our society, schools are increasingly feeling the brunt of public distrust. Impatient with the pace of change, policymakers have set standards for student performance and worked to increase the rigor of those standards over time. They have imposed reporting requirements to reveal discrepancies in outcomes among students who historically have been underserved by schools. And they have offered incentives for states to develop tough new teacher and principal evaluation systems that hold educators accountable for the learning of their students. The common denominator for these various policy initiatives is a lack of trust that educators are doing all that they can to support the learning of their students.

With increasing expectations—and many instances in which those expectations have not been met—trust in our schools has been damaged. In some ways, these dashed hopes and distrust are the result of the very success of public schools, with the increased knowledge and reasoning skills that a better educated public brings to its relations with professionals, experts, and other leaders. The success of our education system has created the very conditions that enable the common person to think critically and to challenge the status quo. Consequently, better education has created greater need for trustworthiness on the part of leaders and professionals.

Pressure for Change

In this time of societal and economic flux, political forces are pressuring schools to make the necessary changes to meet our new, loftier goals for them. There is an urgent need to identify and solve the problems that plague low-performing schools. As Gloria learned, however, urgency is not enough to turn around a failing school. Standards have been imposed on schools because educators have not been consistently accountable, thereby forfeiting the public's trust. Negative publicity has been used to shift schools from complacency to compliance with new accountability measures. Principals like Fred, however, resist and resent these measures when they are not accompanied by the means and know-how to foster a productive school culture. Principals like Gloria become impatient with the slow pace of change and try to force rapid reform on their reluctant faculty, generating resistance and resentment instead of improved outcomes. It takes the wisdom of a principal like Brenda to patiently apply both support and challenge to lead a school toward fruitful change.

TRUST MATTERS

Schools must garner trust and legitimacy at a time when these commodities are in short supply in society at large. Trustworthy school leaders must learn to create conditions in which trust can flourish within their school as well as between their school and their community. School leaders who, like Brenda, earn the trust of the members of their school community are in a better position to accomplish the complex task of educating a diverse group of students in a changing world. Principals and teachers who trust each other can better work together in the service of solving the challenging problems of schooling. These leaders create a bond that helps inspire teachers to move to higher levels of effort and achievement. These leaders also create the conditions, through structures and norms to guide behavior, that foster trust between teachers, and they assist teachers in resolving the inevitable conflicts that arise. Even more important, these leaders cultivate a culture of high trust between students and teachers through their attitudes, example, and policies.

As citizens become increasingly distrustful of their institutions and leaders, the trend away from trust creates a special challenge for schools because trust is so fundamental to their core mission. A school needs the trust of its parents, as well as that of the community that sponsors and funds it. To learn, students must trust their teachers because for much of what is learned in school they are asked to believe what teachers tell them as well as what they read without independent evidence. Students who do not trust their teachers or each other will be likely to divert energy into self-protection and away from engagement with the learning task. Without trust, teachers and students are both unlikely to take the risks that genuine learning entails. Moreover, students who do not feel trusted by their teachers and administrators may create barriers to learning as they distance themselves from their school and build an alienated, rebellious youth culture. They may, in fact, live down to the low expectations of a distrustful school environment. Trustworthy school leaders model trusting relationships with students and parents that serve as examples for teachers as they work to cultivate these trusting relationships as well.

Trust can no longer be taken for granted in schools. It must be conscientiously cultivated and sustained—and school leaders bear the largest responsibility for setting a tone of trust. It is time for school leaders to become knowledgeable about cultivating trust because trustworthy leadership is at the heart of successful schools.

KEY POINTS ABOUT A MATTER OF TRUST

- School leaders that have the trust of their community are more likely to be successful in creating a productive learning environment.
- Trust is a challenge for schools at this point in history, when all of our institutions are under unprecedented scrutiny.
- Much of the responsibility for realizing our society's vision of greater equity is entrusted to our schools. Consequently, higher expectations are especially brought to bear on those who educate our children.
- Without trust, schools are likely to flounder in their attempts to provide constructive educational environments and meet the challenging goals that our society has set for them, because the energy needed to solve the complex problem of educating a diverse group of students is diverted toward self-protection.

- Trustworthy leadership is at the heart of productive schools.

QUESTIONS FOR REFLECTION AND DISCUSSION

1. Recall a time when you worked or studied in a school where trust was high. What was that like, and what effect did that trust have on the learning process? What conditions helped support that trust?
2. What are the signs that trust is either present or absent in your current school? To what extent do teachers trust one another?

To what extent do they trust students? What effects of the presence or absence of trust do you notice?

3. How do you know whether you are taking the appropriate amount of responsibility for continuous improvement in your school? What problems emerge from taking on too much or too little responsibility? What skills and support do you need to provide for teachers so they can assume a meaningful role in the change process?

4. What steps have you taken to cultivate bonds of trust with parents and the community at large? What additional steps might you take to foster a trusting relationship between your school and your community when there is so much negative publicity about schools in the media?

5. To what extent do you trust the teachers and students in your school? What might strengthen that trust?

CHAPTER 2

DEFINING TRUST

*Trust . . . is reliance on others' competence and willingness
to look after, rather than harm, things one cares about
which are entrusted to their care.*

—BAIER, 1994, P. 128

Trust matters because we cannot single-handedly either create or sustain many of the things we care about most. Trust is manifest in situations where we must rely on the competence of others and their willingness to look after that which is precious to us. Because we must allow others to help us care for what we cherish, they are put in a position where they can, if they choose, injure the very thing that is dear to us (Baier, 1994). As a society, we invest much of what we most value in our schools. We send our children to schools, trusting that they will be safe from harm, as well as guided and taught in keeping with our highest hopes for them. Further, a significant share of our collective resources in the form of tax dollars, school buildings, and local employment opportunities is invested in schools. In addition, schools are charged with keeping and promoting our shared values and ideals. They foster and protect our ideals of respect, tolerance, and democracy, as well as the vision of equity in our society. It is evident why trust has become such a pressing issue for schools.

Trust has, paradoxically, been likened to both a glue and a lubricant. As "glue," trust binds organizational participants to one another. Without it, things fall apart. To be productive and to accomplish organizational goals, schools need cohesive and cooperative relationships. Trust is essential to fostering these relationships (Baier, 1994; Goldring & Rallis, 1993; Louis, Kruse, & Associates, 1995). Trust binds leaders to followers. Without that bond, a manager can enforce minimum compliance with contract specifications and job descriptions, but that will not lead a team of teachers to greatness. As "lubricant," trust greases the machinery of an organization. Trust facilitates communication and contributes to greater efficiency when people have confidence in the integrity of other people's words and deeds. Without trust, friction and "heat" are generated that bog down the work of the school. Energy is expended in making provisions against possible or feared betrayal by the other party. Schools need trust to foster communication and facilitate efficiency.

Trust is also a choice. Trust is a judgment based on evidence, but it outstrips the evidence that would rationally justify it. The trusting party makes this leap of faith out of care for the relationship. Solomon and Flores (2001) noted that trust is "cultivated through speech, conversation, commitments, and action. Trust is never something 'already at hand,' it is always a matter of human effort. It can and often must be conscientiously created, not simply taken for granted" (p. 87). They also asserted that it is unethical to withhold trust without good reason, just as it is unethical to treat a person unfairly in other ways. Thus, to be suspicious of a person based solely on his or her race, ethnic identity, gender, or other forms of group membership and not on his or her actions or behavior is unethical.

Trust within a school can be fostered or diminished by the behavior of the leader. Schools that cultivate trust can reap the benefits of greater adaptability and innovation as well as reduced costs (Mishra, 1996; Moolenaar & Sleegers, 2010). Unfortunately, the very conditions conducive to the emergence of trust also allow for its abuse (Elangovan & Shapiro, 1998). Despite the dividends of a culture of trust, organizational dynamics often complicate things because the power differences imposed by hierarchical relationships add complexity to interpersonal interactions. The compliance and reporting arrangements in a hierarchical organizational structure, as well as the capacity of those at higher levels to punish those at lower levels of whose behavior they do not approve, can make fostering high trust relationships across levels more difficult. School leaders can overcome these potential barriers through genuine caring and steadfast commitment combined with thoughtful action and initiative.

WHAT IS TRUST?

Most of us rely on an intuitive feel of what it means to say that we *trust* someone. Trust is difficult to define because the judgments we make in deciding to extend trust to someone are complex. Trust is a multifaceted construct, meaning that many elements operating simultaneously are what drive the overall level of trust. Those drivers, or facets, may vary somewhat depending on the context of the trust relationship. Trust is also dynamic in that it can change over the course of a relationship, as expectations are or are not fulfilled and as the nature of the interdependence between two people changes. For example, when two teachers who have been friends are put together on a team and are expected to engage in joint lesson planning, the nature of the interdependence changes and may evoke a reassessment of the level of trust. As I examined various definitions of trust across the literature in fields from philosophy and psychology to business and economics, reoccurring themes emerged, which led me to the following definition: *Trust is one's willingness to be vulnerable to another based on the confidence that the other is benevolent, honest, open, reliable, and competent* (Mishra, 1996; M. Tschannen-Moran & Hoy, 1998, 2000).

Vulnerability through Interdependence

Trust matters most in situations of interdependence, in which the interests of one party cannot be achieved without reliance on another. Interdependence brings with it vulnerability. Unless parties are dependent on one another for something they care about or need, trust is not essential. Nor is trust an issue in situations where one has complete control over the actions of another. But when parties are interdependent, the uncertainty concerning whether the other intends to and will act appropriately requires taking a risk (Rousseau, Sitkin, Burt, & Camerer, 1998; Solomon & Flores, 2001). The person extending trust recognizes the potential for betrayal and harm from the other. Taking that leap of faith requires trust. This leap may, in turn, lead to further development of trust when the expected behavior materializes. Trust, then, reflects the extent to which one is willing to rely on and make oneself vulnerable to another (Baier, 1994; Bigley & Pearce, 1998).

One of the early puzzles that emerged in the study of trust was whether it is an individual's behavior or his or her attitude in a situation of vulnerability that matters. For example, when a parent leaves her young child at school but holds significant misgivings about doing so, can the parent be said to trust the school? By taking action, the parent has voluntarily increased her risk for negative outcomes, but she has done so with a certain level of anxiety. The decision to place oneself at risk of harm by another could be based on many motivations, including need, hope, conformity, impulsivity, innocence, masochism, or confidence (Deutsch, 1960). Although the behavior of the parent who anxiously leaves her child at school is the same as that of a parent with no such misgivings, the level of trust is very different.

There is growing consensus that trust lies in the degree of confidence one holds in the face of risk rather than in the choice or action that increases one's risk (Rousseau et al., 1998). Trust is therefore the "accepted vulnerability to another's possible but not expected ill will" (Baier, 1994, p. 99).

Schools ask parents to trust in their ability not just to protect the children in their care but also to shape their thinking and behavior. Students are expected to leave school changed, presumably for the better, from how they were when they entered. Schools also ask their community to risk vulnerability by sharing a major portion of its collective resources in the form of tax dollars and school buildings, as well as for control of significant employment opportunities within the community. Schools and school personnel require great trust because of what is at stake if schools perform poorly. Poor school performance has serious negative consequences both for the individual students and for the community as a whole.

The Five Facets of Trust

Teachers and principals are interdependent in their shared project of educating the students in their school. As such, they are vulnerable to one another. Therefore, the principal-teacher relationship provides a window into a school's trust dynamics. In Brenda we have an excellent example of a trustworthy school leader. Her story and those of Gloria and Fred illustrate the various facets of trust that people rely on in making trust judgments. Each of the facets of trust—benevolence, honesty, openness, reliability, and competence—is played out in the relationships within these leaders' schools.

Benevolence

Perhaps the most essential ingredient and commonly recognized facet of trust is a sense of the care or benevolence of another: the confidence that one's well-being or something one cares about will be protected and not harmed by the person in whom one has placed one's trust (Baier, 1994; Zand, 1997). When extending trust, one rests assured in the goodwill of another person to act in one's best interests and to refrain from knowingly or willingly doing one harm. In an ongoing relationship, the future actions or deeds required for continued trust typically are not specified; there is simply the assumption of mutual goodwill (R. D. Putnam, 2000). The sense of care for the person and the relationship are so strong that one can rest easy in the confidence that the other person would not capitalize on an opportunity to enhance his or her outcomes if such an opportunity were to come at the expense of the trusting partner (Cummings & Bromily, 1996). Akin to benevolence is respect, or the recognition of the inherent worth or value of another person and the contributions he or she has to make to the collective. The general orientation of goodwill has also been called personal regard (Bryk & Schneider, 2002). In a situation where one is dependent on and consequently vulnerable to another, faith in the caring intentions or altruism of the other is particularly important. Parents who trust educators to care for their children evidence confidence that the educators will act with the best interests of their children in mind and that their children will consistently be treated with fairness and compassion. Teachers, too, want to feel assured that they will be treated fairly and with respect.

When trust in the benevolence of others is missing, there is likely to be a cost in regard to overall productivity because energy is invested in making mental provisions or alternative plans, or in assessing the recourse available in case of betrayal. Students who do not trust their teachers or fellow students cannot learn efficiently because they invest their energy calculating ways to protect themselves instead of engaging in the learning process. If stories circulate about how an administrator has failed to reliably protect the interests of a teacher or student, a spiral of distrust may start to form as people begin to fear that they, too, might be victimized.

School leaders can promote trust by demonstrating benevolence: showing consideration and sensitivity for employees' needs and interests, acting in a way that protects employees' rights, and refraining from exploiting others for personal gain. Brenda demonstrated benevolence in a variety of ways at Brookside. David, a midcareer teacher who had taught at Brookside for nine years, described the importance of Brenda's goodwill or benevolence and its impact on teachers:

> I think her underlying motivation is to help you be the best that you can be at what you are doing. Her underlying desire for you is nothing but good. . . . She is always looking for ways to build you up, to let you know what your strengths are. And then areas she sees maybe you need to work on—giving you ways to work on those or see how others do it. She expects a lot, but she gives a lot.

Teachers were more willing to go the extra mile to meet the high demands that Brenda placed on them because of the level of support they received.

One of the ways that Brenda demonstrated support for her faculty members was in consistently expressing appreciation for their hard work. Simple expressions of appreciation went a long way toward building satisfaction and commitment among the faculty in Brenda's building. Christy, another teacher at Brookside, described what even small expressions of gratitude meant to her:

> Brenda's expectations are very, very high. We spend a lot of hours after school, on weekends; we work a lot more than some other schools. However, she is always very appreciative. The next day there is always a comment in the bulletin saying, "Thank you, those of you who attended

the program last night." We are in a very thankless job. Parents
don't often say thank you, and kids don't come up and say,
"Thank you for teaching me!" But at least she does it. And
that's all I need. I just need a little bit of acknowledgment.

Because of the support these teachers received from Brenda,
they were willing to accept correction from her and to work hard
to meet the high expectations she had for them. Kathy, a teacher
in her fifth year at Brookside, voiced these sentiments: "Even
though sometimes she gets mad and yells at us, we take our lick-
ings and we go on. Yet, when we have a problem and we ask her
for assistance, she is right there to give it to us."

Reputations serve either to strengthen high trust or to diminish low trust. Social networks tend to drive trust relationships
toward extremes, enhancing strong trust relationships and com-
pounding the effects of broken trust (Burt & Knez, 1996). Where
trust is high, newer members in the social system are encouraged
to extend trust even when events might otherwise have caused
them to be guarded. At Brookside, although Brenda could occasionally be short-tempered or "snippy," new faculty members were
coached by their peers not to let an occasional display of temper
or a negative remark on Brenda's part interfere with their developing sense of trust. They were told that because she cared so
much and worked so hard for the school, it was understandable
that she would sometimes be tired and irritable. Newcomers were
assured that if they ever needed help or support of any kind, they
could count on Brenda.

In situations of high trust, people do not hesitate to seek help
because they do not fear that others will make them feel inadequate or incompetent. They do not worry about being seen as
dependent on another person or about incurring indebtedness to
another person (G. R. Jones & George, 1998). Brenda extended
her care beyond the scope of school, with a willingness to listen,
to advise teachers about issues they faced in the personal realm,

and to be with them in times of sickness and sadness as well as in times of celebration and joy. Principals who hope to earn the trust of their faculty need to demonstrate goodwill and genuine concern for teachers' well-being.

Our principal's eyes popped out when he saw the teachers' year-end evaluation of our new assistant principal. "Wow!" he said. "What has she done with the teachers?" But, you know what? You can always go into her office and talk to her. You can bring her an issue you are dealing with, and she goes right into problem-solving mode. It never, ever comes back to bite you—like you are incompetent or can't do your job. The teachers really appreciate that.

—JOHN, SECOND-GRADE TEACHER

Although there is an emotional element to trusting someone, it is not primarily an emotional process. There is an important distinction between trusting and liking a person. It is possible to like someone you do not trust, just as you may trust someone you do not especially like. The teachers I spoke with at Fred's school liked Fred, but they did not trust him. Because caring is an element of trust and we tend to like those from whom we feel benevolence or goodwill, you may be more likely to like those you trust (McAllister, 1995). Affection, however, is not necessary for trust to develop.

Honesty

Honesty is a fundamental facet of trust (Butler & Cantrell, 1984; Cummings & Bromily, 1996; Rotter, 1967). Honesty concerns a person's character, integrity, and authenticity. When you trust someone, you believe that the statements he or she makes are truthful and conform to "what really happened." You are confident that you can rely on the word or promise of that individual, whether verbal or written, and that this individual will keep commitments made about future actions. People earn a reputation of integrity from telling the truth and keeping promises (Dasgupta, 1988).

Correspondence between a person's statements and his or her deeds characterizes integrity. Integrity is the perceived match between a person's values as expressed in words and those expressed through actions (Simons, 1999). There is no daylight between this individual's talk and his or her walk. When a person says one thing yet does another, trust is compromised. Without the confidence that a person's words can be relied on and can accurately predict future actions, trust is unlikely to develop. Trust might survive a broken promise if a plausible explanation is given along with an apology; however, a pattern of broken promises is likely to pose a serious threat to trust.

When school leaders unveil a new vision or change initiative for their school and then do not follow through, change course again, or do not uphold the principles of their own program, it is worse than if they had not begun in the first place. The "flavor of the month" syndrome creates cynicism and damages trust, rather than leading to positive, sustainable change. When Gloria first arrived at Lincoln, the speeches she gave to the faculty seemed to promise a new day for the school; but as she became mired in conflict, those implicit and explicit promises crumbled.

In an effort to please everyone or avoid conflict, administrators sometimes fail to be completely honest and up-front with individuals. Fred frequently proclaimed that he was not going to tolerate certain behaviors, such as the continual tardiness of particular faculty members or the abuse of sick days. But when his actions failed to correspond to his tough words and nothing was done to address the inappropriate behaviors, the faculty lost faith in Fred's integrity. Failure to follow through on a threat or consequence can be as damaging to trust as a broken promise. The object of the threat may be pleased or relieved not to have the threat fulfilled, but the disconnect between the leader's actions and his or her words damages trust.

The revelation of dishonest behavior may be more damaging to trust than lapses in regard to other facets because it is read as an indictment of the person's character. Once a principal has been caught in even a single lie, and once faculty members have lost faith in the word of their principal, trust can be difficult to reestablish because the communication tool necessary to restore trust is now suspect. Simons (1999) warned:

> Words are one of a manager's most potent tools for guiding subordinates. . . . When credibility is sacrificed, the manager damages that tool, and is forced into additional actions to show when he or she 'really means' what he or she says. (p. 95)

Our principal rarely gets into classrooms to observe
or give feedback. But when we had our accreditation visit,
right in front of the whole team our principal said that
he gets into every classroom at least once a year, if not
more. He said that most were informal, drop-in
visits. We all knew that it wasn't true. We couldn't believe
he would come right out and lie like that! After that,
I never trusted him in the same way again.

—KIM, HIGH SCHOOL SCIENCE TEACHER

Authentic behavior consists of three basic aspects—accountability, avoiding manipulation, and being "real" rather than simply playing a role (J. E. Henderson & Hoy, 1982; M. Tschannen-Moran & Hoy, 1998). Accountability is characterized by an acceptance of responsibility for one's actions and avoidance of distorting the truth to shift blame to another. There is no passing the buck, no scapegoating, no pointing fingers at others.

Authenticity means the willingness to accept responsibility not just for good things that happen but for mistakes and negative outcomes as well. Rather than protecting his or her reputation as hoped, a principal who continually tries to cover his or her shortcomings and mistakes by shifting blame to others will more likely earn the distrust of both teachers and superiors.

Authentic leaders do not exploit or use others, treating them as people who are to be respected rather than as pawns to be manipulated. In addition, authentic leaders are able to break through the barriers of role stereotyping and behave in ways that are consistent with their true self. Their basic personality, not their idea of how to play some prescribed role, is a prime motivator of behavior. Although Gloria had good intentions in regard to turning around Lincoln, she failed when it came to authenticity. She seemed all too ready to shift blame to her teachers when things did not go smoothly. For example, Gloria's teachers felt hurt and betrayed when they overheard her blaming the teachers for a failed grant proposal, even though she had been a member of the committee that had written the proposal and had not carried her weight in the writing process. Her faculty also saw her as manipulative in her attempts to move people around and to remove teachers who were not immediately compliant or did not bend to her will. As tensions mounted, her self-protective move of withdrawal to the safety of her office left her little chance to interact with teachers in informal, congenial ways that would reveal her fundamental personality and character.

Openness

Openness is a process by which people make themselves vulnerable to others by sharing information, influence, and control (Zand, 1997). Teachers see principals as trustworthy when their communication is both accurate and forthcoming (Bryk & Schneider, 2002; Handford & Leithwood, 2013). Adequate explanations of decisions that are made and timely feedback on observations and actions lead to a higher level of trust (Sapienza & Korsgaard, 1996). Openness means the disclosure of facts, alternatives, intentions, judgments, and feelings. When principals exchange thoughts and ideas freely with teachers, it not only enhances perceptions of those leaders' trustworthiness but leads to greater openness on the part of teachers as well. Under these conditions, teachers are more willing to share their thoughts, feelings, and ideas, making these valuable resources available for school improvement. The information teachers share, whether strictly about organizational matters or of a more personal nature, is a giving of themselves (Butler & Cantrell, 1984; Mishra, 1996).

Withholding important information is one technique leaders use to maintain power or manipulate employees (Kramer, 1996; Mishra, 1996). People who are guarded in sharing information provoke suspicion as others wonder what they are hiding and why. Just as openness breeds trust, so too does suspiciousness breed distrust. People who are not willing to extend trust through openness can end up living in an isolated prison of their own making (Kramer, Brewer, & Hanna, 1996). A principal who is secretive about his or her whereabouts and withholds relevant information to retain control over who knows what is unlikely to garner faculty trust. For example, the year the study at the heart of this book was being conducted at Brookside, Lincoln, and Fremont, a new superintendent in the district was gathering all the principals to the central office for weekly, daylong meetings. Whereas Brenda's faculty at Brookside directed their anger toward the superintendent for this disruption because they missed having Brenda in the building, Gloria did not feel that she owed her faculty an explanation of her whereabouts, so the faculty suspected that the meetings were a fabrication and that she was simply shirking her responsibilities.

Openness in communication needs to exist in the context of good judgment. Maintaining strict standards of confidentiality is

a critical element of trustworthy leadership. School leaders may
have to choose not to defend their decisions or actions when to
do so would require sharing confidential information. One of
the more painful experiences some of my administrative interns
encounter on their journey toward becoming school leaders is
that of having to bite their tongue when facing criticism from
others who do not have all of the relevant information. It is also
important at all times to "speak with good purpose" (Reina &
Reina, 2005), that is, to refrain from engaging in gossip, small-
minded chatter, faultfinding, or other forms of negativity. Using
good judgment also means considering the maturity and commitment of those you would share information and influence
with and working over time to build capacity if it is initially
lacking.

Fostering open communication can give schools a strategic
advantage. In schools with a greater level of trust, teachers and
staff members are likely to disclose information that is more
accurate, relevant, and complete when a problem arises. Where
communication flows freely, problems can be disclosed, diag-
nosed, and corrected before they are compounded. Teachers
function as an early warning system, making the principal aware
of problems while they are still small. At Brookside, teachers
perceived Brenda to be approachable and open. Because of her
accessibility, she was made aware of small problems brewing in
the school so that they could be addressed before they escalated.
Brenda made a point of being on the playground during lunch
recess to attend to problems as they arose, rather than engaging
in the time-consuming task of tracking down witnesses and trying
to piece together what happened after the fact. Principals who
want to encourage candor among their staff members must cultivate trust, which means actively encouraging teachers to voice
their frustrations openly, including criticisms of the principal's
decisions.

There is a high level of trust in our whole school district.
It starts with our superintendent, who has an open-door
policy. That sets a tone that is mirrored throughout
the central office and among all of the principals in the
district. There is a feeling that you don't have to be afraid
to take risks here—and if it doesn't work out, you won't
be blasted. He'll just ask you what you learned from
the experience so you don't have to
learn that lesson again.

—BARBARA, CURRICULUM DIRECTOR

Openness in influence allows others to initiate changes to goals, plans, concepts, criteria, and resources. There are two primary reasons for including subordinates in decision making. The first and most common is to win compliance. This motivation often leads to a phony form of shared decision making whereby leaders purport to want teacher input in the decision yet teachers suspect that the decision has already been made. It is just a game that administrators play in an attempt to get "buy-in" and consequently greater compliance with directives. The problem is that teachers see through the ruse and resent how their time has been wasted (not to mention the implicit insult to their intelligence). A more authentic form of shared decision making stems from the belief that the involvement of subordinates will result in higher-quality decisions because these individuals are close to the action and have information and insight that leaders may lack. When administrators share actual influence in decision making, they demonstrate significant trust and respect for their teachers and are more likely to be trusted in return (Hoy & Tarter, 2008; Moye, Henkin, & Egley, 2005; Short & Greer, 1997).

Openness in control is rooted in confidence in the reliability and competence of others and a willingness to delegate important tasks to them. Delegating authority to teachers and joint deliberation in decision making not only foster a sense of trust within schools but also promote a greater spirit of professionalism as teachers are granted the discretion that is at the heart of professional practice (Louis et al., 1995; Marks & Louis, 1997). Trustworthy leaders make themselves vulnerable by sharing authority and accepting the consequences for joint actions taken. Through openness, a cycle of trust can be initiated, leading to increasing levels of trust in the organization. It signals confidence on the part of leaders that neither the information nor the individual will be exploited; recipients thus infer that they can feel the same confidence in return. In taking the initiative to make yourself vulnerable by engaging in acts of trust, the hope is that you may be able to induce others to do the same (Kramer et al., 1996).

Although not all decision making was relinquished to the faculty at Brookside, Brenda included faculty members in decision making in a way that maintained a sense of accountability to the school's mission and goals. Kathy described the process this way:

> She polls our opinions a lot. Sometimes she has made a few decisions on her own that we haven't always agreed with, but for the most part she'll come to us and say, "What do you think?" If we come to her and say we have this idea, we have to have a solution for how it will work. If you come with an idea and a plan for making it work, then she is very open to it and she will think about it. Our input is very important to what happens—because we have to do it. We have to teach it, and we have to implement it.

Brenda's openness to faculty input was evident in a decision concerning the arrangement of classrooms in the school. The faculty, on the one hand, wanted to change the physical layout of the classrooms to enable grade-level teams to work more closely together and share supplies. Brenda, on the other hand, wanted to keep a mixture of grade levels near each other to support the program of having older students "buddy up" with younger students. When the faculty came up with a compromise plan that could accommodate both sets of needs by mixing only those grade levels that partnered together in each hall, Brenda implemented the change.

Reliability

It is not enough to demonstrate benevolence sporadically or to show support from time to time. The sense that one can depend on another consistently is an important element of trust. Teachers may conclude that their principal is a nice person and means well, and even that he or she is very capable and helpful if they can get his or her attention. But if overcommitment, trouble managing the time demands of the job, or being easily distracted means teachers cannot count on the principal to come through for them when needed, trust will not characterize the relationship.

Trust has to do with predictability, or knowing what to expect from others; but predictability in and of itself is inadequate as a facet of trust. We can expect a person to be invariably late, or we can count on someone to be consistently malicious, self-serving, or dishonest. When our well-being is diminished or damaged in a predictable way, our expectations may be met, but we do not really trust the other party, even if our language seems to indicate that we do ("You can trust John to blow it!"). Trust in someone's reliability implies a sense of confidence that we can "rest assured" that this person will do what is expected on a regular, consistent basis. Reliability combines a sense of predictability with caring and competence. In a situation of interdependence, when something is required from another person that has an impact on joint outcomes, the individual can consistently be relied on to supply it (Butler & Cantrell, 1984; Mishra, 1996). The interdependent partners need not invest energy worrying whether the person will come through, nor do they need to make mental provisions for how to manage in case of that person's failure to come through.

We really miss our old principal. When you would
ask him something, he would say, "Let me think about
it and I'll get back to you." And he always would. He was
just very thoughtful and deliberative in his decisions.
Our new principal will make decisions right on the spot.
But then when she gets more information or somebody
complains, she changes it. We never know what
the final decision is or when it might change.
It leaves everybody guessing.

—NICOLE, FIFTH-GRADE TEACHER

Reliability in Brenda's school often meant demonstrating a willingness to address problems no matter what it would take. This meant that Brenda sometimes worked long hours to get everything done. Dependability and a high level of commitment were apparently contagious. Kathy described her principal this way:

> Brenda is a very hard worker. She is here every morning at 6:30, and she doesn't go home until things are done. She may be here until 8:00 or 9:00 in the evening if there are meetings. Seeing her do that, well, the school gives 110 percent. Everybody works hard here.

Sometimes Brenda worked too hard, leading her, as we have seen, to become short-tempered on occasion. Her teachers seemed willing to forgive her, however, recognizing that she had enormous demands placed on her. They appreciated her dedication to them and to the school.

For principals to garner the trust of their faculty, they need to demonstrate enough consistency in their behavior to inspire confidence that teachers can count on them in their time of need. Consistency among the beliefs a school leader espouses, school goals, and actual behavior promotes trust in that individual (Bryk & Schneider, 2002). Teachers have greater confidence when they feel they can predict the behavior of their principal (Handford & Leithwood, 2013). The teachers I interviewed commented that seeing leaders step up to the plate in predictable and occasionally extraordinary ways strengthened their trust in those leaders as well as their own motivation.

Competence

Goodwill and good intentions are not always enough to garner the trust of others. When a person is dependent on the skills and abilities of another, even an individual who means well may not be trusted (Baier, 1994; Mishra, 1996). Competence is the ability to perform a task as expected, according to appropriate standards. In schools, principals and teachers depend on one another's competence to accomplish the school's teaching and learning goals. Likewise, students are dependent on the competence of their teachers. A student may feel that his or her teacher is benevolent and wishes very much to help him or her learn, but if the teacher lacks knowledge of the subject matter or cannot adequately communicate that knowledge, then the student may not trust the teacher. If the lack of skill is evidenced in an apprentice, such as a student teacher, however, it is understood that the person is still learning and expected to make some mistakes—so the lack of competence is not a breach of trust (Solomon & Flores, 2001). In this case, failure should not be confused with betrayal because the person did not claim to have the requisite skill. Presumably the system has safeguards in place to protect others from any harm due to the mistakes of an apprentice.

We expect people whose skill we depend on, especially professionals, to be honest about their level of skill as well as to maintain it. This maintenance effort reflects not merely on their reliability but also on their character and conscientiousness (Solomon & Flores, 2001). The problem is that people are not always honest with themselves (or sufficiently insightful) about their loss of skills and the impairment of their judgment. A superintendent who is fighting a drinking problem, a principal in the early stages of dementia, or a teacher who has "retired on the job" and is no longer effective with students raises serious questions of trust. Reputation comes into play as well when it comes to trust based on competence. A principal who is new to a building, even if she is well intentioned and demonstrates goodwill, may have difficulty earning the trust of teachers and parents if a reputation of incompetence or ineffectiveness precedes her.

Teachers often mention incidents in which the competence of their principal matters. In a study of three high-trust and three low-trust schools, competence was the element most often mentioned as contributing to the trust in, or distrust of, the school leader (Handford & Leithwood, 2013). Skills related to competence included setting high standards, pressing for results, solving problems, resolving conflict, working hard, and setting an example. In high-trust schools, principals are regarded with respect and even admiration. Principals in these schools not only set a high standard but also hold teachers accountable in ways that seem fair and reasonable to the teachers themselves. At Brookside, the faculty was confident that Brenda was on top of things. Kathy talked about Brenda's competence and what it meant for the school:

> Brenda is just very aware of everything in the building. She reads every report card, every conference report. She does recess duty every day herself, with aides, because she wants to be there when the problems happen and stop them. She doesn't want the problems to escalate; she wants to stop them from the minute they start. She is very much an integral part of the school. She *is* the school.

The teachers felt reassured by this level of commitment and involvement from their principal. With caring came a sense of accountability. Kathy continued:

> She rarely takes a sick day; she's always here. She is in every class, every day, between 9:00 and 9:30. She always wears heels. You can hear those heels clicking in the hall, and you know you better put yourself in order. She makes her presence known!

This level of involvement gave the faculty a sense of confidence that the school was being managed effectively, despite the inevitable difficulties inherent in an urban setting. There was confidence that problems would not be allowed to get out of hand. It is not necessary, or even desirable, for principals to have a hand in everything that goes on in their school. But they need to have enough awareness to know when problems are emerging, so they can respond to them.

One way that principals demonstrate their competence is in their willingness to act as a buffer for teachers and handle tricky situations, whether dealing with difficult students or distressed parents, or discretely addressing problems among the faculty and staff (Handford & Leithwood, 2013). One of a principal's primary responsibilities is to protect the core work of the school—the teaching and learning process—which may entail being the first line of defense against disruptions that come from the outside, such as by calming an irate parent who demands to speak to a teacher immediately or by helping create a school culture that is serious about learning and does not condone student misconduct. Fred lost the confidence of his teachers because of the lack of support they felt in dealing with unruly students. Teachers thought his low-key approach sent the message to students that they could do as they pleased and that no serious consequences were likely to come their way. A principal's calm and steady demeanor when responding to an angry parent or a child who is out of control can be reassuring to a teacher who is upset. The good rapport that Brenda built with parents helped the teachers at Brookside in their work. Christy reported:

> People have a lot of respect for Brenda. She knows the families. We have gone on home visits, and she doesn't even have to look up the address. The parents come to her. The parents come back to her after the kids have graduated from Brookside. She is very much into home-school cooperation.

Trust, then, allows a person to rest assured in a situation where something he or she cares about depends, at least in part, on the actions of another person. That assurance has to do with confidence based on the other person's intention and integrity, bolstered by his or her openness, reliability, and competence. Teachers' trust in the principal is based on what they feel they ought to be able to expect from a person who occupies that role. What teachers seem to expect, above all, is a sense of care, benevolence, or goodwill from their principal. Further, principals who have a reputation for integrity and who encourage open communication are likely to earn the trust of their teachers. Teachers, because they feel vulnerable to the problems that emerge from an incompetent or disengaged principal, also rely heavily on competence as a basis of trust. Principals who are disposed to helping teachers solve on-the-job problems also are more likely to be trusted. A growing body of research from schools in a variety of settings has confirmed that all of these facets are important aspects of trust relations in schools (Forsyth, Adams, & Hoy, 2011; M. Tschannen-Moran & Hoy, 2000; Van Maele, Forsyth, & Van Houtte, 2014). The five facets of trust, summarized in table 2.1, are the key ingredients that make for trustworthy leadership.

Table 2.1 Five Facets of Trust

Benevolence	Caring, extending goodwill, demonstrating positive intentions, supporting teachers, expressing appreciation for faculty and staff efforts, being fair, guarding confidential information
Honesty	Showing integrity, telling the truth, keeping promises, honoring agreements, being authentic, accepting responsibility, avoiding manipulation, being real, being true to oneself
Openness	Maintaining open communication, sharing important information, delegating, sharing decision making, sharing power
Reliability	Being consistent, being dependable, showing commitment, expressing dedication, exercising diligence
Competence	Buffering teachers from outside disruptions, handling difficult situations, setting standards, pressing for results, working hard, setting an example, problem solving, resolving conflict, being flexible

DIFFERENTIATED TRUST

Although all of these facets of trust are important, their relative weight will depend on the nature of the interdependence and consequent vulnerability in the relationship. One is vulnerable in different ways to an intimate friend, a boss, an investment broker, or a surgeon. For trust to form, it may not be necessary to have a high level of confidence in all facets, only in those areas where there is critical interdependence. There are crucial thresholds across which trust turns to distrust. Different facets of trust may have different thresholds depending on the level of reliance in a particular area and the consequences of one's expectations' being disappointed (Shaw, 1997). For example, if you are aware that a friend is less than trustworthy in some realm that does not directly concern you, such as that he cheats on his income taxes or is somewhat unreliable in aspects of his work responsibilities, but he is faithful in his interactions with you, you may nonetheless trust him.

As relationships mature, impressionistic and undifferentiated trust evolves into a more fine-grained and differentiated form. As interdependent partners in an ongoing relationship gather experience with one another, they come to have a growing body of trust-relevant evidence to draw on. However, the trust picture that emerges may not be a simple one. Trust becomes more differentiated and may be uneven. Relationships are multifaceted; therefore, a person may trust another in some matters and not in others—so trust and distrust may be present simultaneously in the same relationship (Lewicki & Bunker, 1996; Lewicki, McAllister, & Bies, 1998). For example, consider a situation in which two teachers have taught together for many years and have come to have an abiding trust in one another. The relationship changes, however, when one of the teachers becomes an assistant principal in the school where they have taught together. The teacher is now vulnerable to her former peer in new ways, as that person takes on greater authority and power in the organization. Because the nature of the interdependence has changed, trust must now be reassessed based on the new dimensions of this relationship, especially if the culture of that school emphasizes the differences in orientation between teachers and administrators. This example raises questions about the challenges of establishing trust across the lines of hierarchy, the topic we turn to next.

TRUST AND HIERARCHY

Trust depends, in part, on what one expects of another on the basis of formal roles and informal norms. The reality of life in organizations is that individuals are vested with varying degrees of power and authority. Because of the hierarchical nature of the relationships within a school, the principal exercises considerable authority over teachers and staff members. Within this asymmetrical relationship, it is the responsibility of the person with greater power to take the initiative to build and sustain trusting relationships.

People at different hierarchical levels examine and weigh sources of trust-relevant information differently. They look to one another with divergent expectations of what they owe others and about what others owe them. These differential expectations influence the cultivation of trust. In schools, principals base their trust judgments of teachers more heavily on competence, reliability, and commitment, whereas teachers' views of principals tend to be anchored more in caring, integrity, and openness (Blake & MacNeil, 1998; Spuck & MacNeil, 1999). Teachers, in the lower-status position, are naturally concerned about exploitation and unfair treatment, whereas the principal, in the higher-status position, worries about whether the teachers will shirk responsibilities and undermine the work of the school (Bryk & Schneider, 2002). The principal cannot monitor every class at every moment and has to trust that the teachers are advancing student achievement, whereas the teachers expect procedural fairness, a predictable environment, sufficient resources, and professional support from the principal.

Due to their greater feelings of vulnerability, subordinates seem to be hypervigilant in their trust assessments of superiors, such that even relatively minor gestures take on considerable importance. When subordinate-superior dyads were interviewed about their relationship, subordinates recalled many more trust-related incidents than did superiors, and trust violations tended to loom larger than confirmations of trustworthiness (Kramer, 1996). Even small gestures, such as offering a greeting when passing in the hallway, can be taken by hypervigilant subordinates as significant forms of communication without even being noticed by busy superiors. Because the faculty at Lincoln felt vulnerable to Gloria's whims and did not trust her, they kept a close eye on her moods and actions for clues about how they might protect themselves. The school secretary had a small rubber monster that she perched on her computer monitor to warn faculty when Gloria was in a particularly bad mood, removing it on days when there was smoother sailing.

Schools evidence elements of two competing organizational orientations. Bureaucratic organizations rely on a hierarchy of authority for coordination and control, whereas professional organizations rely on trust in the expertise of the professionals granting them discretion in responding to the needs of clients. Although schools necessarily employ a bureaucratic structure to organize the complex task of educating large and diverse groups of students, there is a danger that school leaders will overemphasize bureaucratic elements, with their implicit distrust of those at the lower levels of the organization, at the expense of cultivating professionalism among teachers (M. Tschannen-Moran, 2009). A professional orientation flips the traditional organizational chart on its head, placing the work of teachers, who are on the front lines of delivering the organizational mission, at the top of the inverted pyramid, with administrators shoring up that work from below.

In productive schools, such as Brookside, principals and teachers are able to work cooperatively across recognized boundaries of authority while retaining their distinctive roles (Hirschhorn, 1997). Teachers feel confident and are empowered to exercise professional discretion. Brenda exercised authority in a way that was flexible, cooperative, and collaborative, in contrast to Gloria, who was rigid, autocratic, and controlling. The degree to which teachers are granted professional discretion has been linked to their level of trust in their principal (M. Tschannen-Moran, 2009). Trustworthy principals help teachers and staff members solve problems, rather than interfering with their work through overly prescriptive policies or cumbersome reporting requirements. In productive schools, principals use their power and authority to design structures that facilitate teaching and learning and buffer teachers from needless interruptions and distractions (Hoy & Sweetland, 2001).

PUTTING IT INTO ACTION

The behavior of the principal has a critical bearing on setting the tone of trust within a school. If you, as a principal, hope to benefit from the rewards of a trusting culture, it is your responsibility to initiate trusting relationships through your own trusting and trustworthy behavior (Whitener, Brodt, Korsgaard, & Werner, 1998). Brenda is an excellent example of a trustworthy principal, but her story is in no way unique. Many other trustworthy principals share the characteristics she exhibited. Like Brenda, they evidence enormous caring for the teachers, staff, students, and parents in their school. High performance expectations for all members of the community grow out of this sense of care. Brenda was both consistent and competent. She was known for her integrity. And she inspired trust by being open in communication and control, keeping the faculty, students, and parents of Brookside informed about matters of importance to them and involving them in important decisions. In extending trust, she was trusted in return.

To be a trustworthy principal is first and foremost to be known as a person of goodwill. Teachers are confident that you have their best interests at heart and that you will do whatever is possible to help them develop as professionals. The form that this caring takes will vary across schools, but it will be evident that you are strongly committed to the well-being of all of the individuals who make up your school community. You need to protect others' rights and welfare, and you must refrain from exploiting others to advance your own interests. You can promote trust by demonstrating consideration for and sensitivity to teachers' needs and interests, listening intently to communicate respect for each person, and engaging in coaching and problem solving if that is what is called for. Making yourself visible and accessible will allow you to more readily demonstrate your support and concern.

To be a trustworthy principal, you must be honest and fair in dealings with the faculty, with students, and with parents. You will need to demonstrate integrity in telling the truth and keeping promises. You also will need to demonstrate authenticity, accepting responsibility for your actions and avoiding distorting the truth to shift blame to others. Trust is also enhanced by a willingness to apologize when you have

(continued)

made a mistake or when a decision you made has resulted in unpleasant consequences for members of the school community (Greenberg,
1993; Konovsky & Pugh, 1994).

You will foster trust through the open flow of information that
allows you to be made aware of problems while they are still small,
as well as by truly involving teachers in making important decisions.
It is important that you be consistent, even predictable, not arbitrary
or capricious. You will need to model hard work and dedication, be
engaged with the faculty, and be aware of what is going on in your
building. By acting in trusting and trustworthy ways, you can create a
school that reaps the rewards of a culture of trust.

KEY POINTS ABOUT DEFINING TRUST

- Trust is a glue that holds things together, as well as a lubricant
  that reduces friction and facilitates smooth operations. Trust
  is also a choice that involves risk.
- In situations of interdependence, when you have to rely to some
  extent on someone else to achieve the outcomes you desire,
  you want to feel confident that the other person is benevolent,
  honest, open, reliable, and competent.
- As relationships mature, trust evolves from being impressionistic and highly undifferentiated to more fine grained and
  differentiated among specific facets of trust.
- Because principals have greater power within the relationships in a school, they have greater responsibility for the
  establishment and maintenance of a culture of trust.
- The principal's behavior has a large influence on the culture
  of the school. Visible and accessible principals can more readily offer support and demonstrate consistency and concern.
- To be trusted, principals need to be willing to extend trust to
  teachers, staff, students, and parents.

QUESTIONS FOR REFLECTION
AND DISCUSSION

1. How can an understanding of the five facets of trust help you bolster the culture of trust in your building?
2. In regard to which facets do you judge yourself to be a trust-worthy leader? In which would you like to improve? What disciplines, habits, and techniques could help you focus on the facets of trust during the school day?
3. Recall an incident in which you felt torn between the need to maintain confidentiality and a desire for openness. How did you handle it? What was the result?
4. Tell about a time when being trusted contributed to your ability to involve others in solving a challenging problem that otherwise would have been difficult to solve.

CHAPTER 3

FOSTERING TRUST

Trust is . . . a human virtue, cultivated through speech,
conversation, commitments, and action.

—SOLOMON AND FLORES, 2001, P. 87

If trust is so essential to the productive functioning of schools, how then is it established? This is a fundamental question for those who would lead schools. The answer is complex. Trust is a multidimensional and dynamic phenomenon. The way trust unfolds will not be the same at all times and in all places. It takes on different characteristics at different stages of a relationship. As trust develops, it "gels" at different levels depending on the type of relationship that has developed as the parties have interacted over time. The nature of vulnerability can change as the level of interdependence increases or decreases and as expectations either are or are not met. Initially, trust relies on assumptions, institutional structures, and deterrents such as sanctions for breaches of trust. However, with a longer history of expectations' being met, as well as the growth of a sense of care for the relationship, trust may deepen. Understanding the developmental nuances of trust is an essential prerequisite for a leader who wants to foster and maintain trust in his or her school.

INITIAL TRUST

Organizations exist to accomplish tasks that are too big, complex, and costly for individuals to accomplish alone. When a
new member joins an organization, a level of interdependence is
established immediately by virtue of the shared purpose embodied in the organizational mission. A new employee's success and
continued employment depends on an ability to forge workable
relationships with the existing organizational players and to serve
organizational purposes. When Christy was hired to teach at
Brookside, she joined an already established school community
with its own history, culture, and norms. Her developing trust was
facilitated by the feeling of camaraderie and good humor evident
at the school. Similarly, as Gloria assumed leadership of Lincoln,
she joined an ongoing operation with a particular history and with
certain expectations and goals for what would be accomplished
under her leadership. Existing members of the school community scrutinized her actions, looking for clues as to whether they
could trust her or not.

As trust develops in newly forming work relationships, an
initial period of impression making is followed by a period of
more intense exploration. Trust between two parties is established through a commitment period during which each partner has the opportunity to signal to the other a willingness to
accept personal risk and not to exploit the vulnerability of the
other for personal gain. A kind of courtship takes place in which
each party is careful not to violate the other's developing trust
(D. L. Shapiro, Sheppard, & Cheraskin, 1992). This commitment
period begins at the moment of initial contact and extends until
participants know each other well enough to predict the other's
values and behavior. As participants begin to feel more comfortable with one another, there may be a tacit testing of the limits
of trust and influence and attempts to arrive at a mutual set of
expectations.

When Gloria became principal at Lincoln, her actions during the commitment period signaled to the faculty and staff that they ought to be wary in their relationship with her. Because of the pressure she felt to make change quickly, she did not invest the time to develop the trust needed to lead people through change. Although it was clear that she had been hired to turn around a failing school, her impatience for change felt disrespectful to those who had invested their professional lives at Lincoln. The relationships had soured before the end of the first year, stabilizing at a point of suspicion and distrust. From there, it was hard to make reparations and to reestablish productive working relationships.

Not long after our new superintendent started work,
I received a phone call from her while I was in class at the
university where I am pursuing my doctorate. I figured it
must be important for her to be calling me in the evening,
so I stepped out of class to take her call. I am the principal
of one of the three Title I schools in our district, and she
informed me that she had been reviewing the test scores
from my school. She stated that the scores from my school
were low and that if I didn't improve them immediately
she would have no further need of my services. I had never
even met this woman! She has since come to value my
work and my strong ties to the community, but after such
a rocky start to our relationship, I will never trust her.

—JULIA, ELEMENTARY SCHOOL PRINCIPAL

Although it makes intuitive sense that trust grows gradually over time, researchers have been surprised to find higher levels of initial trust than expected, even when the parties have very little knowledge or experience of one another. It seems that when people interact with a stranger, they tend to extend provisional or tentative trust until evidence surfaces to suggest a lack of trustworthiness, making defensive action necessary. This preference for provisional trust over initial distrust makes sense because trust is the easier option. Distrust requires that energy be expended in anticipating possible harm and in planning ways to avert it (Berg, Dickhaut, & McCabe, 1995; G. R. Jones & George, 1998). People are inclined to overlook the possibility that the other person may not share their values and consequently fail to meet their expectations in the relationship. As individuals interact, experience either reinforces these trusting assumptions or dispels initial impressions of trustworthiness. Once people have evidence that leads them to perceive differences in values, distrust is likely to emerge (Sitkin & Roth, 1993).

Institutional Supports

High initial trust in schools and other organizations is a function not just of the efficiency of assumed trustworthiness but also of the institutional mechanisms, such as policies, rules, and regulations, that support trust. The belief that the necessary organizational structures are in place to allow one to anticipate a successful interchange and the outcome one desires can support the development of initial trust (McKnight, Cummings, & Chervany, 1998; S. P. Shapiro, 1987; Zucker, 1986). Formal organizational policies as well as informal social structures, such as the norms and values of the culture, support developing trust (Creed & Miles, 1996). These factors can also sustain a cycle of risk taking and fulfillment that facilitates the deepening of trust (Gulati, 1995; Sitkin, 1995).

The mechanisms involved in the hiring process are key institutional supports for initial trust. Schools cannot afford to be naive when hiring new staff members because a failure to detect untrustworthiness is a breach of the trust that parents and other taxpayers have placed in the system. The hiring process is an intentional one of gathering trust-relevant information on both sides of the hiring decision. From the first contact with a prospective employee, a school system not only gathers information about the person's background and checks with references who have known the person but also pays special attention to the nature of the interactions to be sure there is nothing out of the ordinary. Likewise, the prospective employee is judging the feel of the place and is trying to pick up any discrepancies between the espoused values and actual practice. A general impression or an intuitive sense that everything "feels normal" supports initial trust (McKnight et al., 1998). If both sides successfully establish an initial degree of trust, the person may join the organization. Organizational participants interacting with a new employee may feel at ease in extending initial trust, assuming that the proper procedures were in place to root out evidence of untrustworthiness.

Another of the institutional supports for trust in schools is the certification of teachers and administrators. The premise is that a professional must demonstrate a certain level of competence and knowledge to receive certification, and thus that this person is qualified for his or her position. Reliability is addressed to some extent in the contract that spells out the job description and expectations. The other facets of trust—benevolence, honesty, and openness—are not as readily supported by institutional mechanisms but may be supported by the norms of the school or school district because a person violating those norms will risk provoking sanctions and social disapproval (Baier, 1994).

Reputation

In the early stages of a relationship, as two people get to know one another, they may rely on information about the other person's reputation to guide them in assuming an initial level of trust. This is especially true for educational leaders who conduct their career in the public eye. A reputation of trustworthiness is a valuable asset for individuals and organizations alike and can become a self-fulfilling prophesy. Stronger initial trust based on the good reputations of the parties involved may, in turn, lead to a stronger motivation for trustworthy behavior to sustain and build on the benefits of that trust. When Christy applied to transfer to Brookside, it was in part because of Brenda's reputation for excellence and trustworthiness. Christy knew that she would be expected to work harder than teachers at most other schools in the district, but she also felt confident that she would be treated as a professional. Once she joined the faculty, the stories she heard from other teachers about Brenda served to enhance her developing trust.

The trust between two individuals is significantly influenced by the social context in which that relationship is embedded (Daly, 2010). A network of mutual friends and acquaintances can enhance the likelihood that trust in the relationship will develop and grow stronger over time. Such a context, however, can also amplify the effects of a breach of trust. The judgment, observations, and gossip of others can tend to "lock in" relationships at either positive or negative extremes (Burt & Knez, 1996). In a school, stories that are told and passed along through the grapevine can serve to further either a cycle of trust or a spiral of distrust. The stories that circulated at Brookside built trust in Brenda and sustained trust despite an occasional lapse on Brenda's part, whereas the stories told about Gloria reinforced the sense of violation that certain teachers felt, which spread to others who had not been directly affected.

Because trust is only relevant in the context of interdependence and vulnerability, individuals tend to be more alert to negative information and prefer negative gossip to positive (Burt & Knez, 1996). This tendency can be an impediment to the development of trust. Moreover, technologies, such as social media and e-mail, allow gossip to spread quickly and can amplify the impact of broken trust. In addition, misunderstandings introduced in the abbreviated forms of communication often employed in electronic messaging can disrupt trust. Finally, the propensity of the news media to capitalize on the desire for negative information has made the cultivation of trust even more difficult between schools and their publics.

Relationships within schools tend to be ongoing in that people expect to continue to relate to the same network of people over time. Because of this, the social network can exert both formal and informal control that encourages people to act in a trustworthy manner. There is an incentive to behave in ways that are trustworthy, to develop a reputation for trustworthiness, and to reap the benefits of trusting relationships (Coleman, 1990; R. D. Putnam, 1993). When many people perceive that an individual has a good reputation, it is more difficult for a negative event to significantly reduce a high level of trust in that individual (McKnight et al., 1998).

I worked for a man with whom I had a great deal of trust.
Before we even met, I knew of his reputation for the good
things he did in the community. From our very first meeting,
he treated me like a colleague. He treated me with respect.
At one of our first meetings, he challenged an assertion
I made. I reinforced my point. We went back and forth
several times on the point, but he never pulled rank
or insisted that I agree with his interpretation just
because he had greater power. That was the basis
of a strong working relationship over time.

—JANINE, MUSIC EDUCATOR

FACTORS THAT INFLUENCE DEVELOPING TRUST

School leaders need to understand that a number of factors come into play as trust develops. Trust judgments can be influenced by one's disposition to trust; by values and attitudes, especially attitudes concerning diversity; and by moods and emotions. The role that each of these factors plays in the development of trust is explored in the paragraphs that follow.

Disposition to Trust

Some people are inclined to extend trust more readily; they have a disposition to trust. A disposition to trust is particularly pertinent to making trust judgments when two people do not know each other and specific information about the other person is not readily available. A person's disposition to trust may be influenced by a personality trait that inclines that person toward a low tolerance for risk, or from his or her personal history of relationships in which promises have been either fulfilled or broken. A child whose upbringing was consistent may develop a generally trusting disposition, whereas a child who has been regularly disappointed by broken promises or a lack of kindness and goodwill may grow up with a generalized suspicion of people's motives and promises. These early expectations may then generalize to poor psychological adjustment that makes it difficult for that person to extend trust (Hurley, 2012). This generalized suspicion can take a long time to overcome because by being reluctant to extend trust, the person may miss opportunities to accrue positive information about the trustworthiness of others. The process of overcoming suspicion may be accelerated somewhat if the guarded person is helped not only to see the incentives the other party has to be trustworthy but also to recognize the potential benefits of trust as well as the costs of maintaining a generally suspicious stance (Hardin, 2006; Hurley).

A person with a high disposition to trust is more likely to see good points and to overlook flaws in another person that could threaten the development of trust (Johnson-George & Swap, 1982; Rotter, 1980). Such a person is likely to have both faith in humanity and a trusting stance. Faith in humanity has to do with believing that others are typically well meaning and reliable. A person with a trusting stance extends this faith, treating people as though they are reliable and trustworthy in spite of an absence of evidence, based on the belief that over the long run this strategy results in more positive outcomes (McKnight et al., 1998; Solomon & Flores, 2001). Those with a trusting stance believe that even if they are occasionally cheated or taken advantage of, on balance the rewards of being trusting will outstrip the losses. They assume that in the absence of contrary data, extending trust is the wisest course in establishing a relationship. People with a trusting disposition tend to be more trustworthy than others; they are less likely to lie, cheat, or steal, even when they can increase their gain by being untrustworthy. In general, people with a greater propensity to trust are happier, more well liked, and considered better friends than those whose default stance tends toward suspicion. They are less likely to be conflicted, maladjusted, or dependent on others (Moolenaar, Karsten, Sleegers, & Zijlstra, 2010; Rotter, 1967; Wrightsman, 1966).

There are important distinctions between a trusting stance and naiveté or blind trust. Naiveté, on the one hand, is inattention to trust-relevant information, taking for granted the trustworthiness of the other person without paying attention to discrepant information or intuitive warning signs. People with a disposition to trust are not necessarily more gullible or naive; they are able to make use of information about the behavior of others in given situations to recognize when their initial trust assessment should be revised. For example, those with a trusting stance may be more likely to be cooperative initially, but they do not continue to trust once they have been tricked (Schlenker, Helm, & Tedeschi, 1973). Blind trust, on the other hand, is not really trust but willful self-deception. It is a refusal to take stock of the evidence of untrustworthy behavior or to take measures for self-protection. Giving chances even when one has been let down may not be blind trust if one willingly acknowledges the disappointment in regard to trust (Solomon & Flores, 2001). For example, when a teacher catches a student telling a half-truth in covering up for some mistake but gives the student another chance, it is not blind trust if she acknowledges the disappointment. Blind trust is the active denial of the evidence by refusing to acknowledge even the possibility of betrayal.

Values and Attitudes

People make trust judgments partly on the basis of the assumption of shared values as well as attitudes. Values are general standards or principles that are considered intrinsically desirable ends, such as loyalty, helpfulness, or fairness. Attitudes are knowledge structures consisting of the thoughts and feelings individuals have about other people, groups, or organizations. They are the means through which interactions are defined and structured. Attitudes are evaluative in nature, and values are the basis on which people make those evaluations (G. R. Jones & George, 1998). Because people lack choice in the selection of their coworkers, and because relationships within organizations involve interdependence and a degree of uncertainty, people form attitudes toward each other that are likely to contain information about the other party's trustworthiness based on perceptions of shared values. Distrust can arise in a school when an individual or group is perceived as not sharing key cultural values. When a person challenges a school's fundamental assumptions and values, he or she may be seen as operating under values so different from those of the school community that the violator's entire worldview becomes suspect. For example, a teacher who had worked at Brookside the year prior to my study was seen as not having the same work ethic as the rest of the faculty and so was perceived as not sharing the same values about the importance and urgency of the work to be done. That teacher was counseled into transferring to another school at the end of the year.

When evidence surfaces of a lack of alignment in key shared values, it raises concerns because the person in question is perceived as a cultural outsider, one who "doesn't think like us" and may therefore do the unthinkable (Sitkin & Roth, 1993). Thus, anxiety about the threat of future violations increases. A teacher who had been hired at Fremont was distrusted by other teachers because of the harsh and demeaning tone she took with her students, as she was overheard from the hallway. She was perceived as not sharing a commitment to extending dignity and respect to students and this perception of a lack of shared values led to suspicion.

Some schools' values, however, may be appropriately called into question. There may be a valid basis for people's skepticism about whether a school's enacted aims are properly aligned with its stated mission and whether it is legitimately pursing the best interests of students. Pointed questioning might be very appropriate and quite useful to get the organization to focus more clearly on its core values. For instance, given Lincoln's reputation for poor student performance, Gloria had reason to question the underlying values and assumptions about students that led to an acceptance of low achievement at Lincoln. What was missed in Gloria's rush to assert that low student performance would no longer be tolerated was the fostering of relationships and the establishment of a context that would make such a conversation constructive. It takes time to build a productive culture that deals effectively with conflict, encourages open dialogue, and even allows for dissent. Taking a strengths-based approach to conversations about the core mission and values of a school is likely to be more productive than assuming a deficit-based or blaming stance.

People have a tendency to extend trust more readily to those they perceive as being similar to them, based on the assumption that they have adopted similar norms of obligation and cooperation learned through similar cultural structures (Zucker, 1986). The perceived similarity may be based on characteristics such as

family background, social status, and ethnicity. One of the dynamics that contributed to a lack of effectiveness at Fremont was racial
tension among the faculty. Many of the African American teachers had gone to school together, belonged to the same sorority,
and attended the same large church. Teachers in this group had a
long history with one another and shared strong bonds of friendship. They were very involved in each other's lives outside of
school and shared many inside jokes. These teachers hosted big
celebrations for one another's birthdays, with catered lunches,
cake, and balloons. The white teachers were typically not invited
to attend these celebrations. Fred's attendance at such affairs
was taken as a tacit acceptance of these divisions, which to some
white teachers felt like a betrayal. This group of African American
teachers was perceived to be very cliquish by many of the
white teachers. If any of the members ever felt slighted by or was
in conflict with someone outside the group, the outsider was likely
to experience the wrath of the whole group. The teachers in this
group felt comfortable extending trust to one another more readily than to others because other group members could be assumed
to have adopted similar norms of cooperation and obligation
through the cultural structures of school, sorority, and church.

Establishing trust is more difficult in situations of diversity
because people may be uncertain about the cultural norms or
values of others (Kipnis, 1996). Knowledge of one another's culture may be limited and based on partial or misleading images.
Hence, people are often unsure about what to expect. To
simplify the complexity of relationships, people tend to implicitly divide others into two groups: those with whom they share
group membership and those who are outside that group. An
old joke goes that there are two kinds of people in this world:
those who divide people into two groups and those who don't.
In reality, we all belong to the group that divides people into
two groups, those who are in our "in-group" and those who are
not. We implicitly adopt this heuristic as a way to manage the

complexity inherent in relying on and doing business with a large number of people.

Once others have been categorized, people make biased assumptions, based on group membership, about those others' values, preferences, behavior, and trustworthiness. People are more likely to regard "out-group" members with suspicion, and they tend to stereotype them more readily and negatively than they would in-group members. Biased attributions about the capabilities, intentions, and actions of out-group members can fuel feelings of distrust. Individuals tend to use perceived differences in underlying attitudes or values to explain the behavior of out-group members, whereas with in-group members they are more likely to consider situational factors that might have influenced behavior (Allison & Messick, 1985). Thus, an African American teacher at Fremont who made an inappropriate remark might be excused by other members of the clique as just having a bad day, whereas the same remark from a white teacher might be seen as evidence of bigotry or poor moral character. Furthermore, people are more likely to seek information that conforms to their attitudes about their own and other groups and to discount information that disconfirms their biases (Klayman & Ha, 1997).

As African Americans, we learn early that Caucasians are not to be trusted. Consequently, we are always waiting for the other shoe to drop in our professional and personal relationships. The history of poor race relations makes trust very difficult.

—MELODY, SPECIAL EDUCATOR

Group biases can be destructive, not only causing people to regard out-group members with suspicion but also leading them to extend too much trust to in-group members. Members develop a "leniency bias" toward those of the in-group, giving other in-group members the benefit of the doubt when confronted with information that might otherwise be viewed as diagnostic of untrustworthiness (Brewer, 1995). Overconfidence in the collective can lead individuals to "defer too readily to other members, and [they] may inhibit expressions of doubt, or engage in inappropriately severe self-censorship rather than press their claims as vigorously as they might" (Kramer, Brewer, & Hanna, 1996, p. 381). A cohesive culture that perceives itself as being under threat may stifle dissent and result in "groupthink," a dynamic that has been exposed as a factor in some disastrously poor decisions (Janis, 1982).

I was brought up to respect everyone. There are times when I have been the victim of racial prejudice, but I choose not to dwell on it. I have a good relationship with everyone in my school—they trust me, and I trust them. They respect me, because as a black man I can get through to some of the kids that the white teachers can't. To me, trust begins with respect.

—HOWARD, ELEMENTARY SCHOOL HEAD CUSTODIAN

Trust judgments based on similarity or group membership can have very real consequences for how schools function. For example, in one study, superiors expressed less trust in, and were less willing to use participative approaches in decision making with, subordinates who were predominately from a minority group (Rosen & Jerdee, 1977). Research on teachers' trust in students and parents, however, has indicated that socioeconomic status can be an even stronger dividing line than race for differentiating in- and out-group perceptions (Goddard, Salloum, & Berebitsky, 2009; M. Tschannen-Moran, 2001; M. Tschannen-Moran & Hoy, 2000; Van Maele & Van Houtte, 2011). Schools face increasing diversity of languages, ethnic groups, races, and socioeconomic statuses. This diversity brings a richness, but it also carries with it challenges for the development of trust. Diverse groups need time, structure, and support to learn about one another and to come to view themselves as part of the same collective. They need knowledge of one another's culture and values so they can understand the behaviors and attitudes of the other and can come to have confidence that their expectations will be met. Diversity can present an especially daunting challenge to the development of trust when the exploration of cultural expectations reveals very real differences in values. Intentional efforts to develop a strong, shared culture within a school or school system can prevent people from drifting into silos of in-groups and out-groups that promote conflict rather than cooperation (Hurley, 2012).

Moods and Emotions

Although trust is a judgment and not a feeling, moods and emotions provide a powerful context for making trust assessments. Emotions are intense affective states tied to particular events or circumstances that interrupt ongoing cognitive processes and behaviors, whereas moods are less intense, generalized affective states that are not explicitly linked to particular events or circumstances (Solomon & Flores, 2001). Anger is an emotion likely to emerge in response to betrayal, one that intrudes on one's thoughts and may be accompanied by physiological changes such as a flushed face or clenched jaws and fists. A mood of cynicism may emerge after a series of disappointments leads to diminished hope that the situation will improve.

A mood is not simply an emotional response to what has happened but rather an orientation toward the present as well as the future, and consequently toward what is to be done. Moods are our way of being tuned into the world. They are not just occasional occurrences; we are always in a mood. Our moods do not simply "happen" to us. We cultivate our moods through our thoughts and practices. A mood is more akin to a habit of mind than to something that comes over us and over which we have no control

(G. R. Jones & George, 1998; Solomon & Flores, 2001). There are many variations of "bad moods," which include the following (Solomon & Flores, 2001, pp.110–111, italics added):

- There is resignation. *("Nothing is going to improve this situation, and there is nothing I can do to change it.")*
- There is despair. *("Nothing can prevent this looming calamity. We might as well just let it happen.")*
- There is straightforward distrust. *("I don't believe what they told me, so I'm certainly not going to put my heart into it.")*
- There is full-scale cynicism. *("Nothing ever changes, and nothing ever gets better, so it is silly even to try.")*
- There is confusion. *("I don't know what's going on here and I don't know whom to ask, and I can't afford to let anyone know that I don't know what I'm doing.")*
- And there is panic. *("I'll never be able to do this!")*

The most devastating of all bad moods is the mood of *resentment* (*My colleagues don't ever give me the respect I deserve"*).

Just as individuals' orientations toward the world are shaped by their moods, collective orientations toward the world are fashioned by organizational cultures. For example, low morale could be considered one form of the school's being in a "bad mood." When a culture or mood of resignation is pervasive in a school, it functions as a self-protective mechanism, steeling participants against the possibility of further disappointment. In an attempt to avoid disappointment, people refrain from taking any assertive action. They close off the possibility of negotiation and thus the mutual understanding that might lead to an improved relationship proves illusive. When people have lost their grip on hope to the extent that resignation reaches a point of despair, taking preventive action ceases to make sense (Solomon & Flores, 2001).

There are times when an organization adopts a culture of "cordial hypocrisy" (Solomon & Flores, 2001, p. 36) that appears on the surface as a good mood, but that when probed turns out to be a cover for a more deeply pervasive culture of despair, resignation, or resentment. At its worst, this veneer of courtesy and amiability is a collective form of self-deception and denial and thus is immune to easy resolution (Solomon & Flores, 2001). Cordial hypocrisy is evident in schools that suppress conflict instead of creating constructive mechanisms for its resolution (Uline, Tschannen-Moran, & Perez, 2003). A healthy school climate is one in which conflict is seen as a natural and even helpful part of school life and is harnessed for school improvement through the creation of forums for its expression and mediation.

Schools, like individuals, do not need to be trapped by their bad moods. With understanding and effort, those negative habits of mind can be turned into a more constructive orientation that focuses on what is to be done. Once moods are recognized as self-chosen and culturally endorsed ways of being in the organization and the world, the way is open to change them. Solomon and Flores (2001) described the vital role of conversation in changing organizational cultures through a review of the underlying assumptions on which they are based:

> The key to cultivating [better] moods is the revision of these assessments: understanding through conversation just how others see the situation and, just as important, how they see you and your role in the situation. Conversation leads to mutual understanding, and understanding should lead to resolutions and engagements, actions that will bring about new situations and open up new possibilities. (p. 113)

Thus, school leaders who want to cultivate a culture of trust will be aided by an understanding of how trust develops and of the factors that can facilitate or hamper its development and growth.

AUTHENTIC AND OPTIMAL TRUST

Trustworthy school leaders assist in developing authentic trust at optimal levels to support the collective mission of their school. Authentic trust emerges when people have grown to have a deep and abiding trust in one another. Each relies fully on the other, resting in interdependence and vulnerability without anxiety. There is empathy with the other person's intentions and desires, as well as a mutual understanding that leads to effective action in service of the joint work (G. R. Jones & George, 1998; Lewicki & Bunker, 1996).

Trust deepens and becomes more authentic as individuals interact and get to know one another over time (Zucker, 1986). Relationships mature as the frequency and duration of interactions increase, and with the diversity of challenges that relationship partners face together. The more experience parties have, the better the chance that they will come to understand and be able to predict each other's behavior (Lewicki & Bunker, 1996). Reliability in previous interactions gives rise to positive expectations that goodwill will be returned in kind (Creed & Miles, 1996). A self-reinforcing pattern of trust emerges as repeated cycles of exchange, risk taking, and successful fulfillment of expectations strengthen the willingness of trusting parties to rely on each other. A history of fulfilled expectations accumulates and leads to reputations for trustworthiness that can then facilitate and reinforce trust in a wider social context.

An abiding, authentic trust is also robust enough that it can endure an occasional disappointment, disagreement, or difference in values, provided it leaves intact the sense that both parties care enough to protect and continue the relationship. Trust can rebound, particularly if both parties make an effort to restore a sense of good faith and fair dealing in their interactions (Rousseau, Sitkin, Burt, & Camerer, 1998). Each can recognize that the other is human and bound to err and nonetheless make the decision to go on trusting (Solomon & Flores, 2001).

Some scholars have labeled this abiding trust "unconditional trust" (Solomon & Flores, 2001, p. 80); however, trust is almost always bounded and specific. Trust is limited to the context and the capacity expected of the other person. For example, a trusted colleague at work would not necessarily be trusted with one's prized sailboat if she did not have the skill to operate it properly. A trusted spouse would not necessarily be trusted to perform a medical procedure he was not trained to do. At Brookside, the teachers held a deep, authentic trust in Brenda and identified with her vision for the school. This relationship of trust even extended beyond the bounds of professional life, as Brenda was relied on for advice and assistance in personal matters. But even here, there were limits or boundaries to that trust.

So what is the optimal level of trust? More trust is not always better. There are dangers in both trusting too little and trusting too much. Trusting too little is undesirable because schools miss out on trust's potential to confer a competitive advantage through greater adaptability, innovation, lowered costs, and reduced uncertainty (Barney & Hansen, 1994; Mishra, 1996; Moolenaar & Sleegers, 2010). Too little trust can also be dangerous because one's trust orientation can be a self-fulfilling prophecy. Organizational participants may begin to live down to the low expectations held for them. Resentment at being treated with the distrust implicit in many bureaucratic regulations can leave workers feeling that if they are already presumed guilty, there is little reason not to, in fact, be untrustworthy (Fox, 1974).

Conversely, trusting too much can leave open too wide the gates of temptation. It provides too few incentives to deter workers' inclinations toward opportunism (Wicks, Berman, & Jones, 1999) or "looking out for Number One." This could be seen in the poor citizenship of some of the teachers at Fremont who took advantage of Fred's confidence in them to do the right thing and to make decisions in the best interests of the students and the school. The lack of constraints tempted these teachers to cut

corners on their obligations, to lighten their teaching responsibilities, and to shorten their workday.

Discerning the proper level of trust requires wisdom and
judgment on the part of the educational leader. Optimal trust
is prudent, measured, and conditional. Members of the school
community need to know not only when to trust others, and in
what respects, but also when to monitor others closely (Lewicki,
McAllister, & Bies, 1998). A good model for optimal trust is
Aristotle's "golden mean" between excess and deficiency. Trust
levels should be appropriate to the context and may fall any-
where on the spectrum from minimal trust to high trust depending on the person and situation (Wicks et al., 1999). Trust needs
to be tempered by a willingness to confront and punish exploi-
tive behavior. A bias toward trust, shaped by prudence, offers an
appropriate balance for relationships within schools (Solomon &
Flores, 2001).

 PUTTING IT INTO ACTION

As you assume leadership of a new school community, keep in
mind that the first few weeks and months are an important phase
in the process of developing trust with important stakeholders in the
school. You start to establish trust the moment you begin discussions about taking on the leadership of a school building. The hiring
process itself is one of gathering trust-relevant information, and the
offer of an employment contract speaks to the establishment of a
certain level of trust. Your trust relationships with teachers, staff, parents, and even students may begin before any actual contact is made,
if your reputation precedes you and as information is disseminated
about your having been named to assume the leadership of a school.

During the commitment or courtship period, each party has the
opportunity to signal a willingness to extend trust and not to exploit
the vulnerability of the other. Even if trust is not readily extended
to you, it is important to remember that the responsibility for trust

establishment rests more heavily with the one with greater power. Because teachers, staff, parents, and students are vulnerable to you, they are going to be watching you closely to discern if it is safe to trust you. Even small gestures are going to be read as significant as these stakeholders gather information about your trustworthiness.

Fostering trust may be more difficult if you are entering a building where trust is low or where the previous school leader was not perceived as trustworthy. The faculty and staff may have become jaded by a multiplicity of factors, including the failure of past administrators to support them in their work. It is important to recognize that those individuals come by their wariness honestly. It will be important for you to be patient and persistent in earning their trust, rather than taking their suspicion personally.

Fostering trust begins with your willingness to extend trust to the individuals in the school—not blind or naive trust, but as much trust as can be reasonably justified based on what you know. A bias toward trust or a trusting stance holds that the outcomes will be better if you assume people are trustworthy. By extending trust, you may be able to provoke more trustworthy behavior on the part of others than if you were to approach them with suspicion. You will have to discern the appropriate and prudent level of trust, based on the maturity and history of the group as you find it. Trustworthy behavior on your part can cultivate trustworthy norms of behavior among the faculty, staff, and students. In fact, one of the most powerful things a school leader can do in his or her first year on the job is to articulate and enforce norms of behavior that will foster a greater level of trust within the school community. Enforcing the norms means calling people who break those norms to account for their actions, doing so in ways that do not embarrass, humiliate, or demean them but that challenge them to behave better in the future.

Because your actions are going to be scrutinized and mined for meaning as to your intentions and character, it is important to be thoughtful about choosing actions that send a message you want to have received. The first year is not a time to make large, unilateral structural changes, except perhaps to create a mechanism for others to have input into decision making if one does not already exist. Make changes that are symbolic in nature and that communicate your commitment to teachers as well as to students and their families. Think

(continued)

about the message that is sent by the entrance to your school. If it doesn't send a positive message, redecorate to signify that "student learning is at the center of what we do; parents are our partners in this endeavor; and excellence is achieved through the caring, dedication, and diligence of our teachers." If the teachers' lounge is a dingy, dismal place, offer to raise the funds and enlist parent volunteers to refurbish it (under the direction of the teachers, of course!). You may stock it periodically with snacks or fresh flowers to create a welcoming space that acknowledges good work and sends a positive message.

Find ways—both large and small—to communicate your goodwill and caring toward each member of the school community. Be ready to affirm evidence, even glimmers, of excellence from all corners of the school community. But always be sincere in your thanks and praise; even young children can sense a gratuitous compliment. Small expressions of appreciation for extra effort or good citizenship, a kind word or a brief note, can go a long way toward fueling the motivation for more of the same. Make sure that you are true to your word, and be reliable in following up on the concerns that are brought to you. Carry a notepad or smartphone to write them down if you need to. Be truthful, even if the truth is, "I don't know, I'll try to find out" or "I can't share that information with you."

Be as open with information and control as you feel you can afford to be. One of the ways that school leaders can convey a sense of openness is through the use of humor, setting a tone of playfulness in ways that bind a group of people together into a community. Within the bounds of good judgment, engaging in humor and play will demonstrate your trust in students and teachers and your willingness to be vulnerable with them. This should never involve humor that is demeaning, sarcastic, or inappropriate, but it can be a way to build bonds of trust that makes the school a place where people want to be. Finally, demonstrate your expertise by helping members of the school community solve the problems they encounter in getting their work done.

It won't be easy because the demands on school leaders are complex and at times intense. But the trust you earn will facilitate whatever you hope to accomplish through your leadership at the school. One exercise to assist with the development and maintenance of genuine caring uses what Gallwey (2000) called the "STOP tool." STOP stands for Step back, Think, Organize your thoughts, and Proceed.

Gallwey suggested that effective leaders get in the habit of taking daily short STOPs as well as weekly and monthly long STOPs. You can use the daily short STOP, in part, to visualize one person in your school, to think back on recent interactions with that person, and to imagine what that person is dealing with in his or her life and work. Three questions are useful here: (1) What can I do to make this person's job easier? (2) Is there any unfinished business between us that I can clear up? and (3) How can I express kindness and caring to this person? Cultivating benevolence will become more natural and automatic for you as you increase your awareness of the individuals in your school building or district.

Finding time for reflection, whatever the format, is an important discipline for trustworthy school leaders. There is no doubt that educational leaders often function at a whirlwind pace that leaves little time for reflection and planning. But trustworthy leaders make the time. They conceive of reflection as part of their job description, not as an optional extra. Whether they do it first thing when they walk into the building or at another time during the day, trustworthy leaders use their capacity for critical thinking, visualization, reflective writing, intuition, and humor to guide and improve their management of time, energy, resources, and politics.

KEY POINTS ABOUT FOSTERING TRUST

- In the early stages of trust development, the reputation of a school leader plays an important role, but such personal factors as disposition to trust, values, attitudes, moods, and emotions also influence the relationship.
- High trust in educators is supported by such formal mechanisms as certification, job qualifications, hiring procedures, contracts, and rules as well as the informal mechanisms of norms, values, and a school culture that supports cooperation.
- Trust takes root as two parties gain experience and become able to predict how the other is likely to behave in a given situation, and as they develop a sense of care for one another and the relationship.

- As trust develops, it "gels" at different levels, depending on the degree of interdependence, knowledge, and experience.
- Authentic trust emerges when the parties have a deep and robust trust in each other, one that can endure an occasional disappointment or difference.
- Optimal trust is a balancing act, as there are dangers in trusting too much as well as in trusting too little.

QUESTIONS FOR REFLECTION AND DISCUSSION

1. What actions did you take when you first arrived at your school building, and how were they received? Was there a mismatch between what you intended and what people perceived? How has trust developed over time?
2. If you have missed the "golden mean" of optimal trust, have you tended to trust too much or trust too little? What have been the consequences?
3. How has a lack of knowledge of one another's culture created challenges for the development of trust in your school?
4. What is the "mood" in your school building? Is it productive, or does it get in the way of achieving school goals? How might conversation heighten awareness of this habit of mind or orientation toward what is to be done?

CHAPTER 4

BETRAYAL

It is easier to forgive an enemy than to forgive a friend.
—WILLIAM BLAKE

Situations that entail placing something we cherish in the care of another person are ones that require trust. To some extent at least, the outcomes we hope for are determined by someone else. To trust in such circumstances means that we can rest assured, confident that things will turn out all right. But what if they don't? What if our expectations are not met? What if the person we have trusted acts carelessly or takes advantage of our confidence to enhance his or her own outcomes? Situations inevitably arise in which what is cared for is harmed, even if by accident, or in which the trusted person betrays the trust placed in him or her and exploits the other for his or her own advantage.

The dynamics of trust in relationships are such that the nature of the trust can be altered instantaneously with a comment, a betrayed confidence, or a decision that violates the sense of care one has expected of another. When a violation occurs, trust can be shattered, leaving distrust and suspicion in its place (Burt & Knez, 1996). The initial reaction to a trust violation is often stunned disbelief as the victim begins to come to terms with the breach of expectations. Victims report feeling confused and being left with a sense of unreality. On reflection, those feelings often turn to anger and the desire for revenge (Bies & Tripp, 1996).

Although betrayals are possible in every realm of life, the focus here is on how betrayal plays out within schools and school districts and on what trustworthy school leaders can do to manage, mediate, and mend these betrayals. The culture and norms of a school or district can influence the likelihood that betrayals will occur. Organizational norms that emphasize ethical behaviors and a work environment of openness, trust, and respect discourage the violation of trust, whereas organizations characterized by negative internal politics, conflict over goals, and shifting coalitions lend themselves to a greater number of betrayals. Moreover, the culture and norms within a school may not always coincide with the personal expectations an employee holds, causing intrapersonal as well as interpersonal conflict. For example, Brian, a young teacher at Fremont, thought it was important to abide by contractual standards for staying until a specified time at the end of the school day, and he experienced both internal and external conflict over the norms at the school that allowed people to slip away soon after the students were dismissed.

WHAT IS BETRAYAL?

Betrayal is defined as a voluntary violation of mutually understood expectations that has the potential to threaten the wellbeing of the trusting person (Elangovan & Shapiro, 1998). Betrayal involves an action or behavior; for there to have been a betrayal, there needs to have been an actual violation rather than just the thought or idea of betrayal. An act of betrayal has the *potential* to cause harm to the trusting person, even if other factors mitigate the actual harm experienced. And even if the violation is not detected by the trusting person, it still constitutes a betrayal. For example, a betrayal occurs when someone reveals potentially damaging information that was shared in confidence, even if the trusting party never learns that his secret has been shared.

In betrayal, the perpetrator makes a choice to violate the expectations of the trusting party because he or she lacks the motivation to conform to the expectations of the other or becomes motivated to violate these expectations. The motivation to betray results from dissatisfaction with the current situation such that the person believes there is more to be gained than lost by betraying the other person's expectations. Unhappiness with the current situation increases the likelihood of betrayal by lowering the benevolence and integrity of the trusted person. A drop in benevolence implies that the trusted person cares less for the well-being of the other and may be willing to engage in behaviors that might cause him or her harm. Similarly, a drop in integrity implies that the trusted one is less committed to the shared principles at the core of the relationship and may search for justification to switch to an alternate set of principles, even if it means harming the other's best interests. People don't generally like to think of themselves as bad people with poor morals, so they find a way to justify their behavior, at least to themselves, with the hope that they will never be put in the position of having to reveal this (potentially flimsy) rationalization to others. This shift in principles is followed by a decrease in openness, as the betrayer seeks to avoid detection. The guardedness that comes with the need to be ever watchful of one's words and actions to avoid being caught in the act of betrayal can be as damaging to the ongoing relationship as the actual act of betrayal itself. See figure 4.1 for a graphic depiction of this anatomy of betrayal.

In schools, betrayals can be classified as falling into two broad categories: damage to a sense of civic order and damage to one's sense of identity (Bies & Tripp, 1996). Trust violations that result in a damaged sense of civic order involve a breach of rules or norms governing behavior and of expectations of what

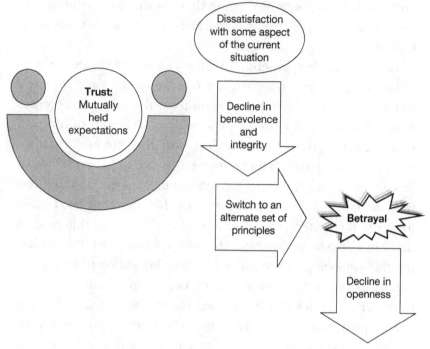

Figure 4.1 The Anatomy of Betrayal

people owe to one another in a relationship. These include honor violations, such as lying, breaking promises, or stealing ideas or credit from others. Such violations could also include shirking job responsibilities or changing the rules "after the fact." A damaged sense of civic order could also result from the abusive exercise of authority, such as coercive or threatening behavior, improper dismissal, favoritism, or sexual harassment (Harris, 1994). In addition, trust can be damaged by the disclosure of private confidences and secrets. Although Fred violated the trust of his faculty mainly by shirking his job responsibilities, Gloria committed betrayals through violations involving the abuse of authority.

I'm really passionate about reading the research literature
and staying up with national trends. Whenever I bring an idea
to our superintendent about something new we might do in
our district, she invariably shoots it down and says it won't work.
Then two or three weeks later, she announces the same idea
as *her* idea, and then delegates it to me for implementation!
I'm really getting fed up with this game.

—HANNAH, ASSISTANT SUPERINTENDENT

The second category of trust violations involves a damaged
sense of identity. One's sense of identity can be damaged as a
result of receiving public criticism; being the target of wrong or
unfair accusations; being blamed by another person for his or her
own mistakes; or fielding insults, either personal or to the collective of which one is a part. When one's dignity has been damaged,
one often feels duty-bound to redress the wrong and may invest
enormous energy in conjuring up a plan to do so. White teachers
at Fremont felt betrayed by Fred's tacit approval of the exclusion-
ary practices of the African American teachers on the faculty. At
Lincoln, Gloria's numerous insults (both explicit and implicit)
to her teachers' professionalism, capability, and commitment, as
well as her habit of apportioning blame to her faculty for personal
mistakes, left teachers feeling wounded and betrayed.

Our principal is all about blame. If there is a problem,
she has to establish that it is someone's fault other
than her own before she can begin to solve the problem.

—MICHELLE, HIGH SCHOOL TEACHER

Whatever its cause, betrayal disrupts trust and damages relationships. The effects of betrayal can be lasting. People generally do not forget, even if they forgive and find a way to move on
(Rachman, 2010). In a study focusing on betrayal in the workplace,

50 percent of the incidents recounted by participants had occurred more than twenty years earlier, and 25 percent had occurred more than thirty years before (W. Jones & Burdette, 1994). The level of trust prior to a betrayal can have an interesting impact on the response to the violation. Where trust prior to a betrayal was high, employees were more likely to overlook evidence of a trust violation, making excuses for the transgression as a misunderstanding, an unintentional event, or a temporary lapse, whereas in low-trust relationships the act was more likely to be seen as intentional and malevolent. However, once the evidence of a betrayal was sufficiently strong that it could no longer be ignored, the emotional reaction of the previously trusting party was much more potent than that of those with previously low trust, resulting in a stronger motivation to seek revenge (Robinson, Dirks, & Ozcelik, 2004). Thus, leaders who cultivate high-trust relationships would do well to be diligent in maintaining that trust.

Although betrayal involves a violation of personal trust, it is not necessarily unethical or antisocial. A trusted colleague may be put in a situation where he or she has to choose between betraying a colleague and violating personal principles or organizational norms. For example, if a teacher learns that a friend and colleague has been skimming school fundraising proceeds or has engaged in inappropriate romantic dalliances with a student, disclosing this information to the administration would constitute a betrayal of the coworker but could be based on the ethical principles of the informant (Elangovan & Shapiro, 1998).

I used to love my teaching job. I was good friends with my principal and had several close friends on the faculty. All that changed, though. Last spring, a few days before our state testing, one of the teachers on my team told me that he had opened the sealed writing prompt to give some similar prompts to his students for practice. He offered to share it with me too. I declined, but one other teacher on our team did look over the prompt. At first I kept quiet, but then I just felt heartsick. My conscience was eating away at me. When I came forward to tell, there was a big ruckus, with a state investigation and a story in the paper. It made our school look bad, so I was ostracized by the whole faculty, especially the principal. No one would even speak to me. It was as if I were the one who had done something wrong.

—AMY, FORMER FOURTH-GRADE TEACHER

Conflict is an inevitable part of life, and it is just as inevitably part of life together at school. It is important not to confuse all conflict with betrayal. School change and school reform are fraught with conflict, with disagreements predictably arising as to not only the best course of action but also the pace and order of change (Fullan, 2003). In addition, some people are advantaged by the changes, whereas others may lose favored positions of power. When handled constructively, conflict does not necessarily constitute a betrayal, but when handled poorly, conflict often results in damaged trust (Uline, Tschannen-Moran, & Perez, 2003).

Conflict, like leadership, has two dimensions: commitment to the relationship and commitment to the task (Thomas, 1976). People who are unskilled in conflict resolution tend to handle conflict with either a "fight" response or a "flight" response. The fight response implies a strong commitment to the task or goal to be accomplished, and the flight response implies little commitment to the task or goal—but both responses are low on investment in the relationship. Gloria demonstrated a fight response to conflict, sacrificing her relationships with teachers in the interest of "winning" her version of reform. Fred, in contrast, demonstrated a flight response, giving up on the task of school improvement as well as relationships in the interest of avoiding conflict. In so doing, he abdicated his responsibility to both the students and the teachers. Fullan (2003) asserted that "conflict avoidance is an act of moral neglect" (p. 32).

The problem with these fight or flight responses is that both extremes tend to do damage to the trust in a relationship. The fight response demonstrates a willingness to bring harm to the other in the interest of accomplishing one's objectives and getting one's needs met. This violates the sense of benevolence required in a trusting relationship. The flight response also does damage to the long-term viability of the relationship: in avoiding the conflict, a person demonstrates a willingness to give up on the goals that fueled the relationship in the first place or to leave the relationship altogether.

In ongoing relationships like those in schools, neither fight nor flight is likely to be productive as the predominant approach to conflict because both responses demonstrate a low commitment to the relationship. Other options exist. Accommodation is a conflict style that implies a stronger commitment to the relationship than to the task or goal and, therefore, a willingness to relinquish the goal. This reflects a "tend and befriend" response to conflict that is often seen among women or people with little power who are unable or unwilling to leave a relationship (Peterson & Peterson, 1990). Although acquiescing in any given situation may be an appropriate and acceptable response, a pattern of acquiescence over time will result in an imbalance in the relationship that sets the stage for eventual betrayal. Compromise is a balance between a commitment to the task and a commitment to the relationship and so implies a willingness to give up part of the goal in the interest of preserving the relationship.

Collaboration implies a strong commitment to both the relationship and the task so that the parties negotiate a solution in which the needs of both are met. This approach can require creativity and a problem-solving focus because conflict, by its very nature, stems from a perceived incompatibility of desires. But even passionately held differences can be negotiated when there is an underlying sense of trust and goodwill—of conviction that the other party will do what he or she can to avoid causing harm to the trusting party. This doesn't just take strong commitment; it also takes skills that many people, adults and children alike, have not mastered. In the next section, we'll see the toll that Fred's poor conflict resolution skills and consequent conflict avoidance had on Fremont.

THE KEEP-THE-PEACE PRINCIPAL

Fred was an affable, friendly man. His congenial mannerisms and easy smile quickly put strangers and children at ease. Fred liked pretty much everybody and wanted everybody to like him. He liked to position himself near the front door each morning to greet the teachers and students as they arrived at school. He especially made a point of greeting the more troubled and troublesome students by name, encouraging them to make good choices and to have a good day.

When Fred became a principal, he enjoyed the status and relative lack of stress of the job. He expected primarily to be a manager, to make sure that the buses ran on time and that the building was maintained in reasonable repair. With the pressures of the accountability movement, however, everyone seemed to be looking to the principal to make things right in the school. There were pressures from above and pressures from below, and Fred felt squeezed in the middle. Fred had always enjoyed his job, so he decided just to do what he could do in the hours he was at school and not to stress about the rest. Fred freely admitted that he was not an instructional leader. He noted that such leadership had not been the expectation when he received his training. He fulfilled his obligation to visit classrooms once or twice a year and to complete a preprinted evaluation form. But having a conversation or giving substantive feedback tended to evoke an uncomfortable response, so he generally gave everyone high ratings and left their evaluation forms in their mailboxes to be signed and returned to him without meeting face-to-face.

Although Fred talked the talk of high expectations, his lack of follow-though when teachers violated even minimum standards, and his leniency with students, led his faculty to discount his words. His motivation seemed to be to avoid conflict at all costs. Fred lost the trust of his faculty not through ill will, but through failure to deal constructively with conflict. He lacked the courage and the skills to manage the inevitable conflicts inherent in running a school, particularly one in an urban setting or one engaged in change.

Fred liked to think of himself as a progressive, collaborative leader. The faculty at Fremont appreciated Fred's openness with information and his willingness to include them in making decisions that affected the functioning of the school. This inclusiveness, however, allowed Fred to avoid some of the more unpleasant aspects of his job, such as holding resistant faculty members accountable to the agreed-on program of the school. The faculty saw Fred's use of shared decision making as an excuse for him to abdicate responsibility and avoid conflict. In the name of collaboration, Fred delegated away most important decisions about the school. Paul spoke for many teachers at Fremont as he expressed his frustration at Fred's inability to make key decisions:

> It's very hard for him to make an executive decision. He'll say, "What do you think?" or "What do we want to do as a staff?" That's fine as far as shared decision making, but if it concerns a really important issue I think he needs to make the decision. There are a lot of decisions we would like to see him make that we don't really feel are staff decisions. They're administrative decisions.

A major problem concerning effectiveness at Fremont was a segment of the faculty that was simply not doing its job. Fred's

continual empty threats and inability to hold teachers accountable to standards of conduct had worn thin with the faculty. Paul
vented his frustration at Fred's empty demands:

> What bothers staff members is that they will identify a prob-
> lem, like test scores at a certain grade level, and he'll say, "I
> won't tolerate this. I'm going to deal with this." And nothing is
> ever done—just so no waves are created. Or if it is somebody
> who is abusing sick time, who has no sick time but just never
> comes—it's, "You know, it's only a matter of time and they'll
> be gone." But it still continues and nothing happens. We have
> people here who have never bought into our program, and
> every year he says, "You may want to consider transferring,"
> but every year nothing happens. He needs to call them pri-
> vately and say, "I will do everything for you; but you are not
> buying into our program. You need to leave." But he won't do
> it. And I think the staff would fall on their hands and knees
> and bow to him if he would do that. You cannot just be the
> facilitator—you have to be the leader.

A failure to follow through with threats can be as damaging
to trust as the breaking of a promise. Although the recipient of
a broken threat may consider the lenient person to be more lik-
able, he or she will likely rate that person as less trustworthy. Trust
may be enhanced by credible, but sparingly used, threats and
sanctions (Lindskold & Bennett, 1973). Principals must have the
courage to exercise controls that punish those who violate trust,
as these controls will have the effect of constraining employee
behavior within acceptable bounds. Brian, a novice teacher at
Fremont, echoed Paul's concerns:

> We have teachers who are late every single day. It's very fla-
> grant with some staff members, and he needs to put his foot
> down and say, "We expect you to be here at 8:30, and I expect
> you to stay until 3:45. And that's the way it's going to be." But
> he won't. He doesn't do that.

Brian was put in a difficult position when he attempted to fill the gap left by Fred's unwillingness to take action. He continued:

> We have people coming in late. That's something that should be dealt with. And it's not; he's not enforcing his rules. I spoke up in one of our meetings, so then I was laughed at. They said, "Oh, now we have to stay late because of you."

Brian felt ostracized and belittled because of his attempts to get the faculty to live up to even minimum contract requirements.

Poorly performing teachers don't just hurt their students; they can have a negative impact on their fellow teachers as well. Having faculty members who neglect their duties, and who do so with impunity, has a debilitating effect on a school, as Fullan (2003) has noted:

> Nothing undermines the motivation of hard-working teachers more than poor performance in other teachers being ignored over long periods of time. Not only do poor performing teachers negatively affect the students in their classes, but they also have a spillover effect by poisoning the overall climate of the school. (p. 78)

Brian was cognizant of the toll the lack of accountability was having on his own commitment level. He was disappointed to watch his own principles slipping.

> The kids leave at 3:15. We're supposed to be here until 3:45. I'll find myself leaving at 3:30 sometimes because it's like, "Why should I stay here? No one else is here." So I find that my moral obligation is less because no one else is doing it. I can say I'm staying because that's the rule. I can have that moral fiber, and I still think I do. But then I also think, "What good is it going to do me to sit here for fifteen more minutes when I could go do something else?"

Fred had a hard time motivating his faculty to stay late and work hard when he himself often left shortly after school ended.

The general apathy in school not only undermined Brian's commitment to his contract but also had an impact in his classroom. The low level of trust in the building and the lack of support were interfering with this novice teacher's developing sense of competence. Brian reported:

> As a new teacher, that kind of lack of accountability, lack of guidance, it hurts. I'm not supported. I need to have an experienced teacher say, "Have you tried this?" I've learned to shoot from the hip, and that's sad. Some of the stuff has already been done, and you don't realize it. You think you're doing something great, and then someone says, "Oh, that's been done." You're like, "Well thank you!" I want to make it real for the kids, and I'm still trying to learn to do that. I swear, if I didn't have to fight discipline all the time I don't know what kind of teacher I would be, but I think I would be a fantastic one. I find myself to a point where, I was always hoping I wouldn't be a teacher that would raise my voice and yell at a child. But I have yelled, and I feel sick.

The lack of support and accountability left Brian disappointed in the kind of teacher he was becoming. This young teacher had a genuine desire to have a positive impact on his students and to create engaging learning opportunities for them. Indeed, he might have been a fine teacher had he started his career in a setting that had offered more support and guidance, not to mention better role models. This young man, who had begun his career with a strong sense of commitment and caring for the low-income children he taught, might well fall short of fulfilling his potential.

There were other ways that Fred's lack of leadership left his teachers feeling unsupported and unprotected. In the name of shared decision making, Fred had delegated all faculty complaints to a building council made up of faculty members.

Complaints were to be made in writing, and the whole process was to be strictly confidential. When Kelli, who taught first grade at Fremont, tried to use the council to address a concern about another teacher, however, the situation became very unpleasant. Kelli reported that often the teacher who was supposed to share recess duty with her simply did not show up. Kelli was put in the difficult position of having to supervise the entire playground by herself. This other teacher was also consistently late to pick up her students at the end of recess, meaning that Kelli and her class lost learning time waiting for the other class to be retrieved. When Kelli took this concern to the council, there was a breach of confidentiality and word of her complaint quickly spread. Instead of getting the help she requested, Kelli was subjected to a harsh tongue-lashing by the other teacher and was ostracized by that teacher's friends. As a result of this incident, Kelli said she had given up on communicating about her problems to the principal or to the building council. She had decided that she would rather do her best to cope with the problem alone than subject herself to a repeat performance of what she had endured.

Another of the ways that the faculty felt betrayed by Fred was in his taking credit for results that almost wholly stemmed from teacher efforts. When Paul applied for and received a large grant for the school, he resented Fred's report to the school board in which he claimed credit for the grant. When the school began to show gains on test scores, teachers resented Fred's boasting about how "we" raised scores although he had provided very little in the way of instructional leadership. These instances might not have seemed like honor violations if Fred had played a more active role in helping teachers accomplish these goals.

Teachers at Fremont distrusted Fred because of his lack of reliability and competence. His integrity was also questioned when he failed to follow through on what he said he would do. Most of the faculty acknowledged that Fred meant well and trusted in his benevolent intentions. But when they couldn't count on him to deal with serious problems at the school, to hold teachers accountable to their obligation to students, and to make difficult decisions, they were left feeling very vulnerable. His desire to keep the peace and to avoid conflict created disharmony and distrust. At Fremont, without the leadership to cultivate and maintain productive working relationships, the environment was strained and difficult for all the participants.

For principals to engender trust, they need to do more than just be nice. Avoiding holding people accountable to their responsibilities within the school may have helped Fred cultivate the perception of his being a pleasant person, but it did not engender trust. Teachers were frustrated by Fred's failure to enforce even minimal rules, such as expected arrival and departure times of faculty, much less to address the abuse of sick time or to rebuke aides who refused to do the work they were assigned. When Fred, in the name of shared decision making, tried to get teachers to be the ones to police their own ranks but did not take action to back their attempts to deal with wayward teachers, the faculty felt betrayed.

A DEBILITATING CULTURE OF DISTRUST

Although we sometimes have no choice but to rely on someone we distrust, those are situations we normally would prefer to avoid. Whether it is a person we once trusted who has betrayed us, or someone we never grew to trust in the first place, it is uncomfortable to find ourselves in a relationship of interdependence in which our objectives cannot be met without the involvement of that person. Distrust is not necessarily an irrational or unwise response in these situations but rather may be based on knowledge, experience, and real differences in values (Barber, 1983). Distrust tends to provoke feelings of anxiety and insecurity, causing people to feel ill at ease and to expend energy in monitoring the behavior and possible motives of others (Govier, 1992).

Distrust can be costly. As trust declines, the costs of doing business increase because people must engage in self-protective actions and continually make provisions for the possibility that another person will manipulate the situation for his or her own advantage (Limerick & Cunnington, 1993). When teachers or students feel unsafe, energy that could be devoted to teaching and learning is diverted to self-protection. In the absence of trust, people are increasingly unwilling to take risks, and they demand ever greater protections to defend their interests (Tyler & Kramer, 1996). People may use various means to protect themselves from possible harm by the distrusted person and to minimize their vulnerability. Subordinates may withhold information, use pretense, or even practice deception to protect their interests. Administrators often resort to stepping up the use of control mechanisms, such as the enforcement of cumbersome rules and excessive monitoring to protect themselves. Although such steps may be necessary and important, they typically are counterproductive (Govier, 1992).

One of the most difficult things about distrust is that once it is established, it has a tendency to be self-perpetuating. In interactions with a distrusted person, even normally benign actions are regarded with suspicion. The negative beliefs about the other lead the suspicious person to discount any evidence that would help overcome distrust (Govier, 1992). The behavior of the distrusted person is systematically interpreted in such a way that distrust is confirmed. The communication that is needed to restore trust is regarded with suspicion, so that suspicion builds on itself. Administrators whose words are not trusted have lost the very tool they need to restore trust.

When I took over as principal at the high school,
I knew I would have my work cut out for me earning
the trust of the faculty because there had been a great
deal of hostility and animosity between the teachers
and the previous administration. I made a point of

positioning myself near the teachers' mailboxes in the
morning to greet and get to know the teachers. I got a taste
of just how tough the challenge was going to be one of the
first mornings, when after I'd said, "Good morning!
How are you?" to one of the teachers, I overheard
her muttering to a colleague on the way out, "I wonder
what she means by that!"

—PAT, HIGH SCHOOL PRINCIPAL

A lack of trust not only makes for an uncomfortable and
unpleasant work environment but also has a negative impact on
the overall effectiveness of the organization. This was evident at
Fremont, where student achievement scores were abysmally low.
Betrayals can damage morale and the ability of workers to collaborate. Productivity and motivation also are likely to suffer. When
broken promises by management were examined in one study,
distrust was significantly related to deterioration in employees'
performance and to intentions to leave the employer (Robinson,
1996). When there was high initial trust between an employee and
the manager, the employee's reactions to a perceived breach were
much less severe; however, when the initial trust was low, the breach
was much more likely to result in poor employee performance and
the desire to leave the organization. The consequences of a spiral
of distrust in a school include deterioration of the quality and effectiveness of communication and shared decision making, as well as a
decline in the citizenship and commitment of the teachers.

Constrained Communication

Schools need open communication to be effective, and distrust
is likely to have a deleterious effect on communication patterns.
When one is interacting with a distrusted person, especially if
that person holds more power within an organizational hierarchy, the goal of communication often becomes the protection

of one's interests and the reduction of one's anxiety rather than the accurate transmission of ideas. One may feel compelled to be evasive or to distort attitudes or information when communicating with a distrusted person. In an organizational culture of distrust, subordinates acknowledge the tendency to withhold information and to distort upward communication (Roberts & O'Reilly, 1974).

Teachers in low-trust schools describe constrained communication networks. The communication between principals and teachers is hampered by distrust. In a climate of suspicion, teachers are guarded as to whom they talk to and what they say. As we saw in the case of Kelli's disastrous run-in with the building council at Fremont, although teachers acknowledged that there were significant problems in their school, they were unwilling to reveal such problems and work to resolve them for fear of retaliation. Communication is often blocked or distorted to avoid confrontation. Where trust is low, teachers may avoid making contact with the principal, rendering it difficult for him or her to gain the information needed to be proactive. When there is a high level of trust between principals and teachers, teachers are more likely to have higher levels of confidence in the accuracy of information coming from the principal, a greater desire for interaction with the principal, and greater satisfaction with communication with the principal (Roberts & O'Reilly, 1974). Such a pattern of productive communication was evident between Brenda and the Brookside teachers. Open communication that flows from the people "in the trenches" can be a tremendous asset to a principal in orchestrating school improvement.

Our principal never has the courage to confront a concern directly with a teacher. He always couches it saying he has had calls "from concerned parents." One time the whole school was gathered on the bleachers for an assembly when we learned that the presenter had not

arrived. The kids were getting restless, so as one teacher
ran to the office to make phone calls and see what
was going on, another grabbed her guitar, and two of
her friends started to dance, putting on a silly,
impromptu performance. The principal must
have seen them from his office window because
later he called in those teachers to say that he had
had "some calls from parents" who thought
their performance was unprofessional. But that
was a lie because where they were wasn't visible
from the street.

—PAM, SECOND-GRADE TEACHER

Confined Decision Making

As mentioned in the discussion of openness, there are two motivations for involving teachers in making decisions concerning the life
of the school. The first motivation is simply to increase teachers'
satisfaction, loyalty, and acceptance of decisions. Leaders recognize that teachers have sufficient autonomy in schools and that if
they do not buy into a decision, they can undermine the effectiveness of an initiative by simply withholding their full effort, or even
by actively sabotaging its implementation. In this model, which
could be called "contrived collaboration," shared decision making is more form than substance; teachers' input is rarely taken
seriously. Often the decision has already been made before teachers are asked to participate. In the second model, principals and
teachers make decisions jointly. This model highlights teachers'
competence and acknowledges that they have valuable knowledge
and insights to bring to decisions. Higher-quality decisions is the
motivation for this more genuine form of shared decision making
that gives teachers actual influence over the outcomes of decisions
that affect them (Pounder, 1998; Short & Greer, 1997).

Shared decision making, as it has typically been exercised in schools, has been criticized as most often being of the first model, affording teachers little real influence over organizational decisions that matter to them (Malen, Ogawa, & Kranz, 1990). This model is rooted in distrust: distrust of teachers' potential contributions to decision making and of their willingness to implement decisions faithfully. The second model requires a good deal more trust in teachers and in their ability to act in the best interests of the school community and not out of narrow self-interest (Hoy & Tarter, 2008). When principals talk the talk of shared decision making but simply go through the motions, as in the first model, they undermine trust by raising teachers' expectations and then creating cynicism when words don't match actions.

When principals extend trust to teachers through shared control, they elicit greater trust from teachers. The level of shared decision making in a school is significantly related to the faculty's level of trust in the principal (San Antonio & Gamage, 2007; M. Tschannen-Moran, 2001, 2009). Paradoxically, when teachers have greater trust in the principal, this trust may actually decrease the need for teachers to be involved in as many decisions. When teachers feel confident that their interests will be well looked after, they may be more willing to extend decision-making authority to the principal and abide by the decisions that are made (Tyler & Degoey, 1996).

In general, teachers appreciate being asked to participate in making decisions about issues that affect them, as they were at Fremont. This pleasure is likely to sour, however, when they perceive that their involvement has no real impact, that they are blamed when the decisions do not work out the way they had hoped, or that the principal is simply using faculty participation to abdicate responsibility for upholding accountability within the school.

Corroded Citizenship and Commitment

Organizational citizenship has to do with instances when a worker spontaneously goes beyond the formally prescribed job requirements and performs nonmandatory behaviors without expecting to receive explicit recognition or compensation (Deluga, 1994; Organ, 1988). Organ (1988) emphasized the importance of organizational citizenship in promoting organizational effectiveness, noting that organizations cannot possibly write job descriptions that encompass all that will be required of an employee. These kinds of behaviors are particularly important for schools, where formal job descriptions can at best delineate broad parameters for the expectations of teachers' responsibilities. When citizenship behaviors such as courtesy, conscientiousness, sportsmanship, and civic virtue are absent, organizational life is likely to be strained. These strains were evident in the frustrations expressed by the teachers at Fremont. If schools attempt, however, to require citizenship activities, they may engender resistance and resentment.

Transformational leadership behaviors are leadership behaviors that are thought to spur employees to go beyond minimum requirements and to give their best for the organization. Transformational leadership describes the behavior of a leader who has articulated a clear vision, who is able to foster acceptance of group goals, and who holds high performance expectations, all while providing an appropriate model for followers to emulate. A transformational leader provides individualized support and intellectual stimulation. Studies have found that transformational leadership behaviors result in greater citizenship among subordinates, but *only if* the employees trust the leader. When employees do not trust the leader, these leadership behaviors do not lead to greater citizenship (Podsakoff, MacKenzie, Moorman, & Fetter, 1990; M. Tschannen-Moran, 2003). The implications for schools are significant. For school leaders to be effective at garnering organizational commitment and citizenship, they must earn the trust of the people who work for them.

At Fremont, organizational citizenship was very low. It was not just that the teachers put forth the minimum required by their contract; they put in the minimum they could get away with.

Teachers reported that many of their colleagues came late and left early and abused the sick leave allotted in their contract. They also reported teacher's aides who spent their time in the office chatting with the secretaries, even during the ninety-minute block of intensive instructional time in the mornings when they were most needed in the classrooms, or who refused to do recess duty even if they were assigned that task. Kelli described her dismay at discovering that the snacks she had prepared for her students to eat during their break from standardized testing had been eaten by an aide! At Lincoln, Allisha reported a veteran teacher who watched television every afternoon while his class was assigned seat work. Because this man was outwardly compliant and often acted as the principal designee when Gloria was out of the building, Gloria turned a blind eye to this behavior, while she harassed much more dedicated teachers who questioned her.

Teachers at both Fremont and Lincoln struggled to maintain their own dedication and commitment in an atmosphere that did not support that effort. For some, poor citizenship led to disillusionment with the whole enterprise of teaching. Allisha, a second-year teacher, questioned whether she would remain in the teaching profession, saying:

> That's why I'm in school now, because I can't see retiring as a teacher. I thought that we would have much more respect as teachers. I was expecting more respect from our principal, and basically we get no respect. She gives more respect to the assistants that work in this building. She gives them something to do, and they won't do it. But let any of us say that and it's a whole different story, you know.

The teachers interviewed at Fremont and Lincoln either had put in for transfers or felt they needed to give a rationalization for staying. They spoke about liking the children and wanting to make things better for their low-income students. Rob, a teacher at Lincoln, described how many of his hours outside of school were spent attending his students' sporting events and concerts. He described lying awake at night thinking about his students and how he could address the difficulties they were having. During the winter months, Rob purchased many sets of hats and mittens for his students. Even students who were not in his class would come to him for these things when word got around. As much as these teachers cared about their students and the work they were doing, in the absence of a concerted effort by the entire faculty, there was a general sense of discouragement.

A teacher in our school made a mistake and used a curse word when she was yelling at a kid. The kid's parents made a big issue out of it, and our principal just buckled under the pressure. She pressured the teacher into taking a leave of absence for the rest of the school year—six weeks before the end of the year. I doubt she'll be back next year. She is a really good teacher; she just lost her temper with this kid. Morale is really low. The whole faculty feels unprotected—like if a parent complained, our principal would not back us up.

—CAITLYN, MIDDLE SCHOOL SPANISH TEACHER

In schools where trust is high, the level of organizational citizenship also tends to be high (G. R. Jones & George, 1998; M. Tschannen-Moran, 2003). At Brookside, not only were teachers considerate of one another, they also went far beyond the minimum required of them. Kathy, a fourth-grade teacher, described the faculty's reaction to Brenda's expectation that every teacher make at least one positive contact with every parent in his or her class within the first two weeks of school:

> We could say no. Contractually we could say no. It's a pain, it takes time and work, and most of it you do from your home or you spend hours here at school. She expects it. She can't force us to do it because it's not contractual. Yet, we have

such a high respect for her, and we want her backing when something goes wrong, so we do it. I mean, we fuss and groan and grumble about things, but most of the time if she says, "Do this," then we try to do our best.

All of the teachers interviewed at Brookside described ways that they willingly responded to requests to go beyond the minimum, from attending an annual Saturday planning retreat in the spring to hosting a fall sleepover, or participating in other extra programs at the school. Brenda had earned the trust of her faculty by being a valuable resource in times of trouble. Whether teachers were struggling with the behavior of a particular student, with how to plan and present a given curricular unit, or with how to cope with a difficult parent, they reported that they could rely on her for help. In exchange, they were willing to work hard and give their best.

Nobody trusts our principal. The way our school office is constructed, you have to walk past the principal's office to get to the faculty mailboxes. But there's a back door near the mailboxes, so faculty will regularly exit through the front door and come around through the back to get their mail. I have to admit, I've even taken that route myself some days!

—BERNIE, HIGH SCHOOL ASSISTANT PRINCIPAL

 PUTTING IT INTO ACTION

To be a trustworthy school leader takes courage. It also takes sensitivity. And it takes a willingness to deal with difficult situations and difficult people in a straightforward and firm manner. A caring stance does not mean that teachers are not held accountable. On the contrary, your caring and commitment to students demand that you hold high expectations for teachers' performance. These high expectations should be bolstered by the support and guidance you offer to help teachers meet these standards.

You need to blend pressing for goal achievement with demonstrating concern for teachers and staff. It takes wisdom and sensitivity to discern how to balance a task orientation with a focus on nurturing relationships, as one or the other may predominate in particular circumstances and situations. But overall, your leadership of the school will need to evidence both support and challenge in good measure. In times of conflict, this same balance of commitment to the task and commitment to relationships will play out when you host productive forums in which differences can be aired and understood, so that constructive solutions can be found. Conflict avoidance on your part may leave your staff and teachers feeling vulnerable and result in their withholding effort and commitment.

To be trusted as a school leader means conducting yourself in a way that is above reproach. You will need to avoid breaches of civic order, such as honor violations or using your authority in ways that are seen as abusive or manipulative. You also need to protect the dignity of every member of your school community to avoid causing any damage to others' sense of identity.

KEY POINTS ABOUT BETRAYAL

- The initial reaction to betrayal is often stunned disbelief that later turns into anger and the desire for revenge.
- Betrayal occurs when dissatisfaction with the current situation causes a drop in the benevolence and integrity of the trusted person.
- Trust violations in schools can be categorized as coming from a damaged sense of civic order or from damage to a person's or group's sense of identity.
- As a leader, avoiding conflict is an act of moral neglect that is likely to garner distrust.

- When forced to work with a distrusted person, people are likely to feel ill at ease. This discomfort may motivate them to protect themselves by withholding or even distorting information.
- In a climate of distrust, teachers are unlikely to give their best efforts to the school and its mission. In such a climate, shared decision making is often a sham.

QUESTIONS FOR REFLECTION AND DISCUSSION

1. When have you felt betrayed at work, and what was your reaction? Did the violation stem from a damaged sense of civic order or from a damaged sense of identity? How did you interpret the motivation of the perpetrator? Was trust ever restored? If so, how?

2. What instances have you witnessed in which a sense of betrayal has lowered people's commitment, interfered with their performance, and increased their desire to leave their school?

3. To what extent does the culture in your school discourage betrayal through norms of trust, openness, and respect? Or is the culture of your school characterized by conflict over goals, negative internal politics, and shifting coalitions that lend themselves to betrayal?

4. How is conflict handled in your school? Is it avoided and suppressed, does it tend to get ugly and out of control, or is it handled constructively? What are the consequences of this conflict management style? How could the quality of dialogue be improved with training in better conflict management skills?

5. Recall a time when working through a conflict in a constructive way led to a positive outcome and perhaps surfaced options that would not have been considered had there not been competing interests.

CHAPTER 5

REVENGE

Revenge is a dish best served cold.
—ANONYMOUS PROVERB

When we have trusted someone, we have held certain expectations of that person in a situation where we felt vulnerable. If those expectations were not met, when our trust has been betrayed, we are likely to feel compelled to respond. Whether the response leads to the restoration of trust or to an escalation of conflict depends on the choices made by the actors in the situation. Trust ebbs and flows as parties choose how to respond to instances of broken trust, either by engaging in the effort required to repair the relationship or by choosing various forms of revenge.

THE DYNAMICS OF REVENGE

When a violation of trust has occurred, the way the victim understands the cause of the violation affects the likely response, specifically whether there is a desire for revenge. When people were asked to recount on-the-job experiences of betrayal, the level of responsibility the victim ascribed to the perpetrator influenced the desire for revenge. When the victim concluded that an action was outside the control of the perpetrator, revenge was not sought;

however, when the victim held the perpetrator responsible for the violation, there was motivation for revenge (Bies & Tripp, 1996). Victims assigned blame and sought revenge when they perceived the behavior to have grown out of selfishness or malevolence on the part of the perpetrator. Victims also assigned responsibility to the system or organization as a whole for hiring or failing to constrain the perpetrator.

Responding to Betrayal

There are a number of revenge strategies that victims may consider. Some people enjoy indulging in revenge fantasies, conjuring up elaborate scenarios of how the perpetrator might be hurt or publicly humiliated. Although they don't intend to act on these fantasies, there is comfort in imagining that "justice will be done." Other victims express their anger and outrage in public ways, recounting the betrayal to others to stir up sympathy and to harm the reputation of the perpetrator. The victim's act of revenge may then lead the perpetrator to feel betrayed in return. This can spark a self-perpetuating cycle of feuding, each side engaging in a tit-for-tat volley of insults, snubs, and betrayal, fueling a spiral of distrust.

Our principal accused some teachers of entering his computer after hours to look at his evaluation records. A few days later, he parked in a handicapped parking space, and one of the teachers alerted the police, who ticketed him.

—TANYA, MIDDLE SCHOOL TEACHER

Some victims simply withdraw, avoiding any social contact with the person who has betrayed them. Others may prefer to confront the perpetrator, although the motivations for the confrontation may differ. Some may arrange a confrontation seeking to expose the misdeeds of the perpetrator and to see this person put to shame, whereas others might arrange for a private confrontation seeking to restore the relationship by making the perpetrator aware of their hurt, anger, and disappointment, hoping to negotiate a resolution. For example, if a victim feels that she has suffered a damaged sense of identity, she might seek the restoration of her reputation. Based on an apology, some form of making amends, or a commitment to behave differently in the future, a victim might be willing to offer forgiveness. There is power in forgiveness because the victim, not the perpetrator, decides whether trust is to be restored. Some harms, however, may be irreversible—in these circumstances the victim may be unwilling ever again to extend trust to the person who has caused him or her harm (Bies & Tripp, 1996). See figure 5.1 for a map of the pathways of revenge.

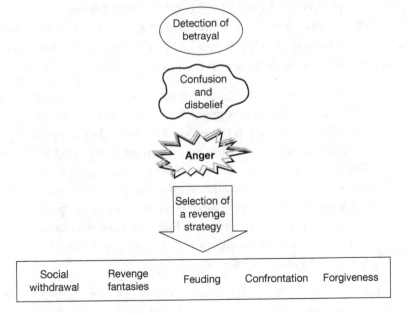

Figure 5.1 The Path of Revenge

The Complexity of Revenge

Revenge is not solely an emotional reaction to a violation; a good deal of thinking and planning go on as well. A victim's initial reaction to learning of a betrayal is often feelings of disorientation and stunned disbelief. This confusion usually turns to anger as the reality of what has occurred sets it. But a study of revenge revealed that, contrary to stereotypic notions, victims' choice of revenge strategy tended to be "cool and calculated, . . . it appeared to be quite rational in both deliberation and delivery" (Bies & Tripp, 1996, p. 259). A complicating factor in the dynamics of revenge, however, is evidence of "different arithmetics" (Bies & Tripp, 1996, p. 259) between victim and perpetrator, each assessing the cost of the perceived damage differently. These different calculations, and the responses they evoke, play a role in the escalation of conflict. On reflection, victims are likely to "discover" more malevolence on the part of the perpetrator, thus enhancing blame, paranoid cognitions, and conspiracy theories that may lead them to seek social support and reinforcement for their perceptions.

Betrayal may lead to not only a motivation for revenge but also to resentment. Solomon and Flores (2001) have drawn a distinction between revenge and resentment:

> Revenge is quick, indeed, sometimes almost instantaneous. (When it is immediate, it might better be viewed as retaliation.) Resentment tends to be slow and simmering, steeped far more in the dream of vengeance than in its actuality. That is precisely what makes resentment so dangerous, for whereas revenge can sometimes indeed restore the balance and provide a level playing field on which to restart negotiation and renew mutual understanding, resentment, because of its clandestine and defensive nature, does not allow for that opportunity. (pp. 142–143)

Resentment is directed not at a situation but rather directly at other people (one's boss, one's colleagues, organizational leaders in general). Resentment can foster distrust because it also tends to be vengeful. A resentful person "allows his own sense of importance and wounded merit to fester inside him until he is poisoned by it and incapable of creative or constructive action" (Solomon & Flores, 2001, p. 112). A school culture that embodies a mood of resentment can lead to deterioration of performance, a lack of initiative, and diminished trust among coworkers. Sabotage and other forms of collective action in defiance of the interests of the institution or its management are typically products of resentment.

My motto is, "Don't get mad, get even." My principal
laid into me in a faculty meeting in front of my colleagues.
I'm going to make him sorry. The next time he
wants anything from me, anything at all, the answer
is just going to be "No!"

—JEFF, HIGH SCHOOL HISTORY TEACHER

Revenge does not have to be seen in an altogether negative light, however; it can play a potentially positive role in organizational life (Bies & Tripp, 1996). Not only can revenge act as a constraint against the abuse of power and injustice, but also it can promote cooperation and be a potent motivator for constructive change. In an act of revenge after a year of being subjected to insults and blame on the part of their new principal, the teachers of one urban elementary school all refused to sign their contracts until they received assurances that the principal would not return the following year. In another instance, teachers in an upscale suburban community got revenge for the demeaning remarks about teachers made by the superintendent during a difficult contract negotiation session by initiating a petition drive to pressure the superintendent to retract the statements. With the assistance of the PTA, the teachers printed the petition with hundreds of signatures in a full-page advertisement in the local newspaper. The superintendent publicly apologized for making the remarks. Revenge has a way of equalizing some of the power differential in an organization. It gives victims a choice of how to respond to a breach of trust, and it affords them some control over if and when they will again offer their trust. The next section details the ways that the faculty at Lincoln felt betrayed by Gloria and the tactics they used to seek revenge.

THE OVERZEALOUS REFORMER

Gloria saw herself as a reformer with the best interests of the children at heart. When she took over the principalship, she was determined to make immediate changes in the way things were done at Lincoln and to get rid of any teachers who didn't want to come along. By pressing ahead before building trust with her faculty, however, Gloria alienated people and became engaged in a power struggle with her teachers. At a faculty meeting early in her first year at the school, Gloria assailed the teachers for their lack of success with student test scores. When the teachers protested about the many challenges they faced in educating the children from this impoverished community, Gloria responded in a matter-of-fact tone,

> OK, fine. I want you each to go back to your classroom and prepare a list of the names of all of the students in your classes that you don't think you can bring up to standard by the end of this school year. I want those lists on my desk first thing tomorrow morning.

Continuing with her voice rising, she added,

> Tomorrow we're going to bring all those students to the auditorium and put them on the stage and take their picture. Then we're going to hold a press conference, because the

parents and the community have a right to know which of
their children *you can't educate!*

This confrontational and condemning stance made it clear
that Gloria was not a resource that teachers could count on to
assist with the many challenges they faced.

Instead of taking the time to invest in relationship building
before embarking on a systematic change process in which she
involved the teachers who were close to the action in their respective classrooms, who understood the culture of the community
and the school, and who would ultimately have to implement any
changes, she forged ahead with a top-down, "my way or the high-
way" approach. Gloria took too much responsibility for change at
Lincoln and failed to recognize that principals get much of their
work done through other people. It is the teachers who do the
central work of the school, and it is the job of administrators to
create the context for teaching and learning. When the teachers
resisted Gloria's initiatives, she asserted her authority, setting the
stage for the ensuing power struggle.

By the third year of her tenure at Lincoln, the power struggle
had become intense, morale had plummeted, and even teachers
who had initially been willing to give Gloria the benefit of the
doubt and work with her began to lose faith. Teachers referred
to the school as a war zone. There was an atmosphere of fear at
the school, and teachers were guarded in what they said for fear
of reprisal. Student achievement had failed to make the kinds of
gains Gloria had hoped for when she took over leadership of the
school.

In various ways, Gloria fell short across all the facets of trust—
benevolence, honesty, openness, reliability, and competence.
Gloria's failure to establish trust was particularly due to a perceived
lack of goodwill or benevolence toward the teachers. Teachers'
complaints centered on Gloria's failure to provide them with
adequate support. Teachers also saw her tactics as manipulative

and dishonest. For example, Gloria lost the faith of her faculty because of the means she employed to remove a struggling young teacher. Gloria initially challenged this teacher about her use of sick days on Fridays and Mondays. The teacher countered that she had used these days to take her young daughter to the doctor and that she was within the number of sick days allowed for in her contract. When the teacher contacted Rob, the union representative in the building, and asked him to be a part of any subsequent meetings on the subject, Gloria responded by questioning the teacher's competence. Gloria initiated an aggressive schedule of observation and evaluation of the teacher. Other teachers were angered by what they saw as the unfair treatment of this young teacher and worried that they could become victims of the same treatment if they were to challenge Gloria. Allisha, a second-year teacher at Lincoln, recounted the incident:

> We just felt after the first observation and evaluation that our principal was on a mission to get rid of her, and nothing she could have done would stop it. She even asked to be placed back in the Peer Assistance and Review program, and she was turned down for that. So there was nothing she could do. When Gloria was telling her that she didn't have control of her classroom, she was asking, "Well, what can I do? You are supposed to be giving me support. Give me advice, what can I do?" But none was offered. So we knew right then and there that she wanted her out. Gloria has always been nice to me, but then she was to the other teacher also. So you never know when she'll turn on you.

Although other teachers acknowledged that this novice teacher was having difficulty with classroom management, they faulted Gloria for not offering guidance and assistance before orchestrating the teacher's removal.

Trust in Gloria was further damaged when she tried to remove several teachers who were informal leaders, well liked and respected by the rest of the faculty, to bring in teachers whom she knew and who would be more compliant with her wishes. Because other teachers identified with the victims, distrust spread among the faculty. One of these informal leaders was Rob Stevens, a popular and well-respected fifth-grade teacher who had taught at Lincoln for a decade. In his capacity as union representative, Rob had come into conflict with Gloria, filing numerous grievances on behalf of various teachers in the school. In response to a reduction in workforce near the beginning of the school year, Gloria announced at a faculty meeting that Rob was being reassigned to teach second grade. Allisha described how the tactic was seen by the faculty as blatantly manipulative, as a means of getting him to transfer out of the building:

> At the beginning of the year we had a staff reduction. We had an opening in second grade, and we had an opening in a four-five split. So we had a staff meeting, and she came in and told us about the staff reduction. Then the next thing we know she goes, "Mrs. Johnson, you'll be teaching the four-five split, and Mr. Stevens (who has been teaching fifth grade for ten years!), you will be teaching second grade. Thank you. That's the end of our meeting. Goodbye." She turned around and walked away. Everyone turned and looked at Rob and asked, "When did she tell you this?" He said, "This is the first I've heard it!" She hadn't discussed it with him; she just announced it and that was that. We just knew instantly that he was going to transfer out. Everyone felt that that's what she wanted. But he didn't. He said he wasn't going to let her pull that one over on him. But he just feels betrayed because of what she did.

The betrayal was motivated by Gloria's negative assessment of the current situation, such that she had little concern for maintaining a positive relationship with Rob, and, in fact, seemed to hope that he would be angry enough to leave altogether. There was also a drop in Gloria's integrity as she constructed a rationale based on a set of principles not shared by Rob and other members of the faculty about an appropriate process for classroom reassignment.

Another incident involved Mary, a teacher who initially had worked very closely with Gloria to see her vision of turning the school around realized. Mary had worked to get a number of grants and special programs for the school. When Mary finally got fed up because of the lack of cooperation and appreciation, she started refusing special assignments. Gloria responded by trying to remove Mary from her position, which left Mary feeling hurt and betrayed. Mary felt doubly betrayed when Gloria's means of doing so was by calling into question her competence.

> I keep on getting things thrown into my mailbox. It is addressed to the principal, and it will be thrown into my box—about grants to write or a committee to chair. Now I just throw it back. So I finally wrote a note back and said, "I do not want to chair this committee, but I will be happy to participate." And that was read at a staff meeting, that that's what I had said, verbatim. Verbatim! . . . I had said to certain staff members that either it would be on the bulletin or she would find a way to let the whole staff know that I declined. After that, she told me I wasn't strong enough in my position and that she wanted someone else.

Although Mary felt deeply betrayed by Gloria, she nonetheless recognized that Gloria's negative behavior was caused, at least in part, by frustration after three years of trying to get the teachers to try new things or do more than the minimum required of them. She acknowledged that Gloria had come to the school with ideas for improving the curriculum but was discouraged by the lack of progress that had been made. Mary said:

> I can understand her frustration, and I can deal with that. I have seen people show an interest and then turn around and

not put in any effort on the follow-through. But I can't take responsibility for all the people on the staff and their unwillingness to learn.

Although Mary recognized that Gloria was both tired and frustrated, and with good reason, she was nonetheless disappointed by the lack of leadership and its consequences for both teachers and students.

There was a breach of civic order at Lincoln when teachers perceived Gloria to be using her authority manipulatively. Teachers wanted reassurance that their principal would be fair and accurate in evaluating them. They also wanted to be sure that fair procedures were followed, whether in regard to classroom and duty assignments or in the hiring of new staff. Integrity is demonstrated by a convergence of actions and words. Integrity, in the sense of consistency in one's statements was compromised when one person was told one thing and someone else was given a different answer to the same question. Teachers resented that Gloria had given negative teacher evaluations to teachers whom she wanted to replace with educators of her own choosing, even though she had previously been complimentary toward these same teachers. The pretense of an open hiring process to fill openings was also suspect when there were indications that she already had in mind the replacements she wanted to hire.

The effects of broken trust were multiplied when the teachers turned to each other, recounting the details of an infraction or an incident in which a teacher did not receive support, so that trust was also broken with all who listened empathetically and worried that they might become victims of the same kind of treatment. The gossip served to broaden the negative impact of these incidents beyond the teachers involved and drive down trust among the whole faculty.

One incident, reported by Rob, entailed damage to both the civic order and a sense of identity. The situation involved a group of teachers, of which Rob was a part, who had served on a committee to put together a technology plan for the school to take advantage of a statewide program. Although none of the teachers had any experience or training in grant writing, they had worked hard to do the necessary research, giving up time after school and during their spring break to write the proposal. Gloria was a member of the committee, but she rarely came to meetings or offered any assistance. Despite all their efforts, the proposal was not funded. When Rob arrived early to a faculty meeting, he overheard Gloria talking to a district official about the plan's rejection. Gloria's harsh remarks about the incompetence of the committee left Rob feeling hurt and unappreciated. He felt especially betrayed because Gloria had not carried her weight as a member of the committee. There was the sense that had the proposal been funded, Gloria would gladly have accepted credit for the process, but when it was rejected she blamed the committee members and failed to acknowledge her lack of leadership. Rob expressed reluctance to volunteer for any future committees.

Openness is another facet of trust with respect to which Gloria fell short. Studies of trust across hierarchical lines in organizations have proposed that openness is key if subordinates are to develop trust in their superiors because the withholding of important information is one means by which superiors maintain power or manipulate employees (Kramer, 1996; Mishra, 1996). At Lincoln, Gloria's lack of engagement with the rest of the faculty was a source of distrust. Rob described the situation this way:

> I see the worker bees and the Queen. The Queen stays in her hive, or in her office in this case. Everyone else is on the front line out here; we are working and getting the job done to the best of our ability. It is almost like two different worlds. And the only time they cross is maybe a discipline issue. It's almost like an island down there. We're out here working, you know, fighting the war, and there's no support.

Gloria was described as inaccessible. When interactions did occur, the tone was often negative and the content unhelpful. Rob continued:

> There is becoming a distinction between the workers and the managers. It is almost like the Wizard of Oz behind the drape, and you can't see, you can't talk to the wizard. You know they're there, but you can't communicate with them.

Teachers at Lincoln were very guarded in their own communication as well. When asked about incidents of broken trust at Lincoln, Allisha began, "I'll be vague about it." Mary switched the public address system to a privacy setting in the room where she was being interviewed. She was visibly shaken when a message from the office came through over the system, and it took several moments for her to regain her composure sufficiently to continue. She was reassured somewhat when she realized that the privacy setting might mean that information could be received in the office but not sent from it. She nonetheless seemed to be mentally rehearsing what had just been said to see if she had said anything incriminating or that she might be punished for disclosing. At the conclusion of the interview, Mary looked around furtively in the hallway and stairwell to be sure they were empty, and she led me out a back entrance to ensure that we would not be seen. All of the Lincoln teachers interviewed wanted reassurance that their confidentiality would be protected.

Although Gloria meant well and genuinely wanted to bring about more positive outcomes for the students in her school, she lacked the personal power needed to lead organizational change. Gloria had positional authority to bring about structural changes, and she exercised that power through the meting out of rewards and punishments at her disposal. She used undesirable class and duty assignments to punish teachers she perceived as not toeing the line, and she rewarded more compliant teachers with lax supervision, looking the other way when they demonstrated a lack of professionalism. But these tactics were insufficient to create the motivation and culture to support innovation and positive change. What Gloria lacked were personal sources of power, including the expertise to be a genuine resource to assist teachers in improving their instruction; nor did she represent the kind of person that her teachers would look up to and want to associate with and emulate. She seemed to lack the self-efficacy or belief in her own capability to bring about the positive transformation that she dreamed of at Lincoln, and therefore resorted to harsh and demeaning tactics.

A pervasive spiral of distrust had set in at Lincoln, making the faculty suspicious of the principal's motives for almost any action. Teachers reported breaches of civic order or what they felt was owed to them and to their colleagues, as well as assaults on their identities as professionals and as people. The incidents had an impact both on the teachers' performance and on their desire to remain a part of the organization. Although these teachers still felt a commitment to the children of their school and wanted to work hard based on their own sense of professionalism, they reported less than full effort by many of their peers. Of the three teachers interviewed at Lincoln, Rob and Mary had put in requests to transfer to other schools, and Allisha, in only her second-year as a teacher, expressed doubts about how long she would remain in the teaching profession. The consequences for the organization of the loss of trust were substantial.

A CULTURE OF CONTROL

One of the most difficult things about distrust in an organization is that it can lead to a culture of control. Schools are both bureaucratic and professional organizations. When schools are pervaded by a culture of control, they overemphasize the bureaucratic nature of the organization at the expense of the professional. Decision making is concentrated in the office of the administrator, and teachers are deprived of necessary professional discretion.

In such schools, the principal uses his or her power and authority to control and discipline teachers. In enforcing a control mentality, the administration obstructs innovation instead of helping teachers solve the problems they encounter in their work. Coercive rules and procedures punish subordinates rather than reward productive practices. Instead of promoting organizational learning, coercive procedures demand blind obedience and force reluctant subordinates to comply.

A bureaucratic orientation on the part of organizational leaders can undermine trust because it is based on an implicit distrust of the workers in the organization. There is an unspoken assumption that at each higher level of the hierarchy, the role occupants are just a little smarter and more capable and more committed to organizational goals than those below. There is also an assumption that workers at the most basic level of the organization want to evade responsibilities and withhold proper and full performance of obligations. In a school with a bureaucratic orientation, systems are designed to monitor and control teachers to enforce compliance with organizational directives they are assumed to resist (Adler & Borys, 1996).

Formal controls can interfere with the achievement of the very goals they were put in place to serve (Miller, 2004). Instead of promoting organizational learning, coercive procedures and excessive control by school leaders are likely to lead to resentment and resistance that can obstruct innovation and motivation (Cloke & Goldsmith, 2002; Hoy & Sweetland, 2001). Standardized controls and rigid procedures have been found to lead to a breakdown in efficiency and effectiveness in situations where a certain amount of discretion is needed for workers to do their job effectively (Fox, 1974; Miller, 2004). In a study of a professional organization in which a system of bureaucratic rules was introduced, conflict and hurt feelings resulted from the use of standardized procedures that threatened workers' sense of professionalism as employees perceived a mismatch between the tasks they performed and the management control systems they had to accommodate (Sitkin & Stickel, 1996).

As professionals they wanted the discretion to make decisions based on their training, not to be controlled by administrators who did not have in-depth knowledge of their work. Rigid rules and regulations are likely to be effective only when the requirements of a task are routine in nature and are understood well enough to be specified clearly and concisely. The work of fostering the learning and development of young human beings, in their infinite variety, does not fit this mold.

The work of schools is complex, changing as the needs of students vary. For teachers to work as professionals, they need the discretion to be responsive to the ever changing demands of their students and curricula. The attempts of principals and central office personnel to improve performance outcomes by instituting standardized, one-size-fits-all procedures often backfire because they strip teachers of the discretion necessary to be responsive to diverse student needs. In schools and school systems with a bureaucratic orientation, school leaders turn to the imposition of rules to assert their authority and try to bring faculty into compliance with their desires for the school (Hoy & Sweetland, 2001). Teachers resent these tactics, seeing them as assaults on their professional status. They become less, rather than more, willing to cooperate on a common agenda. Although teachers may outwardly comply with the rules, many will use their creativity to find ways to surreptitiously sabotage and thwart the leader's efforts (Solomon & Flores, 2001). The resulting power struggle is counterproductive to the development of a professional school community focused on responsiveness to student needs (Miller, 2004). Taken to the extreme, the culture of control leads to micromanagement, rigidity, and a proliferation of dysfunctional rules.

Micromanagement

Distrust by leaders is evident in the all too common practice of micromanagement. Micromanaging is a triumph of perfectionism and ego and a failure of trust. Closely supervising a subordinate, overspecifying job requirements by telling a capable person how to do his or her job, or redoing work that has been done by a subordinate to meet perfectionist standards shows disrespect and a lack of trust in the individual. Subordinates sense this distrust and are likely to become resentful and withdrawn, withholding both ideas and effort (Miller, 2004; Solomon & Flores, 2001). This withholding has a detrimental effect on schools, where ambitious collective goals can only be reached when teachers have the motivation, knowledge, and discretion necessary to be responsive to the diverse needs of students. Teachers tend to resent lockstep, one-size-fits-all curricula designed to "teacher-proof" the work of schools because they view them as an attack on their professional status and as impediments to achieving the goals of fostering student achievement and growth.

One of the harmful effects of the coercive overspecification of job elements is that it keeps teachers in a perpetual state of dependency. A culture of compliance interferes with teachers' developmental need for learning and growth, which may lead them to behave in immature ways (Cloke & Goldsmith, 2002). Indeed, keeping the most capable, intelligent, and creative teachers from exiting the field is a serious concern for the profession. For school leaders to cultivate greater maturity among their faculty members, they must support the learning and autonomy needs of teachers.

Our superintendent is a control freak. It is a small district, so he thinks he can keep his fingers in everything. He'll show up at the school unannounced, and you'll come across him squatting outside a classroom, listening to what's going on inside. When the weather is good, you'll find him lurking around outside under the open classroom windows, listening.

—TODD, ASSISTANT PRINCIPAL

Rigidity

It is not uncommon for an organization to respond to a perceived external threat by exercising increased control over workers and enforcing rigid adherence to standard operating procedures (Daly, 2009; Staw, Sandelands, & Dutton, 1981). These tactics can, in turn, hinder the effective operation of the organization and impair its adaptive response to the threat because communication becomes constrained, resources are hoarded, and workers become increasingly fearful and risk averse. In the midst of the accountability movement, schools are currently experiencing a perceived threat to their legitimacy. Becoming more rigid, however, is likely to be counterproductive. In the face of changing environmental forces, schools need to become more flexible, innovative, and adaptive to respond to shifting external circumstances. Trust is an essential resource for organizations experiencing crisis because it helps them avoid this rigidity and a "hunkering down" mentality (Daly, 2009; Mishra, 1996). Communication flows more easily, and resources are shared rather than hoarded so that they can be allocated in ways that will have the greatest benefit for the survival of the organization.

I can say that for almost all of my twenty-three years as an educator, I have worked for principals who've said to the teachers, "Work your magic!" and left us alone to do what we know how to do. And our students have always done very well. This year we have a principal who doesn't trust teachers a bit. She is very prescriptive about every aspect of what we do, and it's not what we know works for our students. I end up spending hours each week writing up elaborate lesson plans according to her way of doing things, but unless she is in my room, I teach in the way that I know works for my students. It is an exhausting waste of time. I absolutely love teaching, and I am good at it. I am so proud of the impressive gains my students have always made. But I am thinking

I may just retire if I am going to be forced to teach in
ways that I think are harmful to kids.

—MARY, ELEMENTARY SCHOOL SPECIAL EDUCATION TEACHER

Proliferation of Rules

Rules are a necessary part of organizational life. Like all organizations, schools must find ways to balance extending trust to employees at various levels of the organization with creating safeguards
against self-serving, dishonest, or abusive behavior. Schools adopt
rules, procedures, and other formal organizational mechanisms
to guide behavior. However, formal controls instituted to increase
performance reliability can become ends unto themselves and
end up hampering rather than facilitating the achievement of
organizational effectiveness. When trust breaks down, organizations are faced with deciding how to respond. As trust deteriorates
in an organization, one likely response is the institution of rules to
serve as a substitute for trust (S. P. Shapiro, 1987; Sitkin & Stickel,
1996; Zucker, 1986). Taken to the extreme, however, the proliferation of rules is likely to interfere with organizational effectiveness.

At Lincoln, Gloria turned to the imposition of rules to reassert
her authority and to try to bring her faculty into compliance with her
desires for the school. Rob described how over the course of a school
year in which trust took a decided turn for the worse, rules gained
increasing importance.

> I was on the building council. The staff and principal get
> together and talk about issues in the school. At the beginning
> of the year, we would sit around and discuss and come up with
> options, whereas by the end of the year, Gloria would come
> with the teachers' contract book and would say, "Well, it says
> this thing here, and that is how we are going to handle it,"
> even when other options existed or were desirable. It has just
> been going by the book, and a very strict interpretation.

Rob resented going through the motions of a shared decision-making process when the real agenda seemed to be game playing on the part of Gloria, using rules to manipulate the staff. He also resented the arbitrariness with which Gloria exercised her formal authority to assert her power within the school.

The capricious imposition of rules felt like an assault on the teachers' professionalism. Gloria's tactics to improve the performance of what she may have regarded as a lazy or unmotivated faculty seemed destined for failure. Allisha complained:

> There have been many edicts from up above, from the principal. At the beginning of the year, we were told we are no longer allowed to eat lunches in the library unless we have permission. We are professionals. There were no reasons, no input. And just numerous things like that throughout the year. The staff has been really unhappy. A lot of [the rules] just seem petty or trivial. If we could just have input, we might be more accepting of them. But that's never an option.

The teachers resented Gloria's strategies and became less rather than more willing to cooperate with her on her agenda. Although teachers reported that most people complied with the rules, many found creative ways to sabotage and thwart Gloria's efforts. The resulting power struggle did not bode well for the development of a professional school culture or improvement in the school's effectiveness for students.

Rigid and coercive rules negatively influence employees' affiliation with the school and can have detrimental effects on satisfaction and morale. Teachers as well as students may respond to a proliferation of rules with feelings of alienation, resentment, and lack of commitment, which ironically can make dishonesty and cheating more prevalent (Govier, 1992; Kramer & Cook, 2004). A spiral of distrust can ensue as more rules are put in place in response to increasing instances of broken trust. These are precisely the results I saw at Lincoln. Gloria's attempts to improve the performance outcomes at Lincoln by instituting standardized, one-size-fits-all procedures backfired because they stripped teachers of the discretion necessary to be responsive to student needs.

My principal's big thing is that lesson plans have to be done in a certain format—these little books. But I do big units with big ideas—I couldn't fit it all in those little boxes. If you said that you were reading pages 127 through 135 in the history book one week and your plans the next week didn't start on page 136, she'd call you in and ask you what happened. If your plans said that at 10:10 on Tuesday you were going to be doing phonics, if she came in at 10:10, you'd better be doing phonics or she would cream you. She threatened to write me up and send it to the central office. But just when she was about to do that, the letter arrived announcing that I had been named statewide teacher of the year—so she dropped it.

—NANCY, FIFTH-GRADE TEACHER

RULES THAT FACILITATE

The system of written rules, policies, and procedures in schools need not be coercive. Rules and formal procedures can also be facilitative. Policies and procedures can be flexible guidelines to help solve problems rather than constraints that create them. As guidelines, they reflect "best practices," helping subordinates deal with surprises and crises and assisting employees with finding solutions to problems in their work (Adler & Borys, 1996). When policies and procedures are facilitative rather than coercive, organizational participants are encouraged to reflect on innovative ways to respond to novel situations and not to adhere blindly to rules and regulations. Flexibility and professional judgment temper or even substitute for rigid rules and procedures. Enabling procedures invite interactive dialogue; they require participation and collaboration. Facilitative strategies allow problems to be viewed as opportunities, differences to be valued, and mistakes to be capitalized on and learned from (Hoy & Sweetland, 2001). Improvement is the objective.

Trust forms the foundation for this more constructive approach to organizational rules. To foster trust, policies must demonstrate an expectation of trustworthy behavior on the part of organizational participants, and they must be responsive to breaches of trust (Coleman, 1990). When leaders adopted a more professional orientation to rules, it was related to a higher level of professionalism on the part of teachers (M. Tschannen-Moran, 2009). Moreover, principals with this orientation were also more likely to be trusted by their faculty members.

At Brookside, there was a strong sense of accountability, but there was also more flexibility and leniency in response to the unexpected ups and downs of life. When there was a sense of confidence that teachers were working hard and going beyond their minimum commitments, there was a greater willingness to make allowances for teachers. For example, a teacher might be dismissed early to see his own child's school program or to take a sick child to the doctor. Teachers responded by making sure they were worthy of the trust placed in them. They described a sense of urgency to get back after an illness, knowing their absence was placing a burden on colleagues. Instead of minimum compliance, they went beyond the requirements of their contract and district policies. A culture of distrust is likely to hamper a school's ability to be productive, whereas trust can pay off for schools in giving them the flexibility to respond to the needs of their students, faculty, staff, and community.

A few weeks into my midyear appointment as principal of a building where I knew the level of trust with the previous principal had been quite low, three teachers asked if they could meet with me. They said it was important, and they were clearly quite nervous as we began the meeting. After five minutes of hemming and hawing, literally, I assured them that whatever it was, I would listen with an open mind. One of them got up her courage and asked, "Would it be all right if we had a bridal shower for our colleague who is getting married this summer?"

—PATRICK, ELEMENTARY SCHOOL PRINCIPAL

 PUTTING IT INTO ACTION

If you enter a school or a district that is characterized by a culture of control, you will need to take deliberate steps to begin to foster a culture of trust. You need to demonstrate a commitment to the rules and policies of your school and district, and a willingness to deal with those who violate them. However, you can also demonstrate flexibility and a willingness to bend the rules occasionally when a teacher has a valid need. A practice of *strategic leniency*, rather than laxness, is more likely to generate trust by balancing a commitment to fair procedures and a commitment to people (Hoy & Miskel, 2008).

If you take on the leadership of a school that is encumbered by an overabundance of rules, it may help to reframe the rules as parameters for behavior. In the school I led in a low-income neighborhood of Chicago, we learned that you can never specify all of the behaviors that are not allowed; we learned that there will always be those students who use their creativity to find the loopholes in the system. For instance, we had a rule at our school that "we don't use our hands and feet to solve our conflicts with one another, we use our words." One day at recess, a student tearfully reported to the teacher on duty, "I had a conflict with Seneca, and he *peed* on me!" An alternative is to specify broad parameters that articulate the character we hope for in our collective life. In our school, we had just three school rules: "This is a safe place; this is a caring place; this is a learning place." We began each school year with a discussion in which we brainstormed different kinds of actions and considered whether they fell within or outside the parameters we had set. This helped our students begin to learn to exercise judgment in response to particular situations. These three rules were bolstered by procedures, such as how to line up for lunch, where to put the materials away at the end of a lesson, or how to indicate a desire to speak during a class discussion, but these differed from rules. The three rules applied equally to teacher behavior. In a school that has tolerated bad behavior on the part of teachers as well as students, it may take time, patience, and persistence to make it clear that the rules apply to everyone.

One small, symbolic gesture you can make to convey that the school is a professional organization is to flip the traditional triangular organizational chart, putting the teachers at the top of the inverted triangle, with the various layers of administration below. This makes clear that the work of teachers is the raison d'être for the entire system. In this depiction of the organization, the primary work of the principal and other building-level leaders is to support the work of teachers with their students. When such an organizational chart is used district-wide, the work of central office leaders becomes that of assisting the principals in support of their teachers, and the work of the superintendent is to offer resources, encouragement, and inspiration to all whose work rests on his or her leadership. This symbolic gesture may be viewed with skepticism and generate increased cynicism if there are no real shifts in attitude and behavior to accompany it. But if the change facilitates a genuine reorientation of the organizational culture away from a highly bureaucratic orientation to one that honors and supports the work of the key professionals, the teachers, then it has the potential to open the way for new conversations, policies, and practices.

KEY POINTS ABOUT REVENGE

- There is a motive for revenge when the victim perceives a deliberate betrayal stemming from malevolence or self-interest on the part of the perpetrator.
- Revenge may be useful in equalizing the power within organizations and opening up the possibility for constructive change.
- Resentment tends to be clandestine and defensive in nature, making the restoration of trust more difficult.

- Micromanagement is an act of distrust and is likely to lead to resentment.
- A breakdown in trust leads to a proliferation of rules, which can hamper school effectiveness.
- As professionals, teachers need to be trusted and also given the discretion to be responsive to the varied needs of their students.

QUESTIONS FOR REFLECTION AND DISCUSSION

1. Do the rules in your school serve it well or serve it poorly? Do they reflect a culture of trust or distrust?
2. Is there a culture of control evident at your school? What could you do to replace this mentality with a more trusting one?
3. When have you seen resentment lead to sabotage?
4. What would it take to develop a more professional orientation in your school?
5. Recall a time when an act of revenge in response to a violation led to constructive change in a school.

CHAPTER 6

TEACHERS TRUSTING ONE ANOTHER

It is an equal failing to trust everybody, and to trust nobody.
—ENGLISH PROVERB

The culture of a school plays a significant role in supporting and sustaining trust. The actions of the principal certainly help set the general tone of school trust, but teachers' trust in their colleagues has a more direct impact on student learning (M. Tschannen-Moran, 2004). Teachers' trust in their colleagues has been tied to the accomplishment of the central mission of the school in important ways. Where trust is higher among teachers, teachers are more likely to perceive greater professionalism on the part of their colleagues (M. Tschannen-Moran, 2009). Teachers trust colleagues they see as competent, as exercising professional judgment, and as demonstrating a strong commitment to students. Faculty members' trust in colleagues has also been related to higher trust in students and their parents. In other words, it seems that when a culture of trust prevails within the faculty at a school, students and parents may benefit as the recipients of this trust as well (M. Tschannen-Moran, 2004).

And in a triangle of reciprocal relationships, whereby teachers trust students and parents, teachers are more likely to perceive greater professionalism on the part of their colleagues. For professionalism to characterize a school's culture, trust among teachers is required.

Professional learning communities are characterized by the quality, tone, and content of the dialogue among the professionals. Strong professional communities consist of deeply collaborative and meaningful conversations; they are built through joint deliberation and decision making. Fullan (2003) argued for the importance of "disciplined, informed professional inquiry" (p. 11) in bringing about constructive school change. Such inquiry is supported by standards of professionalism as well as norms of curiosity. Principals can influence this dialogue by the example they set. Professional learning communities are based on the trust that both teachers and principals will act with the best interests of students in mind by researching best practices and pursuing data to bolster decision making (Elmore, Peterson, & McCarthey, 1996; Goldring & Rallis, 1993; Louis, Kruse, & Marks, 1996; Wahlstrom & Louis, 2008).

An atmosphere of trust holds promise for transforming a school into a vibrant learning community. To foster the kinds of support teachers need for risk taking and professional growth, they need the trust of their principal and of their colleagues (Moolenaar, Karsten, Sleegers, & Zijlstra, 2010). Cultural norms in a professional learning community can facilitate trust by encouraging cooperation rather than competition between teachers. A cooperative culture fosters trusting and trustworthy behavior not only among teachers and staff but among students as well (Louis, Kruse, & Associates, 1995; M. Tschannen-Moran, 2001; Wahlstrom & Louis, 2008). Building a culture of trust in a given school may require time, effort, and leadership, but the investment is likely to bring satisfying returns.

BUILDING A PROFESSIONAL LEARNING COMMUNITY AT BROOKSIDE

Things didn't start out easily for Brenda at Brookside. When she had assumed leadership nearly a decade earlier, the school was embroiled in conflict. Discipline was inconsistent and largely ineffective. The quality of teaching was far below what she would have hoped to see. It took time and patience to begin to shape the school into a professional learning community. She described her first year:

> My first year was difficult. I learned very quickly that I could not expect to have an open discussion with the full staff. Their meetings had been characterized by conflict. I held team meetings regularly for the first couple of years, saving full staff meetings only for one-way communication. I listened a lot. I sent out weekly memos as a way of organizing the school, keeping everybody up to speed, and expressing appreciation. The staff let me know they appreciated this regular communication.

Part of Brenda's challenge was in changing the culture of the school, especially the teachers' proprietary feelings about their respective classrooms. They were protective of that space and valued privacy and autonomy. Brenda challenged those norms from the very beginning, and she did so with a combination of strength and sensitivity. She described the initial reaction from teachers:

> On the first day of school I visited every classroom. I continued to visit each classroom every day the first week of school just for short visits to get a feel for the building and to be visible. Early the next week I was visited by a teacher who spoke for herself and "others" and explained to me that it was not the practice of that building for the principal to visit

classrooms without an appointment. I explained that I could not make good decisions for the school community without being in classrooms and suggested she pass the word. I showed her the list I had made of things that I could do to improve life for students, things like repairing clocks, moving old books, etc. That changed her attitude.

Over time Brenda was able to improve the quality of teaching through an artful combination of support and challenge. Brenda's affirmation and acceptance of differences in teaching style helped create an atmosphere in which teachers were willing to share with one another. Christy, a teacher at Brookside described how Brenda's leadership helped shape the culture at the school:

> Our principal is very sensitive to everyone's differences. But then she plays on our strengths within our differences, and she treats all of us equally. There is nobody who is put up on a pedestal at any time. That's something that changes the whole atmosphere between staff members because you never have that sense of competition. If you need help in something, you feel comfortable going to your coworkers and asking for help—or sharing what has worked for you or what hasn't worked for you. It is never an embarrassing situation. Brenda will point things out, but she doesn't do it in a way that makes anyone feel inferior because she always brings out that person's strength. That person's strength may not be your strength, so you don't take offense at it. But in the next conversation you may be the person whose strengths she may be discussing. Every person feels valued.

Without a sense of competition or the need to protect their turf, these teachers were able to benefit from one another's expertise and ideas.

The school culture Brenda encountered not only was divided by conflict but also was one in which teachers had adopted an individualistic, "every person for himself or herself" orientation.

One of the ways that the negative culture at Brookside was evident was in the hoarding of supplies. Brenda reported:

> All the returning teachers had placed art orders the previous year. They tucked those materials in their cupboards. The rooms of the new staff were empty of art materials. I entered rooms over the weekend and borrowed from Peter to pay Paul, so to speak. The scarcity of construction paper and art materials became a symbol for me of the general view that there was a scarcity of everything, like appreciation for teachers, and praise for students. I put up shelves in a closet, purchased new materials, and announced that teachers could take what they needed. The closet was empty within a few days, so I reordered enough times to refill the closet and see materials remain until needed rather than being hoarded.

In this way, Brenda communicated her concern for the well-being of the teachers and began to overcome the perception of scarcity.

Brenda wanted to find a way to bolster the sense of community in the school and to move away from teachers' more individualistic orientation. She struck on a school play as an avenue for doing so, but implementing her idea didn't turn out to be easy.

> I felt that it would be good for the school community if we had a school-wide performance, and I asked the music teacher how she felt about doing one. She said she was not willing to put that much time into her job at this time of her life. The assistant principal had informed me that she did not like to handle discipline (and she didn't do an especially good job at it either). She was, however, quite creative, and she readily agreed to visit classrooms, do language experience writing, and write a school play—which turned out to be very clever. It was a major production and accomplished just what I hoped for in building a sense of community with parents, students, and staff. I couldn't help but be amused

at the end of the school year when the music teacher told me that she should have been the one giving that play. I reminded her of our conversation, and she was surprised that she had responded in that manner. The next year she put on a school-wide play.

Brookside's transformation into a professional learning community did not happen overnight. It took several years of steady progress toward that goal. Once teachers learned that they could trust Brenda and her intentions for them, they began to be willing to take risks and to try new teaching techniques. Team meetings grew to be times of true collaboration rather than complaint sessions. Teachers were more willing to invest the extra effort required for excellent teaching and to bring more creativity and imagination to their work life. Bolstered by a strong sense of community, they increased their commitment to the students and the school.

FACULTY TRUST AND THE FIVE FACETS

Whether or not teachers trust one another can have a significant impact on the climate and effectiveness of a school. A collegial atmosphere, authentic relationships, and a high level of involvement of teachers in decision making all play a role in promoting faculty members' trust in colleagues (Tarter, Bliss, & Hoy, 1989; Tarter, Sabo, & Hoy, 1995; M. Tschannen-Moran & Hoy, 1998). Teacher morale is strongly related to faculty members' trust in colleagues as well. High trust in colleagues creates a context for a positive climate, and where distrust is pervasive, morale can be expected to be low (Smith, Hoy, & Sweetland, 2001).

The professional norms at Brookside encouraged teachers to interact frequently, face-to-face and in positive ways, to assist one another in their work with students. When members of the school community interact cordially, they establish a feeling and appearance that everything is "normal" and in proper order, and this feeling helps create a context where trust is more likely to develop (Lewis & Weigert, 1985). All five facets of trust are important in teachers' trust judgments of colleagues. A sense of benevolence or care lays a foundation of trust among teachers. Honesty, openness, and reliability also play a role. An interesting pattern of trust emerges, however, when teachers lack respect for the competence of their colleagues.

Benevolence

A sense of benevolence or caring was the single most often mentioned dimension of faculty members' trust in their colleagues in the schools in this study at Brookside, teachers expressed support for one another in a variety of ways across both the professional and personal realms of life, from helping new teachers get started to taking hot meals to a staff member who was ill. One teacher, Kathy, described how welcome the other teachers had made her feel when she arrived at Brookside:

> My very first year, one of the fourth-grade teachers was constantly giving me things, saying, "Here's an idea." She did my first three days of lesson plans for me. She said, "Here, here's an outline for you. If you like it, use it, if you don't, don't." Just because she knew I was going to struggle. Like those flowers [pointing to a vase on her desk], she just sent flowers around the building to brighten everybody's day. Just because. Just because she wants people to feel good. That's her way of keeping everybody smiling.

Christy, another Brookside teacher, echoed the ways that veteran faculty welcomed and looked out for new teachers, even when the newcomers had previous teaching experience:

> They help new people coming in by . . . when an extra expectation is due, they might say, "You know what? You're new.

> I'm going to take your class for an hour, and why don't you
> work on your writing portfolios." Just because they know that
> the first year you have a lot of extra training and that is all
> on your own personal time—and it is a lot. The principal
> doesn't say, "Go and do this." They just do it on their own.
> It is a wonderful working environment. It balances out the
> hard work.

A spirit of cooperation lays a foundation for trust to develop,
and greater trust helps create greater cooperation. The tradition at
Brookside of cooperative and helpful behavior toward new teachers helped create the conditions for trust to develop. Once trust
was established, those novice teachers were more likely to behave
in cooperative ways, and the cycle of trust became self-sustaining.

In addition to appreciating the help at school, Brookside
teachers exhibited a particular pride in the ways faculty members
looked out for one another beyond the bounds of their work life.
Kathy continued:

> We have collected money at Christmastime to give to people
> because they are struggling a little bit financially. There are
> people who have gone through divorces, and the staff has
> known about that, and they have helped deal with that. We
> have a staff member who was diagnosed with cancer, and every
> Monday they would take dinner over to the family. When a
> staff member had used all of her sick leave, we donated our
> sick leave so that she could continue to stay out. We are very
> caring. Whenever there is a tragedy that has happened in
> someone's life and we know about that, then we respond. As
> well as exciting events like pregnancies and marriages—we
> buy gifts and go and attend.

David, another teacher at Brookside, explained how the atmosphere of caring contributed to a sense of community: "You want
to have that sense of belonging. And you want others to belong.
Just knowing that you're missed when you're not here—it makes

you feel good." The overarching ethos of caring not only made for a more pleasant work environment but also created the context for the development of trust throughout the school community.

Honesty

At Brookside, the teachers took for granted the honesty and integrity of their colleagues. You demonstrate integrity by doing what you say you will, telling the truth, and keeping promises. Further, authenticity, or being "real," accepting responsibility, and avoiding shifting the blame for errors to others, has been found to be significantly related to teachers' trust in colleagues (Hoy & Kupersmith, 1985; M. Tschannen-Moran & Hoy, 1998). For example, a teacher at Lincoln forfeited the trust of her colleagues when she attempted to dodge Gloria's tongue-lashing by pointing fingers at her teammates when she was the one who had dropped the ball in preparing for a field trip, a mistake that resulted in last-minute transportation problems.

The effects of a betrayal are not just intense, they are also lasting. Paul, a teacher at Fremont, described a breach of civic order in a situation where a fellow teacher intentionally distorted the facts to cast Paul in a bad light with Fred. As part of a class assignment, Paul had invited some of his university classmates to engage in a discussion with several Fremont faculty members about the strengths and weaknesses of the professional development activities in the school. Fred was scheduled to be part of the discussion but at the last minute was unable to attend. One of the teachers who had participated in the session called Fred at home that evening to report on the event. The day after the meeting, Paul was called to come to Fred's office. Paul described his chagrin at what happened:

> Fred said, "I heard you all tore me apart yesterday." I was taken aback, and I said, "Fred, what do you mean?" I said,

"No, I have the session taped if you want to listen to the tape recording." That person who'd made the call was the main person who had criticized him! That was real hard to deal with. That's the first time I ever had an administrator call me into his office and shut the door. And I'm thinking, "I don't know what I did wrong!"

Based on the strong personal relationship Paul had with Fred, and thanks in part to the evidence of the tape recording, they were able to work through the misunderstanding and repair their relationship. It seemed evident that the perpetrator thought she could gain an advantage by causing Fred to distrust Paul. Although the rift with Fred was repaired, Paul refused to speak to the colleague who had made the call and avoided any social contact with her. He still maintained his silence more than a year after the incident.

Openness

At Brookside, teachers were pleased to share professional secrets, successful teaching strategies, materials, and equipment in the interest of helping students learn. A spirit of openness allows for greater sharing of both ideas and resources (Kratzer, 1997; Short & Greer, 1997). Openness fosters trust, but it also grows out of a high level of trust; it is thus part of the cycle of trust. Kathy described the openness to sharing ideas at Brookside:

We go to each other for advice on a lesson or if we need resources. We're not afraid to ask other teachers. We'll even go observe other teachers during our specials so we can see what techniques they're using that we can learn. There's an openness. The teachers don't look at you like, "Why are you walking into my room?" We can just walk into each other's room freely, and if there is something I want, like the projector or whatever, I can just take it, and they can do the same.

There is just that sense of trust that it won't be abused, and it will be returned.

Brookside teachers also didn't feel threatened by others' giving them ideas or offering suggestions. Christy elaborated:

> We might say, "What's that I see you hanging outside? That's really neat, can we do it? Do you have extra copies? How did that work?" Or you might go over and say, "I tried this today, and the kids really liked it. You might want to try it with your class." If something worked and your children really benefited from it, why wouldn't you want as many children as possible to gain from that? I think everyone thinks that way.

In an environment of trust, people are more likely to be open with information because they feel more confident that others will not exploit the information for their own benefit. Knowledge (especially when it is hard to come by) can be a source of power (G. R. Jones & George, 1998).

At Brookside, there was an openness not only with teaching ideas and strategies but also in sharing personal information. Teachers were willing to share things that were near to their heart: concerns and joys about family, friends, and life outside of school. With this sharing came vulnerability to the possible misuse of the information in ways that were hurtful. Although teachers at Brookside acknowledged that word about one another was likely to spread quickly, there was a sense of confidence that whatever information people received about one another would be handled with care. The pervasive atmosphere of trust enabled teachers and staff members to ask about and share things that in another context might have been a problem or caused discomfort. David explained, "When you trust other teachers and you know they trust you, you feel comfortable. When they ask about things, you don't feel like they are dipping into your business. You are just happy to talk about it."

At both Lincoln and Fremont, teachers were much more reluctant to be open personally and professionally. Paul explained that at Fremont he had learned through hard experience to be guarded about sharing information about his life outside of school:

> The gossip runs rampant here. It spreads very fast. The best thing I have done—if I have a bit of news that's concerning me or somebody else, I keep it to myself. I don't tell anybody. If I have a problem with me, I keep it to myself. Because if you tell just one person, they'll all know. It's like playing telephone, where you tell one person, and it gets totally distorted by the time it gets around.

Paul's lack of openness was linked to concern about the level of benevolence or goodwill he could count on from his peers. Without the confidence that others would respond in a caring manner, he was reluctant to make himself vulnerable by sharing information about anything of importance to him.

A frequently mentioned breach of civic order among teachers at Lincoln and Fremont was the breaking of confidences. Mary, a teacher at Lincoln, described an instance of betrayal in which another teacher broke her confidence. Mary had been pressured by Gloria to serve on a particular committee, which put her in an awkward position because she didn't want it to be known that she was interviewing for positions at other schools. She confided in Leslie, the alternate to the committee, that she might need to call on her from time to time if her interview schedule were to conflict with the committee meetings. One afternoon, Mary walked into a classroom to overhear Leslie telling another teacher about Mary's plans to interview elsewhere. The other teacher was a close confidant of Gloria's, so Mary knew Gloria would soon be made aware of her plans. Mary described how the scenario unfolded with Leslie: "I walked in and heard her. She knew that that person would communicate with Gloria. When I walked in, she walked out and didn't make eye contact. I called her on it, though. I confronted her."

Allisha, another Lincoln teacher, described what happened when it was discovered that a colleague had made a habit of breaking confidences. Allisha explained how the teacher involved felt the collective wrath of a group of teachers whose confidence she had betrayed:

> There is one teacher who likes to talk about everyone in the building. She and I started together last year, and I really confided in her. But one teacher came and told everyone what she had been saying. Come to find out she basically just repeated everything I had said. So we just snub her. When she tries to talk to people, they just basically turn away or change the subject. She got the message that she wasn't welcome.

So openness needs to be tempered with good judgment and care. But without openness, teachers do not have the opportunity to demonstrate benevolence, reliability, or competence to one another. A lack of openness can provoke a spiral of distrust.

Reliability

Teachers need to feel that they can rely on their colleagues if trust is to develop. Teachers at Brookside talked about the importance of being able to depend on other teachers to live up to their commitments or to take their responsibilities seriously. Being able to count on colleagues in the midst of unexpected circumstances was important to teachers. Kathy described the sense of responsibility to one another that teachers at Brookside felt in emergencies:

> We take each other's kids a lot. Nobody ever says no. The day I had to do that I gave everybody candy bars in appreciation. But they said, "You didn't have to do that, that is just the Brookside way." There is a high level of trust that people will be here unless they are dead on their feet or seriously ill. They won't abandon their room or stick somebody else with

it. If emergencies arise, if one person has to leave because their son or daughter is ill, teachers will automatically take over their students.

One of the ways people help build and sustain a sense of trust in the collective is "compensatory trust," whereby people cover for one another when they become aware that someone may have dropped the ball (Kramer, Brewer, & Hanna, 1996). David reported his confidence in his colleagues' dependability, as well as how compensatory trust was at work at Brookside.

> Off the top of my head, I just can't recall an instance when someone was supposed to have done something and didn't. There is a high degree of professionalism here, and they are committed to what it is they are doing. When they say something, I think they have every intention of following through with that. What I have seen is where others kind of pick up where the other person should have been. Other people fill in. But usually when people have made the commitment to do something they follow through with it.

In schools where reliability is absent, teachers grow to distrust their colleagues. At Fremont, teachers were much less confident that colleagues would show up where they were supposed to or would fill gaps for one another. Kelli, for example, gave up trying to ensure that there would be adequate supervision at recess. Teachers might have been reliable as far as supporting other teachers within their clique, but that reliability did not necessarily extend to the students or to the school program as a whole.

Competence

When it comes to teachers' trust in one another, the issue of competence is not a simple one. The degree to which competence matters to faculty trust is related to how interdependent they feel in the teaching realm. In some cases, this perception is in flux because of the pressures placed on the school due to the accountability movement, or at other times due to moves toward more team teaching or the development of a professional learning community. As perceptions of interdependence increased, judgments of one another's competence may become a more salient part of teachers' trust in colleagues. Principals can influence the degree of interdependence teachers perceive through how they talk about and structure the school program.

Assessments of colleagues' competence may be influenced by teaching philosophy and style. One pair of teachers who were friends and who had taught across the hall from one another for many years had begun the first tentative moves toward teaming but were struggling over issues of teaching philosophy and style. One teacher took pride in having maintained an active schedule of professional development and reading, and in using the most up-to-date teaching methods, whereas her partner employed much more traditional teaching methods. In addition to the differences in philosophy, these two teachers came from different racial backgrounds, which compounded the challenge of working together more closely. Nonetheless, both teachers felt there would be benefits for their students, as well as for themselves, in sharing classes for certain subjects, so they committed to working through the difficulties. This required a deeper level of trust than had been necessary in the previous years of friendship and teaching across from one another.

Understanding teachers' trust in their colleagues is further complicated by evidence of uneven trust. That is, teachers at Lincoln and Fremont felt they could trust one another in some arenas and not in others. Teachers drew distinctions between professional and personal trust, suggesting that there were two different sets of expectations in regard to what teachers believed they owed one another—what they felt they owed one another as professional colleagues and what they owed one another as friends and fellow

human beings. Where teachers did not hold the professional competence of their colleagues in high regard, they were nonetheless able to justify their trust by distinguishing personal trust from
professional trust. Although there was overlap, these two kinds of
trust seemed to be somewhat independent from each other. Rob, a
Lincoln teacher, described the distinction this way:

> Personally, I would trust any faculty member here with any-
> thing, whether it be taking my car, house sitting, anything. . . .
> As far as the professional aspect, I feel some people don't live
> up to their end of the deal. In past years, when I taught in the
> upper grades, I saw children who came to me who were not
> prepared. I have a feeling it is due to some of the professional
> qualities of some of the people I work with. I don't hold that
> against them personally, but I feel that there could be a little
> more dedication among the staff members.

Paul made a similar distinction between professional and personal trust at Fremont, but reported that he held higher professional trust than personal trust:

> I think there are two different levels. The professional deals
> with any issues or concerns at the school level. I think there
> is a high level of trust here because everybody values each
> other's opinions. I think there is another level that surfaces
> among faculty that deals with the interpersonal relationships
> that teachers have that have nothing to do with the school
> per se. There may be outside influences like church, or it
> may be sororities they once belonged to, or they may have
> taught together for a long time. That level of trust can create
> a barrier. There's a lot of gossip that will go around which is
> not really professional gossip; it may be personal gossip. That
> creates mistrust.

In Paul's view, a high level of personal trust within subgroups
or cliques impaired the development of an overall sense of trust

among the faculty as a whole. Fred's failure to intervene to help resolve conflicts or to enforce norms of behavior allowed the sense of community within the faculty to fragment and deteriorate.

Some teachers at Fremont believed that they were interdependent with their colleagues in terms of others' reliability in facilitating the processes that kept the school running smoothly but not necessarily in terms of others' skill in the classroom. Paul reported that he did not feel that judgments about whether colleagues were doing a good job in the classroom entered into his calculation of professional trust because he did not feel that their classroom performance had an impact on him professionally. He said:

> I have seen teachers that a lot of people felt were incompetent or really shouldn't have been teaching. I think the trust was there, but I don't think we as educators took that trust to mean that we are trusting them because they are competent or not competent. We're trusting them because they do help the smooth running of the school. But, to me, competence and incompetence, that's another issue. Now if we were teaming, that would affect me. But we are so isolated right now that it doesn't affect me.

Paul acknowledged that if he had felt dependent on another teacher's skill, if that teacher's abilities had affected him because of a situation of interdependence, then a colleague's professional competence might have been of concern. Even though Paul did not perceive that level of interdependence, some teachers did perceive interdependence and did feel that their colleagues' competence mattered. Brian, a teacher at Fremont, said that he did not trust one of his colleagues, in part, because of the disrespectful tone toward her students that he overheard as he passed by her classroom. This disrespect affected his personal and professional trust in that person.

I have a colleague who came right out and said, "I don't
like boys." As the mother of two sons, I lost all
professional respect for her that day.

—BETH, THIRD-GRADE TEACHER

Each of the five facets of trust contributes to teachers' trust in
one another, although the picture is complicated when it comes
to judgments of competence. As long as teachers are not dependent on the teaching competence of their colleagues, they may be
able to foster trusting relationships with them in spite of negative
assessments of their colleagues' teaching abilities. But with greater
school-wide accountability, the competence of one's colleagues is
becoming more salient in trust judgments. And the level of trust
among the faculty of a school has very real consequences for how
the school functions and for its ability to meet its goals. In the next
section, we will explore some of the important school dynamics
that relate to the level of faculty trust.

THE PAYOFFS OF FACULTY TRUST

Trust plays an important role in overcoming barriers to building a
professional learning community, which include conflict avoidance,
destructive competitiveness, and low levels of teacher self-efficacy
(Leonard, 1999). The payoffs of a high level of faculty trust are
many. These include the facilitation of greater collaboration, a more
robust collective sense among teachers that they can make a difference, and more productive conflict resolution strategies.

Fluid Collaboration

Greater collaboration among teachers fosters a spirit of professional community in schools. Such collaboration is unlikely

to develop, however, in the absence of trust among teachers. Statistical analyses across a large number of schools reflect the patterns seen at Brookside, Lincoln, and Fremont (M. Tschannen-Moran, 2001). In schools where there is greater trust, there tends to be more collaboration. When trust is absent, people are reluctant to work closely together, and collaboration is more difficult.

When trust is high and teachers feel supported and affirmed by their principal, they are much more willing to make themselves vulnerable through teamwork and sharing with other teachers. The spirit of collaboration at Brookside translated into classroom practice, not only in the frequent use of group work in class activities and a conscious step-by-step process for resolving interpersonal difficulties among students but also in a program in which older students teamed up with younger students to read and do projects. Teachers saw this program as helping older students polish their own skills as they used them to instruct the younger students. The younger students benefited from the one-on-one attention of an older friend. Christy described the positive dynamics she observed:

> Buddies are very much an integral part of our curriculum, doing cross-grade-level things. We have a class that we work with, and we may write stories with them, we may do art projects with them, we may write books with them. At the beginning of the year, my students read to the younger students, but by this time in the year [the younger students] read to us. And my kids love it. They'll say, "Hey! This kid's reading at such-and-such a level!" or "They're a good writer!" That creates part of the sense of community too.

Upper-grade students who had struggled with schoolwork themselves took pride in the accomplishments of their younger buddies and became more engaged learners. These positive outcomes would not have been possible if the teachers had not trusted each other enough to collaborate on the planning and implementation of this program.

We have twenty-five regular education students and six
deaf students in our room. Some teachers are not willing
to do this inclusion thing. They want to do things their own
way, to make decisions their own way. They are not willing
to let someone in to work with them. They don't want to
be critically analyzed. On the other hand, there are real
advantages to having two people in the room. It is easier
in a lot of ways. Two bodies are better than one when you
have discipline problems. You can take phone calls.
You can go to the bathroom. It's a lot more fun to
plan together, to come up with some really good things
together. You feel more like a team.

—TRACY, FIRST-GRADE TEACHER

The spirit of teamwork and cooperation at Brookside did not just come about by accident. There was evidence of hard work and a conscious effort toward making it happen. This effort began with the vision that the principal articulated for the school and the resources she provided to make it a reality. The dividends were clear. Teachers, students, and parents benefited from the strong sense of community that resulted.

At Lincoln, teachers cut corners on planning and meeting with other teachers, and they did not extend themselves for each other in the way that the teachers at Brookside reported doing. Mary, a veteran teacher at Lincoln, described her disappointment at her colleagues' lack of willingness to share ideas or try new things:

I would like to see more sharing going on—an openness that
is not quite there throughout the whole staff. If you throw
out an idea, it's not like, "Well, let's consider it. What are the
strengths? What are the weaknesses?" It's not really analyzed.

It's like, "I just don't have the time." I've always been someone who is willing to put in the time, and so I feel kind of
resentful. I have put in a lot of time, and no one is willing to
put forth the effort. That's across the board. I think the children go above and beyond, but the adults don't.

When the sharing of ideas was not reciprocated within teams
of teachers, it led to resentment. Mary continued:

There is a teacher who is leaving her position here because
the other teachers she works with always look to her to do the
work—to do the planning and finding of resources. When
she shares, she expects them to share, and they never share
with her. Then when she doesn't do it for them, they get
upset.

The fact that autonomy is strongly ingrained in the teaching
profession can be an obstacle to collaboration among teachers.
This dynamic was particularly pronounced at Fremont. Reluctance
to give up autonomy was cited as a reason for the difficulty of making collaboration work. In addition to fearing the loss of autonomy,
teachers were reluctant to expose themselves to the scrutiny and
possible criticism of their peers. Paul explained:

We talked about peer observation. We even made a schedule
where there would be peer coaching among the teams and we
would take over their class. But they wouldn't do it. We tried
videotape. Boy, did they buck on that! Because they had to
critique [the videos] after they watched them. Everybody is in
their private domain, and they want to protect that. We have
an open-door policy. The doors are not allowed to be shut in
the building: anybody can come in. But once you try to set
something up where people can observe another colleague,
they are not very receptive to it.

One reason Paul saw for this resistance was that a number of
teachers liked to gain status by talking as though they were doing

a lot of innovative things in the classroom when in reality their teaching remained very traditional.

Teachers not only may be reluctant to collaborate themselves but also may feel threatened when others in their school begin to collaborate. They may communicate this discomfort through social sanctions, as Brian learned to his dismay. Brian, a novice fourth-grade teacher at Fremont, began to collaborate with Kelli, an experienced first-grade teacher, setting up a "reading buddies" mentoring program between the two classes. They also tried collaborating in other subject areas. Brian described what happened:

> This fall, Kelli and I had our classes working together studying trees and fall leaves. That was pretty cool. We were able to mix up both the primary and the intermediate. We took our classes out to some of the parks near here. But then the other teachers asked me bluntly was I having an affair with her! They were joking, I think, but they were also half serious. That really upset me!

As a married man and the father of young children, Brian was deeply hurt by this treatment. He felt that his attempts to work with another teacher were not just noticed but disapproved of by the other members of the faculty. He was put on notice that that kind of teamwork was not welcome. Brian was disappointed that Fred did not step in to support his cross-grade-level collaboration.

Teaching can be such an isolating experience. It really makes a huge difference if you have colleagues that you can count on and share ideas, struggles, and strategies with. Even so, the reality of teaching is that you are often alone with your students for about six hours a day, five days a week. This is a very different feeling from student teaching, when you are surrounded by other adults who watch your responses and are available to give prompt feedback.

—PAIGE, ELEMENTARY SCHOOL TEACHER

Robust Collective Sense of Efficacy

When teachers trust each other, they are more likely to develop greater confidence in their collective ability to be successful at meeting their goals. This collective sense of efficacy is related to greater motivation toward school goals, greater effort, as well as greater persistence in the face of setbacks.

The idea that what people believe about their ability to be successful at the task at hand can make a difference to their motivation and actual achievement is simple but very powerful (Bandura, 1997). There is a large body of research on teacher self-efficacy that demonstrates that what teachers as individuals believe about the extent to which they can influence the learning and achievement of their students makes a significant difference in their teaching behaviors and outcomes (Klassen, Tze, Betts, & Gordon, 2011; M. Tschannen-Moran & Chen, 2014; M. Tschannen-Moran, Woolfolk Hoy, & Hoy, 1998). Teachers with stronger efficacy beliefs are likely to be more enthusiastic and more organized, and to devote more time to planning their teaching (Allinder, 1994). In addition, teachers with a stronger sense that they can successfully have an impact on student learning are less likely to become angry, impatient, or frustrated with a student who is having difficulty; they will stick with that student longer; and they will try more strategies to help the student to understand (Ashton & Webb, 1986; Gibson & Dembo, 1984). Thus, teachers' strong sense of efficacy exerts significant influence on student achievement by promoting teacher behaviors that enhance learning. Indeed, a higher sense of efficacy has been shown to be positively related to higher student achievement (Anderson, Greene, & Loewen, 1988; Armor et al., 1976; Ashton & Webb, 1986; Ross, 1992).

These efficacy beliefs not only operate at the individual level but also can be shared by the faculty as a whole. Such shared beliefs are evidenced in the norms of a school and the small talk concerning expectations about the likelihood of success of a school faculty. Collective teacher efficacy beliefs are the perceptions of teachers in a school that the efforts of the faculty as a whole will have positive effects on students. These perceptions can help explain group behavior and group outcomes (Bandura, 1993, 1997; M. Tschannen-Moran, Salloum, & Goddard, in press). Teachers and schools are more likely to persist in efforts that support goals they believe they can accomplish.

Principals can help to cultivate and to nourish strong collective efficacy beliefs by communicating confidence in teachers' ability to promote student learning, whatever the difficulties and challenges of the particular context of the school. Teachers' collective sense of efficacy has been linked to student achievement, even when taking into account the socioeconomic status of students (Bandura, 1993; Goddard, Tschannen-Moran, & Hoy, 2001; M. Tschannen-Moran & Barr, 2004). This collective belief in being able to successfully fulfill the mission of the school has also been linked to teachers' trust in one another as well as to teachers' trust in students and parents (M. Tschannen-Moran & Goddard, 2001). When a high level of trust prevails in a school, a sense of collective efficacy tends to be evident as well. There was a rise in the collective sense of efficacy among the teachers at Brookside as their level of trust increased and the school grew into a professional learning community. Trust bolstered the risk taking required in trying new teaching practices. This was rewarded with higher student achievement, which, in turn, raised the sense that the teachers could make a difference even among their most disadvantaged students.

Constructive Controversy

One of the primary causes of the disruption of trust in schools is conflict that has been handled poorly. People are in conflict when the actions of one person are perceived as interfering with, obstructing, or in some other way decreasing the effectiveness of another's behavior (Tjosvold, 1997). Conflict can be thought of as a struggle between interdependent parties who perceive incompatible goals, scarce resources and rewards, and potential interference from the other party in achieving their goals (Baron, 1997; Hocker & Wilmot, 1985; Rubin, Pruit, & Kim, 1994).

How individuals respond to conflict can either foster trust or damage it. People make choices in how they respond to conflict, sometimes acting consciously and thoughtfully, other times reacting in the heat of the moment out of fear and anger. Deutsch (2000) organized these common responses across six continua, reflecting a number of choices people make in response to conflict:

- Along the first continuum, people at one extreme tend to avoid conflict (denying, suppressing, or postponing it), whereas people at the other extreme confront it, involving themselves to demonstrate their confidence and courage in the face of discord. Within schools, Peterson and Peterson (1990) found that both children and adults employed conflict avoidance twice as often as confrontation.

- Deutsch (2000) characterized the responses along the second continuum as ranging from hard to soft. That is, people may respond in an aggressive, unyielding fashion at one extreme, or they may be excessively gentle and unassertive at the other.

- A third continuum of choice runs between rigid and loose responses. People may attempt to organize or control the situation on the one hand, or lean toward avoiding all formal responses on the other.

- Yet another, fourth continuum spans the divide between intellectual and affective responses to conflict in that some individuals may respond to conflict with calm detachment whereas others may express intense emotions.

- Individuals at one end of the fifth continuum may attempt to escalate the conflict, expressing it in its largest possible terms, whereas at the other extreme, individuals may seek to minimize the seriousness of the differences between themselves and others.

- Finally, in attempts to communicate with others about the difficulties at hand, disputants at one end of the sixth continuum will choose bluntness, revealing all they think and feel,
  whereas disputants at the other end will hold their cards close,
  concealing what is on their mind.

Individuals' histories and biases affect their tone and style of
approaching and handling conflict along these six continua. As
individuals continue to engage in conflict, learning new strategies for productive resolutions, the range of possible responses is
extended and enriched.

---

*We were trying to resolve a dispute at a faculty meeting,
and one of my colleagues just deteriorated into street talk.
It was very unprofessional. I have never trusted her
since that time. I just keep my distance.*
—MELODY, SPECIAL EDUCATION TEACHER

In schools, teachers often respond to conflict either by acting aggressively to try to force their will on others or by avoiding
or suppressing conflict because they fear the consequences will
be uncontrollable. This avoidance may stem from a lack of skills
and confidence to manage the conflict constructively. School
leaders can reap the benefits of constructive controversy by
understanding common responses to conflict and by supporting
teachers and other members of the school community in moving toward conflict strategies that lead to constructive outcomes.
The principal can play an important role in helping to mediate
between the parties who are in conflict as well as to ensure that
disputants avoid making personal attacks and threats. In fostering lively debate over differences in ideas and strongly held positions about what should be done, a school that functions as a

professional learning community will benefit from improving the conflict resolution skills of the faculty. Schools with faculty members who have these skills will reap higher-quality decisions and improved group functioning (Uline, Tschannen-Moran, & Perez, 2003).

Once teachers at Brookside gained better conflict management skills, those patterns of communication became an accepted part of the school culture, a taken-for-granted sense of "how we do things around here." Teachers became invested in this more constructive way of managing their collective life. Brenda recalled how much the culture at Brookside had changed.

> Teachers were surprised to be reminded later of the behavior they exhibited while they were in the conflict situation. They were so embroiled in their hurt feelings or inability to be productive that they didn't see what was going on around them. One teacher actually told me that it was an adult conflict and had no effect on the students. They could not recognize the environment as the negative force that it was.

When teachers in a school do not trust one another, they are likely to be guarded in their interactions. Energy is diverted from common goals and channeled into self-protection. Collaboration deteriorates. Teachers may go through the motions of grade-level or department meetings, but there is little real joint decision making or collaboration. Teachers' collective sense that they have what it takes to promote student learning is reduced when distrust overtakes a school and motivation consequently suffers. Schools fraught with poorly handled conflict are also likely to experience lower trust. The processes that diminish trust are reciprocal, resulting in a spiral of distrust. Greater collaboration, a stronger collective sense of efficacy, and constructive conflict resolution are more likely when trust is present. Moreover, these elements foster the conditions that make for greater trust.

PUTTING IT INTO ACTION

Although teachers' trust in their colleagues stems directly from their own behavior and not from the behavior of the principal, there is much that you can do to establish a professional learning community grounded in trust. One of the most important things you can do to help foster a productive culture is to be explicit in establishing the norms as to how teachers are to treat one another, and then to address it forthrightly when there is a breach of this agreement. You need to enforce positive norms of conduct and promote and defend the norms that support professional engagement. This takes sensitivity and courage, but without a defender, the culture is likely to tolerate behavior that is destructive to the sense of community. Being available to mediate conflicts and, over time, helping teachers gain the skills to resolve conflicts constructively on their own will go a long way toward bolstering the level of trust among faculty.

As principal, you can make the time and create the structures to facilitate collaboration and allow for professional discourse and shared decision making among teachers. You can foster openness by encouraging teachers to be in one another's classrooms, to observe one another teaching, and to give each other feedback regarding things that are working well rather than to offer constructive criticisms let alone unwanted advice. An observation protocol that focuses on strengths helps to guide teachers in that direction. An example of such a protocol might be as follows:

1. I observed evidence of student learning when . . .
2. I noticed that your students were particularly engaged and excited about learning when . . .
3. I am curious about how . . .

Establishing a successful peer observation program requires planning and training to build the safety and trust teachers need.

There's an adage that says that schools get the teachers they deserve. Rather than starting from a position of blame when teachers do not initially meet the standards of professional performance you would like, it is more constructive to assume that people are, at least in part, behaving as they are in response to their environment. An organizational culture emerges as a pattern of shared assumptions that a group has learned in response to the problems it has encountered collectively, and that are then taught to new members as the correct ways to perceive, think, and feel in relation to those problems (Schein, 2010). To change a distrustful culture into one that better supports the cultivation of trust requires attention to the underlying assumptions and needs that give rise to behavior. It will require patience and persistence as you challenge these assumptions and help teachers find more productive ways to meet their needs and respond to the problems they encounter in their professional lives.

KEY POINTS ABOUT TEACHERS TRUSTING ONE ANOTHER

- Principals set the tone for teachers to trust one another.
- Teachers' trust in one another is facilitated by a principal who promotes a school culture that emphasizes cooperation and caring rather than competition and favoritism.
- Schools with a high level of trust among the faculty are more likely to benefit from teacher collaboration and constructive responses to conflict.
- The effects of betrayal among colleagues can be lasting and can have a detrimental impact on teachers' willingness to openly share teaching strategies, ideas, and resources.
- In the absence of trust in colleagues' professional competence, teachers may nonetheless trust those teachers as friends or based on their contributions to the overall functioning of the school.
- A can-do attitude is more likely to be present in schools with greater trust among teacher colleagues, resulting in greater effort, persistence, and resilience in the face of difficulties.
- A high level of trust among the teachers in a school makes it more likely that the school will function as a professional learning community.

QUESTIONS FOR REFLECTION AND DISCUSSION

1. When have you been a part of a well-functioning professional learning community? What made the experience positive and productive?

2. What specific actions can you take to foster a greater level of trust among the teachers at your school? What structures can be put in place that will bolster trust?

3. What can you do to foster trust between people with different values or passionate viewpoints that simply differ? What would it take for you not only to help your teachers create a culture in which they feel free to visit one another's classrooms but also to foster professional discourse, whereby teachers discuss teaching methods despite possible disagreements and different teaching philosophies?

4. How do you maintain a trusting working relationship with teachers when, as principal, you are responsible for collecting documentation on the mistakes, inconsistencies, or procedural errors of teachers?

5. What kind of teacher induction activities would help new teachers develop a sense of collective trust in each other and in the administrators at your school?

CHAPTER 7

CULTIVATING TRUST
WITH STUDENTS

The only way to make a person trustworthy is to trust him.
—HENRY LEWIS STIMSON

Classrooms are inherently social contexts, and thus teaching and learning in them involve risk, vulnerability, and interpersonal engagement on the part of teachers and students. Much of what inspires children to invest the effort required for learning happens in those interpersonal spaces. Because trust is central to making those spaces generative of learning, trust is critical to the central enterprise of schools. When teachers and students trust each other and work together cooperatively, learning follows from the climate of safety and warmth that prevails. When distrust and competition triumph, however, students and teachers alike are motivated to minimize their vulnerability by adopting a self-protective stance. Disengagement from the educational process results in unfortunate consequences, as safety comes at the expense of students' investment in the learning project. It is, therefore, wise for educators to attend to the dynamics of trust in the classroom because it hits schools' bottom line: student achievement (Howes & Ritchie, 2002; Mitchell, Kensler, & Tschannen-Moran, 2010). Teachers' trust in students and students' trust in teachers are reciprocal processes; indeed, a growing body of research evidence attests to the importance of each.

TEACHERS' TRUST IN STUDENTS

The trust that teachers extend to students is key to the relationships that connect students to each other and to the school itself. Because teachers hold greater power in the hierarchy of the school than do students, it is incumbent on teachers to set a trusting tone in their interactions with students if they hope to build a climate of trust in the classroom. The teachers interviewed for this book, when asked about their trust in students, spoke of students who exercised self-discipline and who were willing to cooperate with the system of school.

The Five Facets and Teachers' Trust in Students

Although a sense of benevolence or mutual goodwill is an important aspect of trust, trust took on a somewhat narrower definition in the classroom context than it did in regard to relationships between adults, most often being characterized as respect. David, a teacher at Brookside, explained, for example, how the sense of respect was related to evidence among students of reliability and self-control:

> I am looking for respect. That is what I am looking for. If I
> see respect, if I see they just behave well; they respect adults;
> they respect others; they know what school is about in terms
> of coming, paying attention, not goofing off, not punching or
> calling names, those are the kids I put my trust in. Those are
> kids who are usually reliable, dependable. They know what
> the system is, and they are working within the system. They are
> not rebelling or trying to go against the system. I can count

on them, and I can trust them. I can walk out that door and not worry about that child standing up all of a sudden and running across the room and popping somebody or throwing something, or yelling out something inappropriate.

Students who were disrespectful or who had a negative attitude were more difficult for teachers to trust. In addition, students who were impulsive and lacked self-control in responding to social situations with other students or with the teachers themselves tended to provoke greater vigilance and suspicion among teachers.

Honesty was a much bigger issue in fostering faculty trust in relation to students than it was in promoting faculty trust in relation to principals and colleagues, perhaps because it was violated in student contexts more frequently. Many of the teachers in the urban context in which these three schools were situated reported that they regularly dealt with problems of students who engaged in lying, cheating, or stealing. Many teachers, like Rob, at Lincoln, reported having students who not only would steal from other students but would, given the opportunity, steal from teachers as well. Rob said:

Most of them I do trust. There's a couple I can't and I don't. A couple of them will go right up and go through the drawers of my desk and take whatever they want. But both of those students I am thinking about take medication [for attention deficit disorder]. It's easier knowing it is a medical condition. Maybe if they weren't on medication I would be a little less forgiving.

On the whole, teachers were more forgiving of dishonesty from students than they might have been of dishonesty from adults because the teachers acknowledged that the students were just children who were still learning the norms of society and self-control. Teachers nevertheless found it difficult to trust students who defensively blamed others for their problems rather than accepted responsibility for their own behavior. This was especially true when teachers attempted to help students learn to accept responsibility as a precursor to behavior change and who experienced frustration in their efforts to enlist parents in this process.

Openness on the part of students was not often mentioned as a problem. As Mary, a teacher at Lincoln, commented, "99.9 percent of the children are willing to talk about themselves if I show an interest in them and take the time to listen." She talked about the importance of making the time to listen to and get to know her students:

> Early on, it is just my personality to establish rapport with the students and with the parents as soon as I can, talking to them often, and letting them tell their stories. I have a sharing time every day, so [students] can say what is on their minds and they are not interrupting at other times. If they have a story that relates to my life, then I will share a little about myself, and they just love to hear that.

Mary also spoke of the reciprocal nature of trust between teachers and students:

> I look for them to open up to me where their personal life is concerned—what they did at home. Sometimes, if a student doesn't share their personal experiences with you, it may be that they are withdrawn, or they may be intimidated by you as an adult. Usually a child just opens up. To me, that's the grounds for trust, because I don't automatically trust a child when they come up to me. I don't think every child is good or not good. It takes time to get to know them. I need background knowledge from them, and they need background knowledge from me. They need to know they can trust me.

For the teachers in my study, competence as a facet of trust in students had more to do with the behavior of students and their willingness to go along with the structures of school than with academic competence. Just as notions of a "good leader" include both task and relationship dimensions, notions of a "good kid" were framed around students who maintained positive relationships and who participated appropriately in the tasks of schooling. Most of the teachers expressed a genuine fondness and caring for their students, even if they were sometimes frustrated by the amount of time and energy they had to devote to disciplining them. In establishing relationships of trust with their students, teachers were above all looking for respect and reliability. For many teachers, there was more leeway in their definition of trust in regard to students because their expectations for them as children were different from those they had for other adults. Simply put, they were willing to cut the students some slack.

Relationship between Teachers' Trust in Students and Achievement

When teachers trust their students, and when they believe that their students are respectful, honest, reliable, open, and competent, they are more likely to create a learning environment that facilitates academic success. There is a growing body of research across a variety of contexts that documents the role of faculty members' trust in students in directly and indirectly fostering student achievement. In a decade-long study of Chicago public schools engaged in reform initiatives, Bryk and Schneider (2002) concluded that trust was a critical factor in predicting which schools would make the greatest gains in student achievement and which would sustain those gains over time. Teachers' trust in students and parents has been found to be strongly related to student achievement in elementary schools (C. M. Adams & Forsyth, 2013; Goddard,

Salloum, & Berebitsky, 2009; Goddard, Tschannen-Moran, & Hoy, 2001); in middle schools (M. Tschannen-Moran, 2004); and across grade levels in an urban context (Moore, 2010). In a European context, Van Maele and Van Houtte (2009) found that the proportion of immigrant students and those from lower socio-economic status was related to the level of faculty members' trust in students and parents. Teachers' trust in students has also been found to be indirectly related to achievement through relation-ships with student attendance rates and discipline referral rates (Moore, 2010).

The powerful role that socioeconomic status (SES) of stu-dents plays as a predictor of student school success has been well documented over the past fifty years. Educational researchers have searched diligently for school factors that predict achieve-ment outcomes above and beyond the effects of SES. And yet, faculty members' trust in students and its close correlates have been found to do just that. Studies have demonstrated a substan-tial relationship between teachers' trust in students and student achievement, even when the impact of socioeconomic status was held constant (C. M. Adams & Forsyth, 2013; Goddard et al., 2001, 2009; Hoy 2002; Hoy & Tschannen-Moran 1999; M. Tschannen-Moran, 2004).

Teachers' trust in students and parents has been found to be closely related to both the beliefs of teachers and the climate of the school, and these three together predict student achievement above and beyond the influence of SES. The sense of collective efficacy of the faculty, that is, the shared belief among a school's teachers that they have the capability to facilitate successful out-comes for all of their students, influences the effort that teachers invest in preparing for and delivering instruction as well as the extent to which they persist in finding new instructional strategies for students who are struggling. In a sample of urban elemen-tary schools, a sense of collective teacher efficacy and teachers' trust in students were strongly related, and the strength of the relationship diminished very little even when SES, race, and past achievement were added as predictors (M. Tschannen-Moran & Goddard, 2001). Collective teacher efficacy beliefs have repeatedly been found to be related to student achievement even when school SES, minority composition, and past achievement were held constant (Goddard, 2001; Goddard, Hoy, & Woolfolk Hoy, 2000; Goddard et al., 2001; M. Tschannen-Moran & Barr, 2004). Moreover, when teachers trust their students, there is likely to be a stronger press for academic achievement. Academic press has also been found to predict stronger student achievement, even when controlling for SES (Goddard et al., 2000; Hoy, Hannum, & Tschannen-Moran, 1998; V. E. Lee and Bryk 1989; V. E. Lee & Smith 1999; M. Tschannen-Moran, Bankole, Mitchell, & Moore, 2013).

These three constructs, faculty members' trust in students, a sense of collective teacher efficacy, and academic press, are so closely linked and such potent predictors of student achievement that together they have been framed as a composite variable called "academic optimism" (Hoy, Tarter, & Hoy, 2006; Kirby & DiPaola, 2011; McGuigan & Hoy, 2006; Smith, Hoy, & Sweetland, 2001). Together, these three variables consistently do what few variables examined by educational researchers have done, and that is to explain student achievement above and beyond the influence of student SES.

When it comes to low-income children whose families are either unable or unwilling to prepare them to access all of the opportunities schools can present, teachers are the primary institutional agents responsible for guiding these students to academic success (Lareau, 1987). Such teachers are in daily contact with students, and thus the quality of their relationships has a large impact on student attitudes and engagement. Building bridges of trust across social class and cultural differences can be a challenge in such situations. Statistical analysis of trust relationships has shown that poverty, more strongly than race or ethnicity, hinders the trust that could lead to achievement (M. Tschannen-Moran, 2001; Van Maele & Van Houtte, 2009). These findings suggests that when teachers draw in-group and out-group distinctions about students, social class is a more salient dividing line than race or ethnicity. Although Brookside, Lincoln, and Fremont each had a diverse faculty, and although some of the teachers had started life in disadvantaged circumstances, teachers had for the most part assumed middle-class values and attitudes that were sometimes at odds with those of the low-income families of their students. Schools with high concentrations of low-income students are likely to benefit from a specific focus on the development of trust.

The evidence is strong that high trust makes schools better places for students to learn. Because of the tendency for trust to build on itself, higher student achievement is likely to produce even greater trust, whereas lower student achievement can be expected to lead to a self-reinforcing spiral of blame and suspicion between teachers and students, lowered collective efficacy, and weakened academic press—all of which could further impair student achievement. As school leaders come to appreciate the importance of trust in learning environments and learn how better to cultivate high-trust schools, greater student success is likely to follow.

STUDENTS' TRUST IN TEACHERS

As we have seen, teachers who trust their students are more likely to create a learning environment that facilitates student academic success. Teachers with greater trust in their students have been found to adopt a more humanistic stance toward the discipline of their students (Karakus & Savas, 2012). When teachers don't trust their students, it is likely to be evident to students in the guarded tone, orientation toward control, and generally negative affect that teachers display in the classroom as well as in informal interactions. It may also show up as a lack of warmth or empathy for students and as a propensity on the part of teachers to blame students for poor performance or behavior.

Teaching is much more than disseminating information and demonstrating skills. Done well, it involves a high level of engagement between teachers and students. Trust facilitates that engagement. The more students are able to trust their teachers, the more willing they are to open themselves up to the risks involved in learning both the academic curriculum and the social and emotional skills they need for academic and life success (Watson, 2003). Without trust, students lose a valuable form of social support and a bridge into the world of the educated. For teachers to help students access the opportunities that schooling can provide, they need to build trusting connections with their students.

Initiation

Teaching involves inviting students into new ways of seeing the world, inducting them into the community of the educated, as well as into habits of mind that include approaching the world with curiosity, asking for evidence, and taking the perspectives of others (Strike, 1999). Central to the transformational processes of education is learning to trust others outside the family, because much of what students learn in school requires them to rely on the written or spoken words of others (Rotter, 1967). A great deal of what we ask students to learn in science, history, and geography, for example, is outside their direct experience. When we ask students to believe that all matter is made up of atoms and molecules, that ancient Egyptians once built large pyramids, or that the island of Madagascar is not just a place in an animated film, we are asking them to accept information that they cannot readily verify firsthand. On the one hand, if teachers are not regarded as credible sources of information, students will have difficulty accepting their guidance. On the other hand, part of what it takes to be well educated is to become discerning about what one believes. So the goal of education may be described as teaching students to be sufficiently trusting but without being gullible and to consider the credibility of the sources of information they accept.

In the best sense, education involves an initiation into a community of practice and traditions of academic thought appraised as valuable. "Initiation into a discipline is initiation into a community of shared standards, virtues, and goods; to accept these goods and standards is an act of affiliation, of joining" (Strike, 1999, p. 231). Teachers derive their authority from embodying the practices, values, and standards of the community. They provide students with the concepts and vocabulary that define the traditions of their subject matter, and they lead students through activities that enable students to gain mastery in the requisite practices. To serve as exemplars, teachers must be motivated by the standards of excellence of that community and must view those standards as valuable. As Strike (1999) observed:

> A mathematics teacher who can solve problems and theorems, but who has no love of an elegant proof and no disposition to rigour, may teach math skills, but such a teacher cannot initiate students in the practice of mathematics in a way that contributes to human flourishing. (p. 230)

When teachers extend to students an invitation to affiliate with a community of practice, they are inviting those students into a community whose values and standards are initially unfamiliar to them. Accepting this invitation requires trust because the students have to begin the process of joining the community before they have the ability to assess the value of doing so or of engaging in the associated intellectual practices that are developed only by achieving mastery (Strike, 1999). Once that trust is earned by one teacher, however, it may come to be transferred to the community the teacher represents. These dynamics may help account for the higher levels of learning and achievement among students with high levels of trust in their teachers.

When trust between teachers and students breaks down or fails to develop in the first place, a number of problems arise. Not only is there insufficient safety to support the kinds of risk taking necessary to learn new skills, but also teachers may resort to more rigid forms of discipline and control as well as the use of extrinsic rewards. Teachers who do not trust their students are likely to rely on inflexible rules and to treat students collectively, as a unit rather than as individuals. Exercising control over the student community, often through the use of extrinsic rewards and punishments, then takes precedence over fostering the conditions for independent thought and induction into a community of practice. Such attempts to control typically diminish rather than increase student motivation, learning, and engagement. As Strike (1999) noted:

> When external goods are overly relied upon to motivate, they can come to substitute for the intrinsic goods, not point to them. Additionally, the consistent and pervasive use of extrinsic motivation may well convey a message of social approval of these motives and of disapproval of intrinsic motivation. (p. 230)

When teachers make use of extrinsic rewards to motivate students, in other words, the students may go through the motions of a practice, but those motions may prove to be insufficient to produce in the students an experience of valuing the practice (or the concepts associated with the practice) for its own sake. Teachers may employ extrinsic rewards to gain compliance without asking for trust; however, such compliance does not generate the engagement in a particular intellectual practice that will foster a sense of the intrinsic value of the practice. The problem with systems of rewards and punishments in a community of learning is that at best they accomplish temporary control and at worst, particularly for students without a strong attachment to school, they confirm students' view of relationships as coercive (Watson, 2003). When such coercive requirements are used to force compliance, student alienation is likely. In contrast, when teachers extend trust to facilitate student learning, it is likely to elicit instructional practices and behaviors based on attraction, engagement, and identification (C. Adams, 2010).

Student Perspectives

An important and promising new development in the research on trust in schools has been the relatively recent addition of student voices and perspectives concerning their teachers. The evidence base for the importance of students' trust in teachers is as compelling as the strong evidence base for the importance of teachers' trust in students. The relationships between teachers and students are reciprocal. When teachers trust their students, students are more likely to trust them in return (Moore, 2010). Learning is a risky business, and students are not likely to take the risks involved in learning unless there is mutual trust. Students' trust in teachers has been found to be strongly and consistently related to student achievement on standardized state exams across a wide variety of contexts (C. Adams, 2010; Mitchell, Forsyth, & Robinson, 2008; Mitchell et al., 2010; Moore, 2010; M. Tschannen-Moran et al., 2013).

In exploring the dynamics that support the strong tie between student trust and achievement, other related constructs have been examined. One such construct that has demonstrated strong relationships both to students' trust in teachers and to student achievement is students' identification with school. Students' identification with school encompasses two thrusts, namely that students value the purposes of school and that they feel a sense of belonging or fitting in. These two thrusts are aligned so closely that they cannot be distinguished statistically and therefore can be viewed as constituting a single construct. When students trust their teachers and believe that they have their best interests at heart, they will be more likely to value the whole enterprise of school and school-related outcomes as well as to feel that they belong to the school community (Mitchell et al., 2010; M. Tschannen-Moran et al., 2013). Furthermore, Mitchell et al. (2008) found that students' trust in their principal and parents' trust in the school were stronger predictors of students' identification with school than SES. In fact, when aggregated to the school level, SES was not found to be a significant predictor of students' identification with school.

In addition to students' identification with school, students' perceptions of the academic press in their school have been found to be related closely to their trust in their teachers (M. Tschannen-Moran et al., 2013). Although student trust, students' identification with school, and students' perceptions of academic press were all found to be significant predictors of student achievement, in a regression analysis student trust was found to be the strongest predictor of student achievement. Students' trust in teachers is influenced not only by the climate in their school but also by their home environment. The level of academic emphasis in students' homes has been found to be a strong predictor of students' trust in their teachers (C. Adams, 2010). When parents trust the teachers, students typically do as well.

Both students' trust in their teachers and their identification with school have also been found to be related to students' feelings of safety (Mitchell et al., 2008, 2010) as well as to their attendance at school (Moore, 2010). When students had low trust in their teachers and school leaders, they felt less safe at school and their attendance suffered. In a study among middle school students in Korea, student trust was found to be related to students' motivation, adjustment to school, and academic performance (S.-J. Lee, 2007). The teacher-student trust relationship contributed to students' performance both directly and indirectly, affecting school adjustment and academic motivation.

Listening to student voices provides an interesting perspective on the development of trust between students and their teachers. In a qualitative study of urban youth involved in a multiyear intervention to support their enrollment and success in higher education, the students reported that they had tested the benevolence and trustworthiness of the adults in the program before they were willing to let down their guard and begin to trust them (Owens & Johnson, 2009). Once trust was established, however, the students began to cooperate with the program structure, to demonstrate leadership in program activities, and to promote the program among their friends and family members. This continuum of behavior was described as moving from calculation to courtship, and finally to contribution. In a study of the perceptions of nine middle school students in a private school setting, the students interviewed described teachers as caring, which included being student focused and demonstrating genuine listening, openness in sharing stories from their real-life experiences, honesty, dependability, clear communication, and flexibility in creating a positive and relaxed learning environment (Kauffman, 2013). A third, mixed-methods study that used interviews and surveys with thirty-two teachers and thirty-two discipline-referred students found a connection between the adolescents' perceptions of their teachers as trustworthy authority figures and the extent to which their behavior was cooperative or defiant (Gregory & Ripski, 2008). In sum, teachers may earn the trust and cooperation of their students if they use relationship-building strategies and persist in such attempts even when the students initially test their goodwill with defiance (Hattie, 2012; Johnson, Perez, & Uline, 2013).

Last year, I had a student who really gave me a run
for my money. He was defiant at every opportunity, and
it seemed that his mission in life was to make me angry
and to try to turn the class against me. I never gave in to
him, and I kept making him behave the way he needed to.
In the end, I was shocked by how it turned out! A student
who had me considering quitting teaching ultimately became a
student who would attend every after-school event I held, from
philanthropy to English remediation. At the end of the year,
I received a very sweet letter from him, thanking me for
teaching him and making him laugh. It was an important
lesson in never giving up on students and that,
sometimes, showing students that you care and
that they can trust you means setting high
expectations and holding them accountable.

—CHELSEA, HIGH SCHOOL ENGLISH TEACHER

EARNING STUDENT TRUST

The old adage, "They don't care how much you know until they
know how much you care," is nowhere more evident than in the
relationships between students and educators. Teachers and principals earn the trust of their students first and foremost by demonstrating that they care, persuading students of their underlying
goodwill and intentions, even if the process of education at times
requires discipline and the correction of misbehavior or misguided
thinking. In the classroom, once teachers have demonstrated consistent and firm caring, they have laid the groundwork from which
they can push students to more ambitious learning goals. David, a
Brookside teacher, for example, talked about the art of knowing

when to push and when to pull students—the tenuous balance between supporting students over an ego-threatening hurdle in learning and challenging them to higher levels of performance. He explained, "Once I have developed that trust, and they really know I care, then I can push them and learning really takes off." When students trust their teachers, they are more likely to take the risks that new learning entails.

Rethinking Student Misbehavior

Fostering trusting relationships with students who are well behaved and act in ways that are expected of them may come easily to teachers, but cultivating trust with students whose behavior is out of alignment with the norms and practices of a school often presents more of a challenge. How we understand the underlying causes of student misbehavior may make cultivating trusting relationships even harder. We tend to assume that school-age children should have the interpersonal skills they need to meet the behavior expectations of school, and if they misbehave, we typically think of it as an act of willfulness or selfishness. Much of our thinking about why children misbehave has been guided by Freudian conceptions of children as pleasure seekers who need to be tamed and civilized through punishment of inappropriate urges, as well as by behaviorism's theories of children as passively responding to a set of externally controlled stimuli (Watson, 2003). From these perspectives, children need to be coaxed to conform to our expectations through a program of external reinforcements. Get the external stimuli right, the thinking goes, and children will behave in accordance with our wishes. These theories have worked well enough to have persisted in schools, but they leave substantial gaps in explaining student misbehavior and suggesting productive interventions for improving student behavior. Attachment theory offers an alternative explanation of student misbehavior and an alternate set of interventions. From this perspective, building collaborative, trusting, and supportive relationships with children and adolescents is at the heart of the work of teaching and socializing students (Watson, 2003).

The problem of student misbehavior is a significant one for schools. Most schools have a stubborn list of "frequent flyers," or students whose persistent misbehavior makes them frequent visitors to the principal's office, in-school suspension rooms, and other repositories for children who seemingly can't or won't behave in ways that are expected of them in the classroom. Even as educators increase the intensity of the punishments and negative reinforcements used to intervene with these students, there may be little improvement in their behavior. The same students who are being sent to the principal's office in second grade are likely to be found in the in-school suspension room in eighth grade, and they may have left school altogether by their senior year.

The reason that traditional means of intervention have such a poor track record of success may lie not with the children but with the inadequacy of the theories we are using to understand their behaviors and motivations (Watson, 2003). The underlying theories of the causes of and remedies for student misbehavior are not as robust as we have supposed because they are based on a basic mistrust of students and even of human nature itself. These theories, rooted in pessimistic and cynical views of human nature, lead us to assume that children will do as we ask only if we offer them extrinsic rewards or praise and that they will not stop their misbehavior unless they experience unpleasant consequences. The interventions for children who are not behaving well that stem from this kind of thinking rely on programs of increasingly unpleasant consequences leading up to and including the removal of uncooperative or defiant students from the social setting of the classroom or school altogether in hopes that the pain of isolation will provide a sufficient incentive for children to exercise greater self-control in the future. Unfortunately, in doing so, schools may unwittingly contribute to the low self-esteem and mistrust that are the underlying causes of the misbehavior and mirror the very parenting strategies that may have led to insecure attachments in the first place. Thus, they add to rather than reduce the problem of student misbehavior.

Attachment theory provides an alternative conception of children as biologically wired to seek a sense of belonging in the social fabric of their community (Howes & Ritchie, 2002; Watson, 2003). As social animals, young people do not have to be forced to affiliate, although those with insecure attachments in the home may need assistance in learning *how* to affiliate in positive ways.

> Disciplining or socializing a child is less a process of *making* a child do what he or she would not otherwise do and more a process of helping a child do what he or she biologically needs and wants to do. (Watson, 2003, p. 280)

Attachment theory suggests that children have an innate need for close attachments to adults, seeking both physical and emotional proximity with the goal of achieving a sense of safety and security. In this view, children are seen as active constructors of meaning who are intrinsically motivated to learn about their social and physical world (Watson, 2003).

For children to feel safe enough to explore their world and to respond to novel events and materials with a sense of openness, according to attachment theory, they will need confidence in their teachers' availability and assistance, should assistance be sought or needed (Howes & Ritchie, 2002). Children with positive teacher-student relationships are better able to make use of the learning opportunities available in the classroom and more readily able to adjust to the behavior demands of the school setting. Children who have a history of insecure attachments to their caregivers at home or at school come to view relationships with authority figures as coercive and to see themselves as unworthy of care (Watson, 2003). These children are less able to navigate the social realm with their peers and to make use of teachers to help them learn. Such distrustful relationships with teachers interfere with their ability to explore and learn in a classroom setting. In describing the continuum of children's orientations, researchers have described four general attachment profiles: secure, insecure anxious-ambivalent, insecure avoidant, and disorganized (Ainsworth, Blehar, Waters, & Wall, 1978; Howes & Ritchie, 2002; Watson, 2003).

- *Secure.* Securely attached children have learned to regard themselves as worthy of care and to trust others to provide the necessary and appropriate care. From this secure base of care, such children generally engage with others in pleasant and cooperative ways and are compliant with teacher directions. They tend to be flexible and resilient, trusting that they can get help from their teachers when they need it. When they seek teacher attention, it is usually for needed help or to share a discovery or accomplishment.

- *Insecure anxious-ambivalent.* Children with an insecure anxious-ambivalent attachment orientation are more dependent on their teachers. In the younger grades, they may be clingy, whiny, and immature. Whining can be annoying to teachers because it is a form of request made with an implied expectation that the request will not be fulfilled. These children tend to be less resourceful, easily frustrated, prone to adopting a passive or helpless stance, and fearful and inhibited in their explorations. Children with this orientation may actively seek unpleasant interactions with their teachers, and may use disruptive behavior to draw their teachers into interpersonal conflict. "Since they expect the adult to reject them, they tend to make 'preemptive strikes,' acting in a hostile fashion before the adult has an opportunity to be rejecting" (Howes & Ritchie, 2002, p. 14).

- *Insecure avoidant.* Children with an insecure avoidant attachment orientation tend to avoid teacher-student interactions altogether. They turn away from rather than seek the comfort of adults because they have experienced rejection and insensitivity from adults in the past. Although they need and want positive working relationships with adults, they are deeply discouraged about their ability to forge such relationships. These children are often hostile and disruptive with peers, engaging in unprovoked aggression, mistreatment, or domination. They may respond to another child's distress in ways that amplify that distress, for example, by taunting, hitting, or laughing at a child who is hurt.

- *Disorganized.* Children with a disorganized attachment orientation have no coherent strategies for interacting with teachers. Their attempts to engage are fragmented and erratic. They do not have reliable means to seek the kinds of assistance and support they need from adult caregivers, and, consequently, they bounce from one ineffective strategy to the next.

If we assume that children have inherent, natural needs and desires to be part of the classroom community, to have positive relationships with their teachers, and to learn about their world, and that what misbehaving children lack are the skills to know how to do so effectively, we will intervene in educative rather than punitive ways when children's behavior does not conform to our expectations. Educators don't need to use rewards and punishments to motivate misbehaving children to become productive members of the classroom community; they need to believe in their capacity and show them how to behave appropriately. A classroom economy based on rewards and punishments is a system whereby the rich get richer and the poor look on with increasing discouragement. The children with secure and supportive relationships at home reap rewards for cooperative behavior that they would have engaged in anyway, while children with insecure attachments at home, where stress or other factors have prevented the parents from providing a secure and consistent base, lose out once again as they watch their more fortunate classmates take home all the prizes. They are thereby left with inadequate social and emotional skills for academic and life success, not knowing how to join the club and collect the rewards.

For students with insecure attachments at home, learning to trust in the context of a caring classroom community can be both challenging and transformative (Watson, 2003). Researchers have found that teachers and children can construct relationships that are different in quality from parent-child attachment relationships. Even if children have not been able to forge prior trusting relationships with adult caregivers, positive teacher-student relationships can provide corrective experiences that compensate for difficult previous relationships (Howes & Ritchie, 2002). Furthermore, studies of resilience among adolescents who have succeeded despite living in highly adverse and difficult circumstances found that they frequently credited a supportive relationship with an adult, usually a teacher, as crucial to their success. When teachers become angry and withdraw their affection, they further alienate insecure students and reinforce the negative views those students have of themselves and of their relationships with others (Watson, 2003). Such consequences isolate rather than integrate children and do not contribute to building their repertoire of prosocial behaviors. What insecurely attached children need, above all, are experiences of secure and nurturing relationships with adult caregivers.

I try to develop trust with all of my students, but it is hard when there are so many of them and just one of me. When I can develop a sense of community in the class so that the other students begin to reach out to the students on the fringes, that's when the breakthroughs really begin to happen.

—DEBORAH, FIFTH-GRADE TEACHER

Creating High-Trust Classrooms

Because teachers hold greater power in teacher-student relation-ships, teachers who hope to create high-trust classrooms must take the initiative in doing so by adopting a trusting stance toward stu-dents. This does not mean being gullible or extending blind trust, but it does mean starting with the premise that students want and need to be a part of a learning community and that, with more or less assistance, all students can learn to function as members of the classroom community. In high-trust classrooms, students will be more likely to take risks, to persevere through difficult situations, to cooperate with teachers, to set challenging goals, and to share the responsibility for their own learning. In contrast, when trust is low, students are likely to engage in self-protective behaviors that can diminish motivation and inhibit learning (Dirks & Ferric, 2001).

Teachers have a choice: they can organize their classroom with an orientation toward either control or commitment. An orienta-tion toward control takes a pessimistic view of students and sug-gests that they must be managed with the skillful use of rewards and punishments. An orientation toward commitment, by con-trast, starts with the underlying assumption that as social beings, children do not need to be coerced into wanting to be in positive relationships with their teachers and peers—they are hardwired to need these relationships. Some students, however, need assistance in finding appropriate and effective strategies for establishing and maintaining these connections. By fostering mutually responsive relationships, there is a diminished need for adults to use power-based, coercive strategies. With this commitment orientation, "classroom management becomes a matter of constructing, main-taining, and sustaining harmonious relationships, rather than of devising strategies for managing and avoiding potential conflict and disruption" (Howes & Ritchie, 2002, p. 41).

Creating a classroom community rooted in commitment to a shared set of norms of cooperation and mutual goodwill requires that children understand that they are part of a larger group and that being thoughtful and cooperative with others benefits both them and the collective (Howes & Ritchie, 2002). Students in such situations rely on the teacher to provide appropriate structure and limits. High expectations are key to the formation and maintenance of high-trust relationships but must be combined with benevolence to be effective. As Howes and Ritchie (2002) noted:

> Many children with difficult life circumstances and certainly children who have prior insecure relationships with their teachers believe that teachers think that they will not be able to do well academically or to regulate their behaviors. When teachers have high expectations, they act as if children will do their best, will follow classroom rules, and will behave in a respectful manner. We observed that only when high expectations were combined with kindness and warmth were they an effective teaching strategy for building positive relationships and disconfirming prior problematic relationship history. (pp. 89–90)

Benevolence

Children learn best when their teachers convey unconditional acceptance and emotional warmth, and respond sensitively to their needs (Pianta & Stuhlman, 2004). Trustworthy teachers embody benevolence through actions that express concern for the overall well-being of students and not just concern for students' academic performance. They demonstrate an interest in students as people, recognizing them as individuals with hopes, dreams, needs, cares, and interests. Receptivity and recognition on the part of teachers lead to responsiveness on the part of students when teachers demonstrate a willingness to invest time and effort in helping to further the students' projects and purposes (Noddings, 2005). When students perceive their teachers as caring and willing to help them succeed, students are more likely to trust the

intentions of their teachers, which can help them to cultivate positive attitudes toward school; to value school; and to develop cooperative, friendly, caring relationships with others.

Honesty

Children are not as gullible as some adults assume, just as
teachers are not as gullible as some school leaders assume. To
establish and maintain high-trust relationships, therefore, it is
important that teachers conduct themselves with honesty and
integrity. Honesty has to do, in part, with the truthfulness or
accuracy of information communicated to students, whereas
integrity has to do with an alignment between one's actions and
one's words. Authenticity is also important in fostering student
trust, requiring that one accept responsibility for one's own
actions rather than searching for scapegoats or others to blame
(M. Tschannen-Moran & Hoy, 2000). When teachers admit to
making mistakes and are willing to apologize, they not only demonstrate authenticity but also act as useful role models to help
students navigate their own missteps. Finally, authenticity implies
a sense of "being real," of not just playing a role but actually letting something of one's unique personality, interests, and passion
show through in appropriate and engaging ways.

Openness

Within the context of teacher-student relationships, openness
begins when teachers adopt an open-hearted and nonjudgmental
attitude toward students, whatever their academic, social, or emotional challenges. Teachers express openness by listening attentively to students' problems and concerns and responding with
empathy. Being emotionally present and listening well convey
caring and help students feel valued (C. Adams, 2010; Noddings,
2005). Openness in this context is less about the completeness
of information shared and more about the quality of caring the

teacher conveys. It is communicated through a teacher's willingness to engage in genuine dialogue with students, and by giving students an appropriate level of influence in making the classroom decisions that affect them.

> Dialogue is open-ended; that is, in a genuine dialogue, neither party knows at the outset what the outcome or decision will be. . . . Dialogue is a common search for understanding, empathy, or appreciation. It can be playful or serious, logical or imaginative, goal or process oriented, but it is always a genuine quest for something undetermined at the beginning. . . . It gives learners opportunities to question "why" and it helps both parties to arrive at well-informed decisions. . . . It also contributes to a habit of mind—that of seeking adequate information on which to make decisions. (Noddings, 2005, p. 23)

Extending trust to students through an openness and a willingness to share small details about their lives outside of school was a strategy that some of the teachers in my study mentioned as being a means they used to foster trust with their students.

Reliability

For teachers to earn the trust of their students and to create a trusting classroom community, they must act with consistency and fairness. Students are in a vulnerable position in relation to teachers, dependent on them to establish the structure and tone of the classroom community, so teacher behaviors that are perceived by students as arbitrary and unpredictable will create an uncertain environment for students. When rules and policies are unevenly or unfairly applied, the resulting lack of safety is likely to preoccupy students and siphon away energy and attention from the learning task. Because teachers serve as attachment figures for students, students must rely on them to provide predictability, support, and security; this is particularly true for students with

insecure attachments or in high-poverty communities where distrust of the education system is high (C. Adams, 2010).

Competence

Competence in teaching involves not just conveying information
but also supporting students' mastery of a set of attitudes, skills,
habits, and concepts. To do this well, teachers must form positive
and productive relationships with students. Certainly pedagogical and content competence on the part of teachers is required if
students are to trust them, but a level of emotional competence is
essential as well. One way that teachers demonstrate this competence is through the modeling their behavior provides. Teachers
model communication patterns, social competence, and coping skills. Teachers also assist students in labeling emotions; in
engaging in help seeking, self-monitoring, and self-regulation;
and in developing strategies to modulate their emotional displays
(C. Adams, 2010; Howes & Ritchie, 2002). In a study of teachers' classroom management strategies, researchers found that the
most effective teachers "were able to preserve classroom rules of
conduct that respected both individual and group learning while
these teachers served as emotional coaches and worked to build
positive attachment relationships" (Howes & Ritchie, 2002, p. 46).

Although the five facets of trust have somewhat different conno-
tations in the context of teacher-student relationships, the basic
underlying structure of trust is the same as what can be found in
the adult relationships within a school. Understanding the benefits of trust, teachers who seek to build a high-trust classroom
can be guided by these five facets in structuring a positive and
productive learning environment.

The school I used to teach at served a primarily low-income
population. When I taught there, the mission statement was all
about creating a vibrant learning community. Since I've left,

there is a new principal, and now the mission statement
is all about the kids' abiding by a behavior plan. I am
alarmed and dismayed by the distrust and low
expectations embodied in that guiding document.

—PAIGE, ELEMENTARY SCHOOL TEACHER

UNDERSTANDING TEACHER AGGRESSION

One of the major obstacles to creating the conditions to foster
student trust in classrooms is the problem of teacher aggression.
Teacher aggression includes teachers' yelling at students, using
sarcasm or humiliation as a means of control, and punishing
the whole class for individual misdemeanors. Attachment theory
offers not only a potentially more powerful way to understand
student misbehavior but also an explanation for these forms
of teacher misbehavior as well. Outnumbered by the students
in their classes, teachers may feel vulnerable to the potential for
student behavior to get out of hand. In these situations, teachers tend to be reactive and may fall into maladaptive patterns of
interaction with difficult students. Examining the causes of such
maladaptive patterns may help principals and teachers better
understand why they occur and provide teachers with strategies
to deliberately change them (Howes & Ritchie, 2002).

Attachment theory suggests that all human beings seek a
sense of "felt security" to navigate their lives and manage anxiety.
When their needs for safety and connection are not met, people
will engage in behaviors intended to cope with the resulting insecurity. Teachers, too, have these needs and will employ strategies
to cope with their own anxiety when they feel stressed by unmet
needs. Riley (2010) noted that teachers with unresolved attachment issues are at risk for aggressive behavior when they feel
rejected by students.

An insecurely attached teacher, who may be consciously or
unconsciously looking for students to provide a corrective
emotional experience through attachment to her, is vulnerable to rejection by those students. Therefore, the threat of,
or actual rejection by students may be an experience likely
to activate the attachment behavioural system in the teachers (Bowlby, 1988). This would inevitably lead to protest
behaviours [by teachers] directed at students to reduce the
separation anxiety caused by the actual (or perceived) rejection. The kind of self-reported aggressive behaviours that
appear in the literature—yelling, sarcasm, humiliation and
punishing the whole class for individual misdemeanours—are
typical of protest behaviours. . . . Making the world a safe and
predictable place, even if unhappy, is a set goal of attachment.
But without a secure base, the teacher only succeeds in recre-
ating her insecure way of relating to students that she sought
to avoid by becoming a teacher. The resultant unhappiness of
this situation may be unconsciously blamed on the students,
who might then be punished for causing the teacher's internal distress. This in turn creates "difficult students" who feel
unsafe with the teacher, a no-win situation. (pp. 61–62, 95–96)

Clearly, intervention by administrators, counselors, and other
support personnel is needed when teachers and students fall into
separation protest behaviors that threaten their emotional safety.

Whether or not teachers choose aggressive means of coping
may depend not only on their own emotional controls but also on
the context in which they are teaching. When principals are supportive, for example, they may function as a secure base for teachers, and teachers may be better able to avoid aggressive behaviors.
In contrast, when school leaders are perceived as threatening to
teachers, the likelihood of teacher aggression is increased (Riley,
2010). Administrators who provide a secure base of support have
been found to offer the corrective experience necessary to assist
teachers with developing more constructive coping behaviors.

In studies of the management of student misbehavior, a number of common features have been found in classrooms where student misbehavior was well managed; primary among the protective factors was a high degree of support offered to teachers by their principal. Teachers' positive perceptions of principal support were consistently related to caring and empathetic behaviors on the part of teachers (ISQ Briefings, 2007; Riley, 2010). The more visible and supportive the principal was in the school, the lower the incidence and intensity of student misbehavior. Riley (2010) noted:

> When teachers felt they had a secure base, in this case a principal who would be available and supportive, they could more easily become the secure base for the students; responding early and flexibly addressing the situation at hand, offering emotional scaffolding for the students and modeling the behaviours they were encouraging the students to also display. (p. 116)

Teachers who felt supported by their principal were less threatened by rejection by students, as their security resided solidly with their relationship with the principal. Although the hierarchical elements that characterize relationships in schools can promote insecurity and defensiveness, including inflexible rule following on the part of teachers in an attempt to create greater safety, the dependency inherent in relationships with both school leaders and students may also afford teachers opportunities to have corrective emotional experiences (Riley, 2010).

In working with teachers who self-reported their own aggressive behaviors in the classroom, Riley (2010) was able, through a series of six structured interviews, to get such teachers to reflect on their own attachment history and issues and to "re-story" (p. 109) their classroom experiences to develop more adaptive classroom management strategies. He found that all of the teachers interviewed had insecure attachment patterns, and that all were able to identify patterns within their family of origin that contributed to their current aggressive behaviors in the classroom. Each reported experiences of having been betrayed, making it difficult for them to extend trust. Most perceived using fear to be the most effective means of controlling students. "Having experienced this type of 'control' in their family [of origin], they each felt that it was their turn to take on that powerful role. Freud called this behaviour 'identification with the aggressor'" (Riley, 2010, p. 91). Riley found that once these teachers had learned about their attachment history and how their attachment issues played out in themselves, they were able to take corrective action to learn more effective strategies for use with their students. All of the teachers reported improvements in their relationships with students, and these improvements were corroborated by principals and assistant principals. For the five teachers in an early cohort of Riley's study, less aggressive behavior patterns had been sustained over a period of five years following the initial interviews.

I have a student who I've been working with all year
to get him to trust me. Then, the other day, my principal
stopped by my room between classes and barked at
me: "I saw the latest benchmark tests for your class,
and they were terrible! I don't know what you're doing,
but you'd better get those scores up." I was so upset
by this unexpected attack that just came out of nowhere!
I was doing my best to hold back my tears as the students
in my next class came in, which included this boy.
But then in the middle of the period he did one of his
little annoying behaviors that I usually ignore, and I blew
up at him. Now he won't look at me, and he avoids me.
It was a huge setback. I feel terrible.

—ASHLEY, EIGHTH-GRADE SOCIAL STUDIES TEACHER

PUTTING IT INTO ACTION

School leaders and teachers need to build trusting relationships with their students to accomplish their essential goals of fostering student achievement and equipping students for citizenship. As principal, you play a critical role in setting a tone of trust in your school. Your attitude toward students, especially misbehaving students and students who fall outside of the mainstream culture, is likely to be contagious. You have the opportunity to demonstrate both your caring and your competence as you engage in proactive strategies to support students for success in regard to both academic performance and behavior. This may involve a reassessment of the school-wide discipline policies and practices as well as the mechanisms for intervening when students begin to fall behind. Earning a reputation for consistency and fairness will pay dividends as you help maintain discipline and exercise your responsibility to shape the character of the young people in your care.

It is incumbent on you, because of your position of power, to take the lead in establishing trusting relationships with both teachers and students. How you understand and respond to teacher aggression is also important in establishing a school-wide tone of trust. You cannot afford to ignore teacher aggression, lest you compromise student learning and leave students in a vulnerable position without an ally. It is also unlikely, however, that taking an aggressive posture with aggressive teachers will have the desired effect. Aggressive teachers may be acting based on their own insecure attachment history; they may, therefore, require assistance not only in finding more effective ways to handle their own and their students' needs for belonging and a sense of community but also in understanding the needs that student rejection stimulates in them. Riley (2010) asserted that "the best way to help students is to meet the needs of their teachers so that they, in turn, can meet their students' needs" (p. 44). When you are supportive of teachers and are able to provide a secure base from which they can operate, you create the conditions for them to serve as a secure base for their insecurely attached students.

KEY POINTS ABOUT CULTIVATING TRUST WITH STUDENTS

- Teachers' trust in students and students' trust in teachers are reciprocal processes. Teacher trust seems to be a necessary precondition for student trust.
- Both teachers' trust in students and students' trust in teachers are strongly related to student achievement.
- Fostering trust can be more difficult with low-income students because teachers may be less confident that such students share the same cultural values and ethical standards.
- Teachers' trust in students is related to other important social processes in schools, such as a sense of collective teacher efficacy and academic press.
- Students' trust in teachers is strongly related to students' identification with school, their feelings of safety, their perceptions of academic press at school and at home, and their attendance rates.
- Attachment theory provides an alternative conception of the underlying causes of student misbehavior and offers potentially more robust and lasting interventions.
- Attachment theory also provides a useful explanation for teacher aggression, and positive interventions stemming from this framework have been found.
- Teachers can create high-trust classrooms through attention to the five facets of trust.
- Principals can help set the tone for trusting relationships with students by modeling constructive attitudes towards students, even those whose behavior and attitude reflect difficulty with adapting to the behavior expectations in the school.

QUESTIONS FOR REFLECTION AND DISCUSSION

1. Think of a time when you visited or participated in a classroom where trust between the students and the teacher was

high. What did you notice? How did it feel? What were the implications of the high level of trust that was present?

2. What specific strategies do you employ to assure students that you care about their well-being and are a trustworthy adult? How do these strategies relate to the five facets of trust?

3. Bring to mind the name and face of a specific student whose behavior is troublesome.

   a. How would attachment theory explain this student's misbehavior?

   b. How does that explanation align with your own perceptions?

   c. How might you intervene differently if you were to conceive of this student's misbehavior as a form of separation protest behavior?

   d. How do the tenets of attachment theory change your thinking as to future interactions you might want to have with this student?

4. Bring to mind a specific teacher you have supervised who has evidenced some level of teacher aggression.

   a. What supervision and coaching strategies flow from attachment theory?

   b. How do those strategies align with what you have tried already or with your own sense of what might work best?

   c. How do the tenets of attachment theory change your thinking as to future interactions you might want to have with this teacher?

   d. What might be done to intervene early in or even to prevent instances of teacher aggression if you, as an administrator, were to understand the underlying cause of teacher aggression to be teachers' own insecure attachments?

5. What is one new strategy with which you might experiment to foster greater trust with students? Which facet of trust most needs to be emphasized or amplified?

CHAPTER 8

BUILDING BRIDGES OF TRUST WITH FAMILIES

The best way to find out if you can trust somebody is to trust them.
—ERNEST HEMINGWAY

Researchers and policymakers alike have increasingly recognized the importance of the quality of the relationships that connect schools and families. Relationships between families and schools have, indeed, become the focus of many federal and state educational policies. For example, the National Policy Forum for Family, School, and Community Engagement (2010) wrote:

> Families and communities can be a force for turning around low-performing schools. Family engagement entails thoughtful effort on the part of districts and schools, so that evidence-based frameworks and practices are adopted, external resources such as community and intermediary organizations are used, and student data become a tool for honest and transparent conversations between families and schools. Underlying these strategies must be a continuous effort at relationship building so that trust binds families, schools, and communities to change the trajectory of underserved students. (p. 17)

Building and extending high trust between families and schools lies at the heart of cultivating productive relationships between home and school, and doing so proves to be particularly important for the education of disadvantaged children (C. M. Adams & Forsyth, 2013; Goddard, Tschannen-Moran & Hoy, 2001).

The role of families in the educational process has traditionally been seen as one of supporting their children's education by sending them to school well rested, fed, clothed, and equipped with their completed homework—in other words, ready to learn. Today, however, parents increasingly conceive of their role as also involving advocating for their children when they feel that their children's needs are not being adequately met by the school system. This may seem to put parents at odds with school personnel, whose job it is to balance the needs of many students. These competing needs point to a crucial interdependence that makes the establishment of trusting relationships with families an essential task for school leaders.

Trust has always been key from the standpoint of families. The trust required to send one's child to school is far different from that required to entrust one's financial assets to a bank or a broker. When people turn over their life savings to a financial institution, they do so with the hope that their assets will be well managed and, through wise investments and strategic efforts, will grow over time. But particularly if those investments are covered by government deposit insurance, much of the element of risk is eliminated. To turn over one's child to an educational institution involves significantly more risk and vulnerability. There are no guaranteed "rates of return," and yet there is the clear understanding that what one holds most dear will be fundamentally changed. Education is a transformational process that has to do with the development not only of skills but also of habits of mind (such as being curious, demonstrating healthy skepticism, and evaluating evidence); habits of heart (such as engaging in the learning process); and habits of will (such as persisting in the face of challenges). Whether or not these skills and habits are developed will inevitably have a profound impact on a child's current well-being and functioning as well as on his or her future opportunities and choices. It's no wonder, then, that trust matters a great deal to the parents of schoolchildren. For productive working relationships between school and home to emerge, educators need to pay attention to those things that make for trust—a key aspect of managing risk in any context.

Principals play an important role in risk management, working to enable and empower productive connections between families and schools. School leaders create the framework and structure for these relationships and, by example, may set the tone for the associated interactions as well. At Brookside, for instance, Brenda set an example for positive relationships with parents and created various social gatherings as opportunities for teachers and parents to engage in important, trust-building dialogue.

THE FACETS OF FAMILY-SCHOOL TRUST

When I began investigating the nature and role of trust in schools, I conceived of teachers' trust in students and trust in parents as being separate from one another. However, when I developed measures on which teachers were asked about their trust in students and their trust in parents as separate variables, I was surprised to find that the answers were statistically indistinguishable. This meant that the faculty did not make clear distinctions between the trust they felt in the students and the trust they felt in the parents. Teachers who rated trust in students as high also indicated high trust in parents; in cases where trust in students was low, trust in parents was low as well. My interviews with the teachers at Lincoln, Fremont, and Brookside reinforced these statistical findings linking teachers' trust in students with their trust in parents. David, a teacher at Brookside, explained that when a child was seen as trustworthy, the trust engendered was extended through the child to the parents:

> This just may be a quirk of mine, but I have a great deal of respect for those parents of the students who have earned my trust. Because those qualities are coming from somewhere, and I say those qualities are coming from home. That's what I say.

Research on trust between schools and families has identified the same five facets of trust found in other relationships explored in this book. In addition to benevolence (and respect), these facets include honesty, openness, reliability, and competence to meet the specific needs of individual students.

Benevolence

Benevolence, or an authentic sense of care for the well-being of another, involves trusting in the intention of another to demonstrate actions that are in the best interests of the person whose trust they hold. Further, benevolence includes believing that something that one cherishes will be taken care of by the person in whom trust is placed. In the relationships between teachers and parents, for example, the differences in the power dynamics had an impact on how the first facet of trust was characterized. Although parents sought a sense of benevolence among teachers to ensure that they would look out for the well-being of their children, teachers more often spoke of respect among parents, rather than benevolence, as the basis of their trust in those parents.

Parents' trust in schools rests heavily on the perceived benevolence of school personnel. Parents want to feel confident that educators care about their children's well-being and genuinely want to see them be successful in school and in life beyond school. This is true for all students, but benevolence takes on particular significance for parents of children with special needs and parents of economically disadvantaged students, who are especially dependent on the skills and motivation of school personnel. Parents who trust educators to care for their children are confident that such educators will consistently act with the best interests of their children in mind, and that their children will be treated with both fairness and compassion.

When parents serve as active participants in their children's education, they develop perceptions of teachers based on how those teachers watch over their children's progress and intervene, when necessary, in the best interests of their children. These interventions, when seen by parents, are opportunities to generate positive perceptions in regard to the benevolence of the teachers and their desire to help each child as an individual.

For their part, the teachers in my study were attuned to whether or not parents were committed to their children. In making judgments about how much trust to place in parents, teachers often mentioned wanting to see a commitment to the child's well-being and to his or her education. They were also looking to see whether or not respect was extended to them as teachers. It was more difficult for teachers to trust parents who were rude or disrespectful. David noted:

> I usually trust parents if they are sincere about their child's education. If they come into the building and they don't pose a threat—where they're wanting to look for the negative. When they give you some positive hints or comments, or some positive body language—that makes me feel comfortable. To me that's very important because the better the lines of communication, the better it is for the child. If the child sees that you don't pose a threat to their parents and they don't pose a threat to you, the child fits into that link and then they can feel more confident to come in and share even personal matters.

When teachers felt that parents shared their commitment to acting in the best interests of their children, even if they occasionally disagreed over what that looked like, they were willing to extend trust to those parents. When teachers were not confident that parents had a child's best interests at heart, they became angry at those parents and did not feel they had the basis to develop trust with them. Rob, a teacher at Lincoln, described the challenge he faced with one of his students:

> I have one little girl whose parents, for some reason, play games and don't give her her medication in the morning. But as soon as she takes her pill at 11:00 she is fine. She is terrible in the morning. She gets so frustrated. She spits, she throws things, she slaps, she gets up, she screams, she leaves the room. At times you get frustrated, but when you think about it, you understand it is not entirely her doing. And then my anger goes to the parents. It has been a long year with this particular family. They don't want to be called at home when the child misbehaves. They want the child identified as disabled, and when the child wasn't identified they got up and stormed out of the room. Personally, I think they wanted money. I think they are using the child. I've heard rumor that they are selling the medication they are supposed to give her in the morning. The child was adopted, and I have my suspicions about why they adopted her.

Teachers also had a sense of what they were owed by parents, and they felt hurt or betrayed when parents did not meet those expectations. Teachers wanted parents to respect their expertise and felt hurt when parents questioned their competence. When parents expressed confidence that a teacher cared, the teacher in turn found it easier to establish an atmosphere of cooperation and mutual respect. Teachers also wanted parents to deal directly with them rather than with the administration when problems arose. Christy, a teacher at Brookside, described an incident that bothered her, in which a parent complained to Brenda about discipline problems in Christy's classroom without discussing the issues with her first:

> I did have some trust issues with a couple of my parents at the beginning of the year that I have not forgotten. The first day of school I must have started out wrong because discipline was a real issue for me. It was a very frustrating situation for me as an educator. Really that first month was really hard on me and took a lot out of me. So, one of my parents came in at 2:00 and stayed in our class for the rest of the day. She had always been very supportive of me. She knew the makeup of the class, and she admitted that it was a very difficult group. Well, she went to the principal later and said I didn't have good discipline. It really hurt me that to my face she seemed all supportive, and then she went and did that. But it is interesting that as the year has gone on, of course, these parents have changed their whole tune about it. They say, "Oh, my child is reading better than he ever has." But I still remember that [incident] because I don't feel it was handled right. I would have preferred it if they had come to me instead of going behind my back and talking to the principal.

Christy's anger increased when she learned that the woman's son had had a reputation as a troublemaker at his previous school. Brenda helped by encouraging the parent to deal directly with Christy and by offering to be a part of the conversation if the parent felt she needed assistance. Christy felt vindicated by the progress she was able to make with this boy as well as with several other troubled students in her class that year.

> As a family, we were very committed to public schools and actively involved in our local school. Then a new principal was assigned to our school that had little administrative training and no experience in an elementary school.

That same year our son was assigned a young,
inexperienced teacher. Instead of looking for the best in
our son, the two of them just saw him as a troublemaker and
a problem. He was sent to the principal's office repeatedly.
They punished him and shamed him in front of his class. He
was isolated, made to sit away from the class, in the hallway, or in
other classrooms. Of course, as this went on he became angrier
and angrier and acted out more. No one questioned that
his behavior might be linked to a learning problem, and
they said they could not help it if some of the
behavior was brought on because he was bored. It
was devastating to watch our charming, clever,
if sometimes mischievous, little boy transformed into
an angry, hostile, and unhappy child. In the end
I felt that I had no choice but to remove him
from school and teach him at home.

—ZOE, HOMESCHOOLING MOTHER

Honesty

A person's honesty has a bearing on whether his or her word can be counted on to be true and on whether commitments he or she has made will be carried out. Honesty is a particularly important facet of trust because it is seen as an indicator of a person's character. Integrity, a component of honesty, has to do with unity between a person's words and his or her deeds. Educators exhibit honesty and integrity in collaboration with families when they demonstrate that their actions align with their words. If parents are told that early intervention will be provided for a struggling learner, for example, and subsequently receive regular updates as to what is being done and how the student is responding to that intervention, trust will increase. Trust is bolstered when educators do what they have committed to doing, whereas distrust is generated when educators fail to follow through on promises or fail to communicate with parents about steps that are being taken.

Authenticity in terms of accepting responsibility for one's behavior is another important aspect of the trust between families and school personnel. Parents who blame others for problems instead of accepting responsibility for their own behavior are difficult for teachers to trust; parents who communicate a shared sense of responsibility are easier for teachers to trust. Likewise, parents find it easier to extend trust to educators who come across as real people, as opposed to those who are so guarded that they come across as people simply filling a role.

In my study, although faculty members' trust in students was mediated by the recognition that they were children and still learning how to get along in the world, their observations of student behavior contributed to a blurring of the lines between trust in students and trust in parents. Several teachers said that when a child misbehaved it was not the child they mistrusted but the parents of that child. Christy made this distinction clear:

> At this age level, I feel that if the child is not trustworthy, it is as a result of the parents. The responsibility isn't really on them at this young age. I tend to get angry with the parents and lose trust with the parents. I don't think I ever lose trust with the child. I get very angry with the parents.

We had a parent who had been very active in fundraising
and helping out at the school over a number of years
as his children came through. But then it came out that
he had been embezzling some of the money he raised.
Over all that time, it added up to quite a bit of money.
There was a series of articles in the paper about it. I used
to feel proud to say where I worked. Now whenever

> I say the name of our school, that's all people want
> to talk about. His wrongdoing has overshadowed
> all of the good things we're doing.
>
> —EMMA, MEDIA SPECIALIST

Openness

Teachers are the first line of communication between a school and its families. Parents rely on this communication, and thus openness is another critical element of building trust with families. Openness, which refers to the sharing of information as well as influence, leads to a greater willingness to share ideas all around. This sharing can generate a greater willingness to pool valuable resources in the name of school improvement. In addition, open communication may confer an advantage on schools because in schools with a high level of trust it is more likely that problems will be shared while they are still small, which allows them to be more easily resolved.

As educators bring parents into the discussion about how a child is performing, parents can see how educators care for and respond to their child's idiosyncrasies and needs. Parents, if they sense both caring and competence on the part of educators, are more likely to become contributing partners in outlining solution strategies for addressing areas of difficulty. Traditional parent-teacher conferences can be fraught with anxiety and a sense of vulnerability on the part of both teachers and parents (Lawrence-Lightfoot, 2003). New technologies are emerging that have greatly facilitated the sharing of information with families, such as Web-based systems for conveying homework expectations and posting grade books. These technologies can be helpful in opening up lines of communication between home and school, but they are more likely to engender trust if their use is preceded by face-to-face communication, telephone communication, or both that establishes rapport with parents, communicates shared goals for student success in both short-term and long-term contexts, and identifies goals for the parent-teacher relationship itself in terms of partnership.

I was chatting with a parent about something fun we
had done in the classroom and what her daughter
had contributed when the mom looked at me and said,
"You really like my daughter, don't you?" I said, "Of course
I do!" She said, "That's all I need. I need to know
she is spending her days with someone who
likes her."

—CINDY, SECOND-GRADE TEACHER

Most of the teachers interviewed at Brookside, Lincoln, and Fremont wanted to have partnerships with parents, but they acknowledged that they did not often initiate contact with parents unless there was a problem with a student. Brenda insisted that every teacher make a positive contact with the parents of each student in his or her classroom before initiating contact of a problem-solving nature. Another program at Brookside aimed to increase the number of positive contacts with parents by sending out a postcard to a child's parents when he or she had done something commendable. At Brookside, students were also expected to attend the quarterly conference between home and school. Students were even expected to lead a portion of the conference, a task that, although challenging, helped each child to accept responsibility for his or her learning and to trust that his or her needs and concerns would be addressed. In such conferences, the student was the direct recipient of praise for whatever progress had been made but also now became the center of the effort to resolve any difficulties. In being made "responsible," each child became more "able to respond."

Parents' willingness to communicate with teachers enhanced the sense of trust between teachers and parents. When a parent was willing to convey his or her trust in a teacher, that sentiment was often reciprocated. In contrast, when parents discounted what teachers said, narrowly taking their child's side and blaming the teacher or other students for the child's misbehavior, distrust was generated. Mary, a teacher at Lincoln, recognized that she could facilitate openness on the part of students and parents not just by showing interest but also by being willing to share information about her own life. She noted:

> Anytime the parents come in for any reason, I try to take the time to talk with them, try to pull information about their lives, what kinds of jobs they have, what kinds of things they do with their children. When I tell them about myself, then I think they feel more comfortable with me. I remind them that I have children because then they say, "Oh, you do understand!" I think that really helps.

In contrast to teachers at Brookside, teachers at both Fremont and Lincoln described discipline that was more reactive than proactive. They reported minimal involvement or communication with parents, and they also noted that whatever communication existed revolved mostly around problematic student behavior. Brian, at Fremont, for example, described his attempts to work with the parent of a child who started the year as a model student but who came back changed after the winter break: hostile, unruly, and unkempt. Brian said the mother had come to the first couple of conferences to address this problem but then stopped coming or even returning phone calls. There were very few social encounters between teachers and parents at Fremont and Lincoln. Even when events were planned, attendance was minimal.

When school personnel have a high level of trust in parents and students, a high level of collaboration between parents and the faculty is also more likely to be evident. Moreover, when students can be counted on to respect the systems and structures of a school, and when parents can be trusted to engage constructively with teachers, a climate of openness in decision making is more likely to be evident. When school personnel have greater trust in parents, educators are less defensive in regard to problems as well as more willing to share authority. And with a greater sense of shared purpose, there is more room at the decision-making table (Hoy & Tschannen-Moran, 1999; M. Tschannen-Moran, 2001). Thus, trust facilitates open communication, just as trust is fostered by communication.

A mother of two middle school students moved into our area. She announced to me that she was not going to send her children to the neighborhood school. I explained that she had a legal obligation to make sure her children were educated, and her only other option was to teach her children at home. The woman declared that that was what she wanted to do. But when she read over the documents I requested from the state on what would be required, she had to admit that she was not prepared to homeschool her children. When I probed further about her resistance to sending her children to school, she declared, "I don't trust the principal." Puzzled, I asked, "You just moved here, how can you know that you don't trust the principal?" The woman replied angrily, "I know because he was my principal when I was in junior high!"

—ROBERT, SOCIAL WORKER

Reliability

Reliability is an important facet of trust because without it you must continually make mental provisions in case people do not come through in the ways that you expect them to. Even if one has confidence in the good intentions of the other party, the benefits of high trust will not be reaped and the penalties associated with low trust will be paid if one cannot rest assured that the other party will do what he or she has committed to doing or what is needed. Parents want to be able to rely on teachers and other school personnel to provide timely feedback on their child's progress and behavior, for example, and they want this feedback to be delivered in a manner that is both respectful and helpful. Parents must also rely on school personnel to fulfill their commitments in terms of the interventions or services to be provided to students. Just as one expects thorough and appropriate assessments to be made in devising medical treatment plans, with reliable, consistent, and even-handed medical practitioners making competent decisions based on evidence, so too do parents expect such reliability in education (M. Tschannen-Moran, 2009). Ongoing, rigorous professional inquiry in regard to how best to educate a child requires joint deliberation on the part of all parties as participants pursue data to bolster decision making and devise educational treatment plans (Elmore, Peterson, & McCarthey, 1996; Fullan, 2003). As for the educators, teachers sense that parents are reliable when they make sure not only that a student arrives at school ready to learn but also that her or his learning is supported at home through proper rest, nutrition, and positive attitudes toward school and schoolwork.

Homework is one topic around which concerns about unreliability are regularly expressed, and it is often a point of contention between schools and families. Educators often want to extend the learning time for their students beyond the school day by sending home extension and practice activities for students to complete either independently or with family members. In many instances, these activities provide an opportunity for family members to be involved in a child's learning and contribute to this important part of his or her life. For parents under stress, however, homework can become a battleground, both with their child and with their child's teachers, when it is not completed and returned reliably.

Schools can be sensitive to families' differing capacities and needs around homework by building flexibility and support into their expectations for work to be completed outside the classroom. Asking parents about the capacity and context for completing extension work at home and offering to help them invent good homework strategies and plans, rather than assuming a one-size-fits-all stance and telling parents what to do, is an approach that may be met with greater reliability on the part of parents in terms of their participation in student work.

Competence

The final facet of trust is competence. This refers to someone's ability to meet expectations in regard to the successful completion of a task. Parents want to feel confident that teachers and other school personnel are competent in their respective jobs because the stakes—their child's present and future success—are so high. They want to be assured that their child's teachers have not only subject matter expertise but also pedagogical and classroom management skills. As parents see their child overcome difficulties through teachers' implementation of effective instructional strategies and interventions, they are more likely to have confidence in the school's ability to meet their child's needs. Teachers and school leaders also demonstrate competence when they maintain control of themselves in ways that parents respect, even in stressful situations. If teachers or school leaders lose their temper in interactions with a student or a parent, it is likely to be read as evidence of a lack of competence. It is also likely to undermine a parent's overall sense of safety about the school setting because school personnel have the power to punish children in ways that can affect their overall life trajectory. The stakes, in other words, are high, and parents are rightfully on guard.

This works the other way around as well. In making trust judgments about parents, teachers pay special attention to the level of competence evident in their basic parenting skills. When teachers perceive that parents lack the competence to provide basic necessities, structure, and support for their children, trust in parents is more difficult to establish, and that gets reflected in teacher attitudes as well as classroom dynamics. Furthermore, when parents seem unable to control their temper, educators are understandably wary.

I had a little boy last year that came from a poor, dysfunctional family. He was the oldest of five children, and everybody had different fathers. They did a lot of moving.
I think he could have learned easily if he had been in a stable environment and had emotional support. He was very hyperactive, always trying to threaten the other children, hurting them when he got the chance. No respect for other children, not even respect for adults. Although I would get angry at him for his behaviors, I was so mad at the mother.
I directed all my frustration at the parents. There was nothing else wrong with him other than that he never had the consistency of a normal family. It was so frustrating.

—BARBARA, SECOND-GRADE TEACHER

At times, the teachers I interviewed were willing to give parents the benefit of the doubt, expressing empathy for their situation. They recognized that some parents were at a loss as to how to discipline or care for their child. David recognized the complexity of the parenting task when he noted, "Some are to the point where they don't know what else to do. They say, 'I tried this, I tried that.' I'm sure in their own way they will do what they can." Other times, teachers appeared to resent the ways in which their job was made more difficult by incompetent parenting. Such resentment can create a vicious, self-fulfilling spiral in which trust becomes difficult to establish and, as a result, teachers, parents, and students are not able to reap the benefits of trust.

TRUST AND FAMILY ENGAGEMENT

Forming a support system that is responsive to children's needs is the shared responsibility of schools and families. Caring teachers and supportive home environments help students internalize the values of education, and schools are more effective at cultivating student commitment to and involvement in the learning process when families support and cooperate with teachers (Ryan & Stiller, 1994). Although parents' engagement with schools has largely been a taken-for-granted part of schooling, researchers have only recently begun to recognize the critical role that trust plays in the relationships that connect families and schools. The quality of trust in these relationships and the impact of that quality on school environments and student achievement have taken on increased importance. Broadly speaking, these relationships seem to be yet another area in which the rich get richer and the poor get poorer. Research has demonstrated that trust between families and schools is more likely to develop in schools where student achievement is higher and where the student body is more stable. In schools with transitory student populations and where student achievement is lower, trust and the benefits of trust are more difficult to cultivate. Overall, research on trust between families and schools has found trust to be positively related to a family's commitment to the school, the school's outreach to parents, and the collective sense of responsibility shared by families and the school (Bryk & Schneider, 1996).

Teachers' Trust in Families

Schools typically assert a stance of partnership with parents, yet the cultures of schools vary widely in their attitude toward families. A study that examined educators' beliefs about family involvement found significant gaps between the practices educators believed were important and what they actually did, revealing a discrepancy in espoused versus enacted values (Barnyak & McNelly, 2009). Many factors play into this discrepancy. Good intentions to forge partnerships may be inhibited, for example, by time constraints on both sides of the relationship. Attitudes toward parents based on the level of trust also contribute to this discrepancy, as partnerships with families rise and fall with trust. Although schools typically profess to value parent engagement, research has demonstrated that outreach efforts are likely to flounder when trust is low or poorly developed (Bryk & Schneider, 2002). When the level of collective trust in parents is high, schools reach out to parents more robustly. Conversely, the sense of partnership is likely to be inhibited when trust between educators and parents is impaired (Karakus & Savas, 2012).

Some schools actively cultivate family involvement, the collective attitude of teachers and administrators being one of openness and welcome. In these schools, school personnel genuinely believe that families have a valuable contribution to make in regard to their children's education. As a result, these schools have developed policies, practices, and traditions that communicate to parents not only that their involvement and input are valued but also that the school is willing to be flexible in working around obstacles to that involvement, such as parents' work schedules or the needs of younger children. In many schools, however, although parent involvement is an espoused value, the reality is quite different, and the tone is anything but welcoming. Outside of a narrowly prescribed set of behaviors, such as helping with homework and attending parent-teacher conferences, parents in these schools are seen as more of a hindrance to the educational process than as an integral part and a help (Epstein, 1988; A. T. Henderson & Mapp, 2002; Mapp, 2004). Parents may even be seen as intruders who interfere with the important work being done in the school or who think they know more than the educators about how to educate students

(Lareau & Horvat, 1999). In such situations, antagonism between parents and the school may be high while trust is low.

Reluctance on the part of educators to engage with families may also relate to their lack of confidence in their own ability to build the requisite bridges with them. It may be that their intentions to establish partnerships are good, but that they just don't know how to forge those partnerships effectively. Teachers with high self-efficacy and schools with a strong sense of collective efficacy are more likely to extend support to parents and seek them out as partners in a student's education (Bandura, 1997). Furthermore, frequent and productive communication between home and school has been found to be more likely in schools with a strong sense of collective efficacy (Epstein, 1988). In a study of organizational trust in urban elementary schools, greater trust was positively related to teacher self-efficacy in terms of stronger perceptions of the ability of the faculty to plan and implement actions leading to student success (Hoy & Tschannen-Moran, 1999). This trust helped foster a stronger learning dynamic both at home and in the school environment.

A deeper form of family engagement, namely, that of collaborative problem solving between parents and teachers, has also been linked to faculty trust (Karakus & Savas, 2012). In one study of urban elementary schools, faculty members' trust in parents and students was notably found to explain nearly two-thirds of the variance in regard to parent collaboration in school decision making (M. Tschannen-Moran, 2001). This finding indicates that the more faculty members trust the parents, the greater the likelihood that the parents will participle in decision making and influence important school decisions. Furthermore, a widespread culture of trust between the principal, teachers, students, and parents was found to predict more widespread collaboration across all constituencies. Of the various forms of trust measured in this particular study, faculty members' trust in students and their parents was most influential in predicting the set of collaboration variables (M. Tschannen-Moran, 2001). Thus, the inclusion of parents in decision making was more likely to happen in schools where trust levels were high across all constituencies.

It is likely that teachers' and school leaders' level of trust in parents, whether high or low, is quite evident to parents. Attitudes about trust are not easily faked. Thus, the trust that educators extend to students and parents will set an important tone for these vital relationships. When high trust is extended to families, that trust is likely to be reciprocated on the part of parents toward teachers and the entire school community. Conversely, low trust from teachers toward students and parents may spark widespread suspicion and even contempt among parents.

Parents' Trust in Schools

Although limited studies are available on the direct impact of parents' trust in schools, the few that do exist highlight some important findings. In exploring the factors that influence parents' involvement in a school, specifically those parents coming from economically distressed circumstances, relational school factors have been found to have a major impact (Abdul-Adil & Farmer, 2006; A. T. Henderson & Mapp, 2002; Mapp, 2004). In a study by the Consortium on Chicago School Research, the educators at 210 schools were surveyed in an attempt to identify the characteristics shared by the schools that were improving. Parent-teacher relationships at the top 30 schools were found to be significantly stronger than at the bottom 30 schools, leading the authors to conclude that trust as a quality of the relationships between families and schools is a key factor associated with improving schools (Payne & Kaba, 2001).

How parents and community members are viewed and treated by school personnel, namely, as assets to the process of raising student achievement levels rather than as liabilities, has surfaced as a factor influencing educational outcomes throughout the studies that have been conducted. A. T. Henderson and Mapp (2002), for example, concluded that when a school community welcomes parents into the school, fosters caring and trusting relationships with parents, honors their participation, and connects with parents through a focus on the children and their learning, parents are then more likely to be involved in the school, with consequent benefits for the students. Payne and Kaba (2001) took this further when they stated that the level of trust in a school community, including the quality of relationships between teachers and between teachers and parents at a school, can predict not only the quality of a school environment but also its educational outcomes.

Parent trust has been found to vary considerably from school to school (C. M. Adams, Forsyth, & Mitchell, 2009). Fortunately, trust is not dependent on social and contextual challenges, and school leaders in various contexts have been able to build and sustain parent trust by aligning policies and practices to address the pressing concerns and needs of parents. Doing so reduces parents' perceived vulnerabilities and risks within the parent-school relationship. Trust was also developed through the social interactions of parents and educators, as well as through the ways in which both parents and teachers met the expectations and responsibilities they held for one another.

In multiple studies, parents' trust in teachers was found to be higher than teachers' trust in parents (K. S. Adams & Christenson, 1998, 2000; Van Maele, Forsyth, & Van Houtte, 2014). The trust of parents and teachers was also determined to be higher at the elementary level than at the secondary level, with parent trust declining measurably between elementary and secondary schools. It is important to note that parents who reported low to moderate levels of trust also engaged in parent involvement activities less frequently than did those who reported high levels of trust (K. S. Adams & Christenson, 1998). The amount of special education services children were receiving led to significant differences in parents' trust in their school. Parents whose children were receiving higher levels of special education services reported greater trust in their school. Researchers speculated that this was due to more interactions and exchanges between the family and the school, in addition to the benefits of the services themselves. At the high school level, performance measures such as the number of credits earned, grade point average, and attendance correlated significantly with parent trust (K. S. Adams & Christenson, 2000).

Communication

When it comes to communication between home and school, quality seems to matter more than quantity. In a study of trust in family-school relationships, the tone and helpfulness of parent-teacher interactions was a better predictor of trust than was the frequency of those interactions (K. S. Adams & Christenson, 2000). Improving the quality of communication between home and school was noted as the best way to build trust between families and a school. In building trust, conveying respect proved to be more important than maintaining the regularity of contact, although the latter was not totally unimportant. When the regularity of contact dropped below a certain critical threshold, the quality of the relationship itself began to suffer measurable harm. Quality and quantity are, therefore, both important aspects of communication, with quality being the more pivotal of the two.

Family-school partnerships enhance student success when the goals of those partnerships are centered directly on improving educational outcomes for students (K. S. Adams & Christenson, 2000). In addition, it is important for partners to operate with the understanding and belief that parents and teachers share the responsibility for educational outcomes. This orientation fosters two-way communication and increases parent participation in educational activities. Equipping teachers with the skill of perspective-taking toward parents, such that they adopt a nonblaming stance in their interactions with parents, and providing a range of options for meaningful parent participation at school also contribute to higher parent-teacher trust. In sum, cultivating high-quality, respectful communication, at regular intervals, is an essential task of school leadership.

Partnership and Collaboration

Parents' desire to be involved in their children's education is enhanced when teachers and principals recognize and value parents as partners in the educational development of their children. Whether parents perceive that they have a voice and can influence school decisions and whether their children feel a sense of belonging at school both influence parents' trust in a school to a much greater extent than contextual conditions, such as a school's poverty status, size, diverse ethnic composition, and grade level (Abdul-Adil & Farmer, 2006; C. M. Adams et al., 2009). This suggests that school leaders can build and sustain parent trust by aligning policies and practices to be responsive to the needs of families and to reduce the sense of vulnerability they perceive in the parent-school relationship.

Effective family and community engagement in low-performing schools often must begin with intensive efforts to rebuild trust, given long-standing dynamics of miscommunication and distrust between these schools and their surrounding communities. Efforts to help facilitate improvements in school-community relationships and foster a sense of trust and collaboration among families and school personnel provide the necessary foundation on which to build meaningful partnerships between home and school (National Policy Forum for Family, School, and Community Engagement, 2010). Building such partnerships is a primary job for school leaders. "In the absence of trust," C. Adams (2010) observed, "individuals protect themselves from potential negative outcomes by withdrawing from relationships" (p. 265). It is essential for school leaders to cultivate a spirit of partnership and collaboration because these elements are essential for student achievement.

Whenever we had an event at school, my principal would
drive into the projects where many of our students
came from, and drive slowly through the streets.
The kids and parents would come out and get in her
car for a ride to school. When her car was full, she
would drive them over to the school, and then
go back to get another load.

—PAIGE, ELEMENTARY SCHOOL TEACHER

Student Achievement

There is a growing body of research documenting the powerful role that fostering mutual trust between families and schools has in relation to student achievement. A number of studies have pointed to the way strong family-school relationships enhance student achievement (Conway & Houtenville, 2008; A. T. Henderson & Mapp, 2002; Jeynes, 2005). This even proves to be true after accounting for the cognitive ability of students and the socioeconomic status of families (Epstein, 1988; Mapp, 2004; Purkey & Smith 1983; Westat and Policy Studies Associates, 2001). In an analysis of data from the elementary schools in an urban school district, for example, Pennycuff (2009) found that when parents trusted school personnel, they were more likely to be engaged at school and to be physically present for school functions, such as parent-teacher conferences and student performances. They were also more likely to perceive that the school was a safe place for their children and that there was a strong emphasis on academics. By promoting engagement, safety, and an emphasis on academics, trust facilitated increased student achievement in reading, even when controlling for the effects of the socioeconomic status of students.

The attitudes that parents convey to students about school may be the most powerful outgrowth of parents' trust in schools. In a meta-analysis of research on parent involvement in middle schools, Hill and Tyson (2009) found that although almost all forms of parent involvement were positively associated with achievement, strategies reflecting academic socialization in the home had the strongest positive association with achievement. The authors suggested that socialization to value and take responsibility for academics is consistent with the developmental stage and tasks of early adolescence. Similarly, C. Adams (2010) coined the phrase for this form of socialization as "home academic emphasis" and found that students were much more likely to trust teachers when there was a strong emphasis on academics at home.

Diversity in Socioeconomic Status and Race

Research has provided a mixed record in terms of the impact of socioeconomic and racial diversity in a school on the trust present in the relationship between teachers and families. Lareau (1987) asserted that social class explains much of the variation among schools in the ways in which they expect parents to partner with them. In one study, the proportion of students receiving meals for free or at a reduced price was found to explain approximately two-thirds of the variance in trust levels across schools (Goddard et al., 2001), indicating that low socioeconomic status (SES) takes a negative toll on the relationships between students, parents, and teachers. In contrast, another study found that the income level of families, their ethnicity, and student enrollment in special or regular education had no significant effects on the quality of family-school trust relationships (K. S. Adams & Christenson, 2000).

The combination of race and ethnicity with SES compli-
cates the picture of trust between families and schools. When
SES and race or ethnicity were examined in the same statistical
analyses, trust was found to be affected more significantly by
SES than by race or ethnicity (Goddard et al., 2001; Van Maele
et al., 2014). Because poverty was found to hinder trusting relationships, developing relationships built on the facets of trust
is particularly important for educators working with families of
low SES. Establishing trust with families is important because
trust has been found to be related to a strong press for academics as well as to the faculty's collective efficacy beliefs, and these
are strongly related to student achievement (Hoy, Tarter, &
Hoy, 2006; Kirby & DiPaola, 2011). After controlling for race,
gender, SES, and past educational achievements, researchers
have found that educators' trust in parents and students has the
potential to be strong enough to overcome the negative effects of
poverty on achievement (C. M. Adams & Forsyth, 2013; Goddard
et al., 2001).

Trust matters most, then, in distressed communities. Yet
social class, race, and cultural differences can present challenges
to fostering trust between families and schools. In a study that
examined the dynamics of race in the relationships between
families and schools, Lareau and Horvat (1999) found significant
differences between how educators saw their efforts to engage
parents and how those efforts were perceived by black and
white parents. The educators thought that they had been very
welcoming of parent involvement and believed that their requests
for parent involvement were effective and focused on promoting
higher achievement, but the parents perceived those efforts differently. From the parents' perspective, the teachers wanted them not
only to be positive and supportive but also to trust implicitly their
judgments and assessments. Parents thought the teachers preferred
parents who deferred to them and accepted their opinions about
their children without question. Many black families felt excluded

by this narrow frame of acceptable behaviors. They often had a keen sense of race relations and how those dynamics pervaded the school, leading black families to conclude that their attempts to advocate for their children were viewed as destructive or unacceptable. The white parents who participated in the study did not exhibit the same level of suspicion, distrust, and hostility toward schools as that found among some of the black parents. However, even among the black families, there were important social class differences in how they managed their concerns. Middle-class black parents were much more likely than the low-income black parents to find ways to advocate for their child's needs that were accepted by teachers. Among white, working-class parents, there were also conflicts with the school, but these parents were more likely to focus on their own child's experience and to discuss the problems in terms of one teacher, rather as concerns about the school as a whole.

Schools serving increasingly diverse student populations may have to work especially hard to cultivate trust with parents. Latino parents who were interviewed by Finders and Lewis (1994) wanted to be included in the schooling of their children and to have a positive, constructive relationship with the school. Issues of language and cultural barriers, conflicting work schedules, and attitudes stemming from Latino family members' own negative school experiences, however, have been found to present barriers to cultivating trusting relationships between Latino families and schools (Linse, 2010). In an urban elementary school serving a largely Latino student population, Peña (2000) found that parent involvement was heavily influenced by the attitudes of school personnel. She emphasized the importance of school personnel's being welcoming, taking the time to gain the trust of parents, and informing them of how they could be involved. School personnel communicated respect and benevolence when they worked to find ways around the many barriers to parent involvement, such as the lack of availability of child care, language differences, and cultural influences that colored parents' expectations of how they should interact with school personnel. Taking proactive steps toward fostering trust took on even greater importance for parents whose educational level was below that of the teachers.

When talking with educators, the message
I often hear is, "We wish we could find ways to get
parents more involved." As a parent, though,
the message I get from the school is, "Keep out,
keep out, keep out!"

—MARK, PARENT OF TWO ELEMENTARY SCHOOL STUDENTS

FOSTERING TRUST WITH FAMILIES

Faculty members' trust in students is inextricably linked to trust in families. Thus, if we hope to foster greater trust with students to reap the rewards of trust described in chapter 7, we need to work to foster greater trust with parents and other family members as well. Parent engagement is a variable that can be influenced by the practices of the teachers and school leaders. Cultivating trusting and respectful relationships with families starts with working to change the attitudes of school personnel so that they recognize the advantages of teachers and parents' working together and embracing a philosophy of family-school partnership (A. T. Henderson & Mapp, 2002).

Through helpful interactions, educators can raise the level of trust in their relationships with families. It is important to make parents feel welcomed. This often requires perspective-taking on the part of school administrators and staff. It is also important to consider the educational level, language, culture, and home situation of parents. Recognizing that most parents—regardless of income, education, or cultural background—are invested in their children's learning and want their children to do well is a helpful place to start (Abdul-Adil & Farmer, 2006). Even if parents cannot be present at school, educators can recognize that parents' helping their children at home is a valuable contribution to students' learning and growth. Educators should design programs that will support families in guiding their children's learning, providing a range of involvement opportunities. Whenever possible, teachers should also consciously and directly recognize any and every effort made by families to support student learning, whether at school, in the community, or in the home.

School leaders can prompt teachers to plan and organize parent activities by emphasizing the importance of teacher encouragement and by giving teachers time to figure out how best to involve parents. When planning activities to promote parent engagement, teachers should take parents' interests and needs into consideration. Schools that succeeded in engaging families from diverse backgrounds shared three key practices. First, they focused on building trusting, collaborative relationships among teachers, families, and community members; next, they recognized, respected, and addressed families' needs, as well as class and cultural differences; and finally, they embraced a philosophy of partnership whereby power and responsibility were shared (A. T. Henderson & Mapp, 2002). It is important to be responsive to the special challenges of low-income households, as the problems they face are often overwhelming. Educators need to recognize the importance of flexibility and creativity when striving to establish trust between school and home, especially when working with low-income families.

That said, it is understandable that teachers who invest themselves in their students want to feel that their caring and work are acknowledged and shared by parents. They want to feel that there is a unity of purpose between school and home. It is important, therefore, for teachers to work to build trust with parents by communicating their commitment to the learning and success of all their students. Educators need to demonstrate to families not only that they care about their students but also that they are competent to foster student learning. Teachers should be open in sharing their teaching methods and practices. By including parents in open and honest discussions about their particular child's present levels of performance as well as the instructional strategies and methods they recommend for improvement, they help parents become valued and valuable partners in the educational process. Asking for input from parents, talking about possibilities, sharing research, soliciting advice from experts, and otherwise exploring alternative approaches to improvement are all part of teachers' framework for building trust with parents. When the importance of building a high trust relationship is seen clearly and put into action effectively, teachers and parents can become successful partners in working toward the learning, growth, and development of the young people in their care.

This year we placed family advocates in some of our schools. The family advocates made an average of 525 individualized contacts with parents (not including attending school events). That says a lot about how closely they communicated with parents to bridge the gap! In one of the schools where there's a large Spanish-speaking population, we hired a woman who was fluent in Spanish, and that has made a tremendous difference! The school has significantly reduced the level of truancy, including tardies and early dismissals, just by educating the parents about how much learning time their children were missing. And they have increased parent involvement through parent workshops and other activities. Because this advocate earned the trust of the families, the school was able to learn about and respond to many needs of the families that had been invisible before.

—MARY BETH, TITLE I COORDINATOR

PUTTING IT INTO ACTION

As principal, you set the tone for building trusting relationships with families by the example of your own attitudes and behaviors in regard to families. In a five-year project studying the social qualities of trust, respect, and caring in Chicago's public schools, principals with leadership styles that were viewed as facilitating the involvement of teachers and parents in the decisions affecting their school garnered greater trust (Bryk & Schneider, 1996). Similarly, among the families in an urban district, parents' trust in the school administration was strongly correlated with parents' trust in teachers, family engagement, and parents' perceptions of school safety and academic press (Pennycuff, 2009). And among a sample of ninety-seven high schools in Ohio, educators who trusted in their principal were also more apt to trust the parents and students in their school (Hoy & Tschannen-Moran, 2003). These studies make clear that the example you set for trust in students and parents radiates as ripples in a pond.

You can help foster trusting relationships between teachers, students, and families by creating structures and opportunities for teachers to engage in positive and productive problem solving with families. If you want to build bridges of trust with families, you must also demonstrate a willingness to share power with them. This starts by making sure that all parents, school personnel, and community members understand that you view educating children as a collaborative enterprise. To that end, it is important to develop the capacity of faculty members to work with families (A. T. Henderson & Mapp, 2002). One suggestion for educators working to build trust with families is to provide assistance to boost parents' confidence in their ability to support the education of their children—a process that is facilitated when educators discuss instructional strategies with parents that help them become partners in their children's education. Cultivating the knowledge to be culturally responsive to the sensitivities and values of the populations served by a school is also important, as are efforts to extend welcome to parents whose primary language is not English.

To increase opportunities to build parent trust, educators must find ways for parents to be involved as trusted partners in the school community rather than as adversaries or consumers. You need to ensure that you and your teachers are reliable in following through on
(continued)

commitments made to students and parents as well as scrupulously honest in dealings with families. Withholding important information or telling half-truths, not to mention outright lies, to avoid conflict only serves to damage trust in the long run.

Principals are often asked to intervene in situations where teachers are experiencing disrespect from a parent. When principals are able to intervene constructively in these difficult situations, it can help initiate a process of building or rebuilding trust. If you are heard complaining about how a parent or parents relate to the school or their child's education, let alone speaking about them in disrespectful ways, it sends the message to other adults in the building that this is an appropriate way to think, feel, and talk. It may also communicate frustration, giving the impression that you doubt your ability to bring about productive change and that you do not know what else to do, which may damage the sense of collective efficacy among your faculty.

When families fail to support the learning of their children as expected, they need to be confronted with kindness and understanding rather than judgment and disdain to foster norms that support mutual respect and trustworthiness. Families also need to be guided in understanding what they can do to support their child's learning more effectively in the future. Learning to use coaching methods can help you diminish the sense of defensiveness on the part of parents that often interferes with productive conversations (B. Tschannen-Moran & Tschannen-Moran, 2010). By inviting parents and teachers to describe student behaviors that are the cause of concern in as straightforward and direct a way as possible, and by avoiding judgmental words and tone, school leaders can help replace finger-pointing with a search for strengths. By establishing empathetic connections with parents and other family members through accepting their feelings and needs in a particular situation, educators contribute to an emerging sense of understanding and common cause. By looking for strengths, especially in situations where strengths are not immediately obvious, educators bolster students' and parents' sense of their own capabilities. By making requests to imagine and design possible new ways of moving forward rather than using words and phrases that communicate demands, educators increase the likelihood of both a cooperative and a creative response from parents. Fostering cooperation should be the goal of every conversation between educators, families, and students. Such are the benefits of cultivating a sense of trust with families.

KEY POINTS ABOUT BUILDING BRIDGES OF TRUST WITH FAMILIES

- Parents, above all, want to be assured that school personnel are deeply committed to the well-being of their children and will be reliable in fulfilling their commitments to students. They also want to feel confident that school personnel are competent to achieve their important mission, and that they are honest in their dealings with students and parents.
- For teachers, the lines between trusting students and trusting parents are blurred. When they don't trust students, they tend not to trust the parents either.
- Teachers want to feel that their professional competence is respected and that their caring for their students is acknowledged.
- Building bridges of trust may be more difficult between educators and low-income families or families from cultural backgrounds that differ from those of teachers because both sides may be less confident that they share the same values and ethical standards.
- Efforts on the part of teachers and principals to foster more open and frequent communication with parents and more opportunities for parents to be involved in decision making have been linked to greater trust.
- Educators' trust in parents and students can be strong enough to overcome the effects of poverty.
- Principals can help set the tone for trusting relationships with parents by engaging in proactive strategies to support student success and by making positive connections with parents.

QUESTIONS FOR REFLECTION AND DISCUSSION

1. What activities have been the most successful in engaging families at your school? What made these experiences so positive?

2. How are parents made to feel welcomed as valued partners in the educational process at your school?

3. What supports are offered at your school to parents who are struggling with the challenging and complex task of raising their children?

4. What specific strategies could you employ to assure parents and members of the community that you care and are trustworthy?

5. If you had all of the time, personnel, and money that you needed, what kinds of bridges with families would you like to see developed at your school?

CHAPTER 9

RESTORING BROKEN TRUST

Hold a tight rein over the three T's—Thought, Temper
and Tongue—and you will have few regrets.

—ANONYMOUS

There is both good news and bad news when it comes to restoring broken trust. The good news is that damaged trust can be repaired. The bad news is that trust repair is an arduous process that requires humility and effort and may extend over a long period of time. What is required to restore trust will depend on what caused the disruption of trust in the first place. Whether distrust has grown from hurt pride over a perceived insult, disillusionment that grows out of broken rules or norms, or the recognition of real differences in basic values, attention will need to be paid to such issues in the restoration of trust. In every instance, the beginning of a transformation from distrust to trust with a person with whom you are engaged in an endeavor of mutual interest requires conversation. This conversation best starts with a clear description of the situation that has provoked distrust, avoiding language that suggests evaluations, judgment, or blame, as well as revealing your feelings and needs in regard to what happened. Such conversations are by no means easy or comfortable;

being willing to initiate and engage in them is a concrete and powerful way to show that you care, and it is the only way to repair broken trust (Solomon & Flores, 2001).

To that end, when going into such conversations, it is important to recognize the distinction between disappointment and betrayal. Teachers may be disappointed in a decision made by their principal in that their preferred option is not selected, but differences of opinion do not constitute a betrayal. Betrayal is an intentional act that has resulted in possible or actual harm to the victim. Furthermore, failures are an inevitable part of human relationships because human beings are imperfect and fallible. Solomon and Flores (2001) warned that "to confuse failure with betrayal is to set yourself up for no creativity, no innovation, no adventure, no intimacy, no trust, and no life at all" (p. 130). If trust is diminished due to failures, a lack of reliability, or because a person's competence has proven to be inadequate for the task at hand, this may or may not constitute a betrayal. A betrayal implies that the lack of follow-through grew from a lack of sufficient caring or that the incompetence had been hidden through an act of dishonesty. A betrayal therefore represents a much more serious problem, and a much more difficult thing to overcome in repairing trust, than occasionally falling short of one's good intentions.

TRUST REPAIR

In running schools, principals often find themselves between a rock and a hard place, with the needs of one constituent played off against the needs of another. As mid-level managers, they are often caught in a vice between initiatives and mandates from the central office and being attuned to the needs of their teachers and students. Even within a given school building, there are many competing interests to be balanced. It can feel as though every possible course of action will in some way damage the trust of one group or another. This was the situation that Brenda found herself in when salary negotiations reached an impasse in Brookside's district. The union called for the teachers to impose a "work-to-rule," meaning that they would fulfill contractual obligations to the letter but do nothing more. This can be one of a union's most powerful tactics, because schools rely on teachers to go far beyond minimal obligations to function effectively and to serve students well. Kathy explained the tough spot that both Brenda and the teachers found themselves in as a result:

> With the work-to-rule at the beginning of this school year, we weren't supposed to stay for any after-school meetings. But then we had a huge debate about Grade-Level Night because that's the night where parents get to talk to their child's teacher about what's going to happen in the classroom. Brenda felt very strongly about having it, so we gave in because we understood her reasons. She came to us with a very pleading heart. She told us that she wouldn't force us to do things but just to talk about it. We said we understood where she was coming from, so we gave in. I don't know if we should have, but we did.

The hard feelings that resulted from this conflict put a strain on Brenda's relationship with her teachers. Some felt that they should not have been put in the position of having to choose between loyalty to the union and loyalty to Brenda and the school. Those teachers felt it was a betrayal of the care they had come to expect from Brenda. More than six months later, the effects were still being felt in the relationship. Kathy continued:

> Just last week somebody said, "Regardless of all she does for us, she is still an administrator." As much as she values us and will make concessions for what we need, she still has to run her building. It's hard. That's the only time I really felt bad here.

As a result of this conflict, Brenda was put in the position of having to repair damaged trust and mend relationships with her teachers.

Trust repair is a two-way process in which each side must perceive that the short-term or long-term benefits to be gained from the relationship are sufficiently valued to be worth the investment of time and energy required by the repair process. Each party must decide that restoring the relationship is preferable to finding other ways to meet the needs that once were met by the relationship (Hurley, 2012; Lewicki & Bunker, 1996). The violator and the victim have different roles and responsibilities in the reestablishment of trust. Trust repair often is initiated by the victim, who verbally or nonverbally confronts the violator and makes him or her aware of the sense of betrayal. But it can also be initiated by the perpetrator, who feels contrite and wants to make things right again in the relationship. Regardless of how the repair process is initiated, the violator then has the opportunity to engage in the "four A's of absolution"—Admit it, Apologize, Ask for forgiveness, and Amend your ways. The teachers who felt it had been inappropriate for Brenda to ask the teachers to go forward with Grade-Level Night as planned rather than to reschedule after the labor dispute was settled found various ways, both subtle and not so subtle, to let Brenda know that they were harboring hard feelings. Finally, Brenda raised the issue at a faculty meeting to clear the air. How she handled this situation illustrates well both how the four A's work and why they are worth the effort.

Admit It

To begin with, the violator must acknowledge that a violation occurred and that harm was done. The violator begins by listening attentively to the victim, which is a sign of respect and signals a willingness to engage in the process of rebuilding the relationship. To dismiss the harm as insignificant is disrespectful to the experience of the victim as well as to the risk the victim may have experienced in arranging the confrontation. Brenda explicitly opened up the topic for discussion, noting the changes in attitude and behavior that she had witnessed that caused her to suspect there were unresolved feelings. She listened to what the teachers had to share about the difficult position she had placed them in when she decided to go forward with Grade-Level Night, when all the other schools in the district had canceled theirs. Although teachers reported that they were normally proud to say they taught at Brookside, they said that they had taken flack during that time from teachers in other buildings, as well as from the union, for breaking ranks.

In admitting wrongdoing, the perpetrator accepts responsibility for the effects of his or her actions. The violator must admit not only to having caused the event but also to the fact that the event was, in some way and to some degree, destructive. Even if the harm was unintentional, the violator needs to acknowledge that the way events unfolded left the victim, in some sense and to some degree, feeling harmed. People who immediately discount the extent of the violation, make excuses, or shift blame to someone or something else provoke frustration and wariness rather than signal a willingness to reestablish a trusting relationship. The energy they spend in self-protection would be better spent facing up to the damage they have done and looking for solutions. The need to absolve oneself from legitimate guilt will interfere with rebuilding trust when actual harm has been experienced. Although Brenda was stung by the accusation that her wanting to go forward with Grade-Level Night on the scheduled date was motivated as much by the desire to enhance her own reputation as by a desire to start the year with good communication with the parents, she avoided becoming outwardly defensive or lashing out at those calling into question her commitment to the school. Nor did she remind the teachers that she had left the final decision to them. Instead, she accepted responsibility for the ways in which her request had forced teachers to make a painful choice in a situation where they felt divided loyalties.

Apologize

To apologize is not only to admit that harm was done and that one's actions contributed to that harm but also to express regret for that harm. Trust is enhanced by a willingness to apologize for the unpleasant consequences of one's actions (Greenberg, 1993; Konovsky & Pugh, 1994). Solomon and Flores (2001) have reminded us that "an apology is a statement of an intention to redeem oneself and the beginning of a conversation about how this can be done" (p. 133). Brenda apologized for how the request and the decision to go forward with Grade-Level Night had both caused dissension and hurt feelings within the school and diminished their pride in being Brookside teachers, at least temporarily, because their loyalty to the school became a cause for derision among their colleagues across the district. Because the labor dispute had not been protracted and had, in fact, been settled not long after the event in question, Brenda admitted that Grade-Level Night could have been rescheduled without undue loss to parent-school communication.

An apology can, in some cases, be sufficient to restore the relationship because in admitting wrong there is an implicit understanding that one will endeavor to avoid repeating the error in the future. But the perpetrator should not assume that the apology automatically erases the error for which it has been issued. To rush too readily to the conclusion that all is now well violates the sense of care that undergirds the trusting relationship as well as the sense that one will take the feelings and needs of the other seriously. It is often important for the perpetrator to ask for forgiveness and to demonstrate a willingness to make amends for his or her errors.

Ask for Forgiveness

If trust is to be repaired, some form of forgiveness is required. Forgiveness can be transformative, but it is not easy to achieve, especially when the extent of the violation is great. Forgiveness is a process in which the victim reaches out to the betrayer and expresses a willingness to once again lower his or her guard in the context of interdependence or vulnerability. Forgiveness is not simply a state of mind; it is an action—or a sequence of actions—and a ritualized releasing of the feelings associated with the betrayal. Forgiveness can be facilitated when the perpetrator makes an explicit request to be forgiven. Solomon and Flores (2001) discussed the importance of spoken statements in the process of forgiveness:

> Forgiveness does not always have to be verbally articulated and formally expressed in the public realm, but in practice, this is what happens. One can indicate that one has forgiven a betrayal, for instance, by simply acting toward the betrayer as if there is nothing wrong, although this carries with it the liability that such behavior may well be interpreted as mere artifice, to trick the betrayer into lowering his or her defenses before getting even in some equally hurtful way. Or the absence of explicit forgiveness may indicate that the person betrayed simply does not take this particular betrayal—or the betrayer—seriously, which may constitute an offense in its own right. For such reasons, an explicit verbal act, paradigmatically some form of "I forgive you" or "Forget it," is particularly desirable. (p. 140)

Forgiveness may restore trust, but it will probably not return the relationship to its former state. Even if the victim is willing to extend forgiveness to restore the relationship, it is unlikely that he or she will forget what has happened. Victims can often recall vivid details about a significant betrayal at work even decades afterward (Hurley, 2012; W. Jones & Burdette, 1994). It is possible, however, that if the betrayal is placed firmly in the past and overcome (but not erased) by forgiveness, the commitment to and trust in the relationship on both sides may be strengthened and deepened through the subsequent greater care and attention paid to relational dynamics (Solomon & Flores, 2001).

Amend Your Ways

Because it is the victim who determines what is required to restore trust, the power in determining the future of the relationship is in his or her hands. The restoration of trust often entails specifying acts of reparation designed to show that the violator is sincere in the desire to rebuild the relationship and to demonstrate the violator's willingness to incur a certain amount of personal loss in doing so. Open offers made by the perpetrator that allow the victim to determine the terms of trust repair are more powerful than specific targeted offers (Hurley, 2012). The acts of reparation set by the victim may seem in the eyes of the perpetrator to be either reasonable or unreasonable, resulting in either a willingness or an unwillingness to meet them. If the acts are undertaken, the victim then has the opportunity to judge the commitment of the violator as he or she carries out these actions. Reparation also creates an opportunity for the violator to work out any guilt that she or he may have over the harm that was done, whether that harm was intentional or unintentional (Lewicki & Bunker, 1996).

It may be that the victim refuses to accept any actions, terms, or conditions for reestablishing the relationship. The victim may perceive the damage done to be so extensive that he or she is no longer willing to continue the relationship and risk being subjected to the possibility of further harm. Or it may be that the effort required to rebuild trust is just too arduous, considering that the victim has sufficient alternatives to get his or her needs met elsewhere. Should the victim refuse to extend forgiveness, a continued interdependent relationship, such as an ongoing work relationship, is likely to be fraught with tension, poor communication, and lower productivity.

Another fall tradition at Brookside was the annual Camp Night, when the students remained at the school on a Friday afternoon for a series of activities and then stayed for an overnight sleepover. Each teacher, including resource teachers, hosted a mixed-grade-level group of students and engaged in fun, hands-on learning activities. The parents came and joined in the fun, and the PTA provided a meal. At the end of the evening there was a program, and then everyone slept at the school. Although Camp Night was a lot of work, it was an important community-building event for the school. It was also very important to Brenda. The teachers especially disliked sleeping at school with the students, however. So in light of teachers' having stepped up for Grade-Level Night, and as a way to make amends, Brenda conceded the sleepover aspect of Camp Night that fall.

Although the conflict over Grade-Level Night had accentuated the differences in role responsibilities between Brenda and her teachers, it had also caused a reassessment of how much both sides valued their normally cooperative relationship and in many ways strengthened their mutual resolve to care for the quality of that relationship in the future. Brenda's forthright and open handling of the situation made her a role model for the teachers in their own disputes with one another. Setting a betrayal aside but not out of mind, and moving on through the public act of forgiveness, can bring healing even after a very painful episode.

FACTORS THAT FACILITATE RESTORING TRUST

Trust is fundamental to cooperation, and yet it can be difficult to establish once a cycle of suspicion, competition, and retaliation has begun. Even in the midst of tension and conflict, however, trust can be fostered through the conciliatory initiatives of one party acting unilaterally, signaling the desire to establish trust without sacrificing the genuine need to protect his or her interests (Fisher & Brown, 1988). Trust repair is facilitated by a balance of inquiry and advocacy, seeking to understand and communicate empathy to the other party while assertively articulating one's own position and needs (Hurley, 2012). This process is aided by unconditionally adopting constructive attitudes and actions, establishing clear boundaries, and communicating promises and credible threats. It is also facilitated by working for good communication by using constructive conflict resolution strategies, being meticulously reliable in following through with commitments that are made during this process. Each of these skills and orientations will be considered in turn.

Unconditionally Adopting Constructive Attitudes and Actions

Although relationships necessarily have at least two parties, it takes only one party to change the quality of the relationship. Even in situations of mutual suspicion, each side has the opportunity to improve the level of trust in the relationship. Each person has the opportunity to adopt unconditionally constructive attitudes and actions (Fisher & Brown, 1988). These include inquiring to try to understand the other side's interests, attitudes, and beliefs as well as adopting a nonjudgmental attitude of acceptance toward the other side. There are many contexts in which we have to interact with individuals and groups of whose conduct we do not approve. But we can work to understand their behavior even if we do not condone it or become convinced of the correctness of their point of view. In trying to understand others and their motivations, one should assume that others do not see themselves as bad people pursuing immoral ends through illegitimate means, but rather that they have what they consider to be good reasons for doing what they do. Their justification may grow out of a value system that differs from one's own, but it can help create a context for conversation about their rationale for the behavior one finds offensive. When communicating to foster trust, it is important to convey only clear observations of what was seen and heard and to assiduously avoid communicating evaluations, diagnoses, judgments, and blame (Rosenberg, 2005).

> I took over a school that was filled with conflict and a total lack of trust. It was divided between those who were loyal to the previous principal and those who opposed him. That first year, I had mugs printed with the slogan "Children are not things to be molded but gifts to be unfolded." I wanted to put the emphasis on the children as a way to create some common ground.
> I began a tradition of hosting a barbeque at my house four times a year. That was neutral ground. Had we had it at the home of a teacher from one faction or the other, some teachers would not have come. Those turned out to be important occasions where teachers met family members and got to know each other away from the building. Teachers shared with me how much they appreciated those events and the emphasis on students.
>
> —PEGGY, ELEMENTARY SCHOOL PRINCIPAL

Establishing Clear Boundaries

Feelings of violation can result in a sense of betrayal. We assume that others understand how we want to be treated, but what we want is not always clear or obvious. People differ according to their personality, as well as according to cultural norms and understandings about what is acceptable. In creating a context for trusting relationships, it is important to set clear boundaries about how one expects to be treated. There are four stages or levels in the establishment of clear boundaries: inform, request, insist, and leave (Coach U, 2003).

The first stage is to inform the other party about how one wants to be treated, and perhaps about how his or her current behavior violates those desires. Too often, we assume that others know or should be able to figure out what we want through the interpretation of our nonverbal cues and signs of irritation, hoping to spare ourselves the effort and discomfort of having to articulate our needs and desires. But this strategy leaves open the possibility that the other party simply will not get it. He or she may have a different set of understandings about how people are to be treated, perhaps because of coming from a different cultural background or having different personal preferences. A person raised in the rural south of the United States, for example, may hold assumptions that are altogether different from those of a person from New York City about what are considered to be polite or acceptable ways of interacting with one another. Each may misinterpret or be at a loss as to what is meant by the nonverbal cues sent by the other.

The second stage is to make an explicit request for the behavior that is desired. Ideally, this request is communicated in a firm, even tone. Editing out anything that might read as irritation or annoyance in one's voice or body language has sometimes been referred to as communicating in a "charge-neutral" manner. A common mistake that people make is to skip over the first two stages, letting anger build with each breach until they reach the third stage, to insist, making it the starting point instead of a late stage in a four-part process. Each violation is here counted as a betrayal, based on the assumption that there has been a mutual understanding of common principles, when in fact this may not be the case at all.

The fourth and final stage, if continual requests and insistence have not created a situation where one's boundaries are respected, is to leave. It may be inconvenient and disruptive to leave a relationship and to figure out how to have the needs that were met by that relationship met in other ways, and it may even mean giving up on a cherished joint project; but if the level of violation is serious enough, it may be worth all that it costs.

I worked with a man from the Middle East who was
very aggressive and, it seemed to me, very judgmental.
It seemed like he had to challenge everything I said. The
relationship finally reached a breaking point, when I told him
how hurt and angry I was feeling all of the time. I told him the
negative impact it was having on my enjoyment of my work life,
to the point where I was ready to put in for a transfer. He was
surprised to learn I was so unhappy. He explained, "Where I
come from, everything's an argument. There isn't anything
in my culture that is not an argument. It's the way we express
affection, acceptance, prices, news—you know? Everything."
He had never before told me that, or invited me into
that knowledge of his culture. After that conversation, he
was able to tone down his argumentativeness with me,
and I was able to be less sensitive to his remarks so
we could work much better together.

—JANINE, HIGH SCHOOL SPECIAL EDUCATION TEACHER

Communicating Promises and Credible Threats

In situations where we are attempting to build or restore trust, it is important to be mindful of our words, because language is a primary vehicle used and needed to establish trust. Specifically, we must be very careful when making either promises or threats. Neither should be spoken unless we have every intention of following through. In fact, in a situation of repairing broken trust or of fostering initial trust, it is a good strategy to "underprom- ise and overdeliver." If some unforeseen set of circumstances prevents the fulfillment of a promise, the one who made the promise owes an explanation and an apology to the one who was disappointed.

The use of promises is important in building a strategy for mutual cooperation. To overcome distrust, one party announces a clear, conciliatory initiative—a promise grounded in goodwill toward the other that is intended to aid in the mutual project of renewing a sense of connectedness and interdependence. It is then crucial to carry out this promise reliably and to invite (but not require) the other party to reciprocate (Fisher & Brown, 1988). The point is to achieve an explicit and well-defined concili- ation that both parties accept.

Making credible threats can be as important to building trust as keeping promises. Violations are likely to occur in any ongoing system, if only by chance, but the system of interchange will break down if those violations are frequent and go unchecked, as they did at Fremont. Each person must have a way of reacting to viola- tions: there must be a credible threat that is known to the other party and can serve to inhibit violations. Without that threat, with the perception that the other party is powerless and either unable or unwilling to retaliate for inappropriate behavior, systems of exchange invite exploitation. Threats can be made credible and trust can be supported by even one example of the willing- ness to retaliate for broken trust. At Fremont, Fred's continual threats that he "was not going to tolerate" certain behaviors, in the absence of any action year after year to end those behaviors, caused him to lose credibility. His unwillingness to follow through on threats led to a lack of trust.

Although making credible threats can be important in build- ing systems of trust, it is important that this be done discretely and in ways that preserve the dignity of the persons being corrected.

Gloria's willingness to publicly humiliate teachers who had challenged her authority or to make an example of poorly performing teachers by treating them badly in front of the faculty was seen as a betrayal of the rules of fair play within the school. Such behavior cost Gloria the trust of her teachers. In rebuilding trust, the golden rule of treating others as you would want to be treated is a good guide to behavior, especially in a time of conflict. Going a step further and honoring how *they* want to be treated is even better.

Offering blind trust, or extending trust beyond what is reasonable given the available information about another's actions and motivations, is dangerous and does not rebuild trust. Because each party always has the opportunity to be completely trustworthy, there is no good reason to insist on blind trust. Such insistence on the part of the other party might even raise suspicion that the he or she is harboring negative intentions, leading to an escalating spiral of defensive actions to protect one's interests. When such a spiral of distrust and competition ensues, it interferes with the ability to collaborate and work together effectively. Ending this spiral involves protecting one's interests while signaling to the other the desire to negotiate a mutually beneficial relationship. New rules of engagement must be found and embraced with a sense of mutual satisfaction and acceptance.

These rules do not require exact reciprocity in a relationship because such an expectation risks disillusionment or even triggering or aggravating a conflict (Fisher & Brown, 1988). A tit-for-tat strategy or threat does not work in most situations because in real-life relationships, the meaning of particular actions—whether they are in the interest of cooperation or obstruction—is not always clear and may be an issue of dispute. Exact reciprocity is hard to gauge because victims and perpetrators often use "different arithmetics" in assessing the harm done to them as opposed to that inflicted on their opponent. Seeking such reciprocity can lead to a cycle of feuding and an escalation of the conflict as each side continually attempts to even the score.

Using Constructive Conflict Resolution Strategies

Because trust is hard if not impossible to reestablish in the absence of effective communication, having and using good communication skills are central aspects of restoring broken trust. Without honest communication, once suspicion has come to characterize a relationship and a spiral of retaliation and revenge has set in, it is extremely difficult to negotiate new rules of engagement that both parties accept and trust. Yet without trust, negotiating a bilateral agreement to reverse a cycle of betrayal and revenge can be quite difficult and perhaps impossible. Conflict resolution is a problem-solving process designed to negotiate a solution that each party can embrace and live with.

When setting up a conflict resolution process, the first decision to be made involves finding a time and a space conducive to beginning the conversation. Both sides need to feel comfortable with the arrangements, and the risk of interruptions should be minimized. There are various ways that the parties in a dispute can signal a cooperative attitude as a prelude to the initial or subsequent conflict resolution meetings. One such cue is for each party to address the other using the name or title by which that other person prefers to be addressed, as a sign of respect. In some cultures, making eye contact is a sign of openness, although in others it may be interpreted as a sign of aggressiveness or disrespect if the parties are of different social standing. Being aware and respectful of such cultural differences is important.

A formal conflict resolution session can be facilitated by starting with an agreement to abide by a set of ground rules with which each party feels comfortable. These rules typically include a commitment to speak truthfully and respectfully and to wait for one's turn to speak rather than interrupting. There may be other, culturally specific rules to articulate and honor as well.

In most formal conflict resolution sessions, the first to present is the person who initiated the meeting or whose feelings are running the highest. Such feelings need to find voice and be expressed. If there is a difference in status or position, however, it can be helpful for the one with the lower position to begin first. Addressing the other disputant directly, the speaker begins with a "just the facts" description of the situation, the feelings that have been stimulated by the situation, as well as the underlying needs that have been stirred up (Rosenberg, 2005; B. Tschannen-Moran & Tschannen-Moran, 2010). It is important for speakers to use "I messages" to reveal information about their own reactions rather than asserting information about the other person ("you messages"). Defensiveness and resentment can be provoked when one person asserts what another person thought, felt, or intended. These emotions may lead that person to be less willing to engage productively in the process or to expend effort in cooperative endeavors. Each person wants to be the expert on his or her own intentions, feelings, and thoughts. Revealing one's hurt or pain, without aggression or blame, can create a context that is more conducive to the other person's responsiveness. Further, sharing the underlying needs that provoked these negative emotions deepens the possibility of establishing an empathic connection. These expressions are followed by an explicit request for communication that conveys the hearer's understanding of what has been shared.

When the first person has finished sharing, the second reflects what he or she has heard, being careful to be accurate while nonetheless editing out any evaluations or judgments that may have been relayed. The second party then reveals his or her own feelings about the situation along with the needs that may have been aroused. This is followed by a request for the listener to share what he or she has heard. Only after there is a mutual understanding of the needs that have been stimulated by the conflict is there a conversation as to what is to be done to restore the relationship. Each party should clearly request the actions he or she would like to see happen. Then both parties engage in problem solving, offering solutions that they believe will meet both of their needs. If, after considerable effort, a solution that is fully satisfactory to both sides is not discovered, then the parties generate and explore compromise alternatives that at least partially meet the needs of each side. After agreeing on an acceptable solution, both sides make an explicit commitment to abide by the agreement. It is, of course, extremely important to honor that agreement going forward so that trust is further reestablished and strengthened over time.

We have a strong emphasis on conflict resolution skills at our school. Our school is in an urban neighborhood known for violence, so we are very committed to giving our students the skills for resolving differences peacefully. The returning teachers are always the ones to train new teachers in the process we use. We let them know it isn't just for the kids— we expect them to use the same process for the difficulties we have with each other, too. Once they learn it, they get all excited and come back and tell how it has worked with other people in their lives outside of school!

—ANNE, INTERMEDIATE TEACHER

Repairing trust can be a difficult and time-consuming process. However, by adopting constructive attitudes, establishing good boundaries, clearly communicating promises and reliably fulfilling them, and engaging in conflict resolution strategies that honor the feelings and needs of both parties, individuals can work toward a relationship that is once again characterized by trust.

CREATING A CONTEXT FOR TRUST REPAIR

Schools are social systems, and thus the interpersonal relationships in them are embedded in a social context. That social context not only reflects but also shapes the trust relationships therein (Daly, 2010). The effect of the social context and the gossip that takes place in an organization is one of pushing trust relationships to extremes: enhancing high trust and driving low trust even lower (Burt & Knez, 1996). In a trusting environment, people may give one another the benefit of the doubt about questionable behaviors, whereas in an atmosphere of distrust similar actions or behaviors may serve to even further diminish a low level of trust.

Examples of broken trust were not limited to the low-trust schools in the study on which this book is based. Almost all of the teachers interviewed could give an example of a time when their trust had been broken either by a principal or by a colleague. The difference was that in the high-trust school, the rift was eventually repaired, whereas in low-trust schools, the resentment festered, sometimes over long periods of time. In trusting contexts, it was more likely that people would take the risk of repairing trust because they were supported by greater hopefulness about a positive outcome. In the low-trust schools, there were fewer reports of attempts to repair damaged trust. Feuds were carried on from year to year. Ongoing distrust was a drain on energy, imagination, and vitality at both Lincoln and Fremont, and faculty members were therefore less able to respond to the needs of students. These schools were not places where people looked forward to coming to work each day. In these schools, a self-perpetuating spiral of distrust seemed to drive trust even lower. Once distrust has taken hold in an organization, even innocent or neutral comments or actions are often read with suspicion (Govier, 1992).

Although Brenda was highly respected at Brookside, she was known on occasion to be short-tempered with faculty members. People were willing to overlook this shortcoming and forgive her because of her overall dedication and level of support for them.

Kathy described how Brenda's caring created the context for forgiveness:

> I think people are willing to go to bat for her because she will go to bat for them. When she may not be having a good day and it just seems that she is upset with you personally, people are willing to step back and say, "This is not how she operates. This is not the norm." I am willing to step up and give her the benefit of the doubt that there is something external to me. I have even heard [that] when she has responded negatively, the person was able to go back to her and tell her that they didn't think it was right. She apologized, admitted her mistake, and everything was fine. We all coach each other, and with the new teachers we tell them, "Don't worry, that's just the way she does sometimes. She'll be fine. She is not out to get you." There is that support there to help that person understand.

Brookside teachers were willing to extend forbearance when Brenda was having a bad day and was unnecessarily short-tempered. The story that circulated of Brenda's willingness to apologize when confronted by a teacher built trust even among teachers who had not received such an apology themselves. As a consequence of the trust invested in this principal, new faculty members were encouraged and coached to not take any outbursts personally and to let them go. This is an example of how a cycle of trust builds even greater trust, and how the involvement of third parties can strengthen trust in a high-trust environment (Burt & Knez, 1996). Trust, in other words, is self-reinforcing. Incidents that might be interpreted as a breach of trust are neutralized when the overall sense of trust is soundly established.

At Brookside, in contrast to schools with a lower level of trust, it was more likely that when trust was damaged it would be repaired. Teachers were more willing to talk with the person who had violated their trust, even when their usual tendency would have been to not say anything and just avoid that person. Because they had a stake in maintaining a positive work environment, and because they could anticipate a caring response, they were willing to risk sharing their feelings and needs with the person who had offended them. Once aired, these grievances could be dealt with, and trust could be restored. Kathy described a situation in which her feelings had been hurt, and in which she let her colleagues know what was bothering her, with the expectation that her feelings would be taken seriously:

> There was one time this year where two of the other fifth-grade teachers started rotating students for certain subjects with each other and I felt kind of excluded, I guess. Once my feelings were known, we talked about it and got everybody's feelings out in the open. It wasn't done intentionally at all. They told me that they had done it on a whim because they needed to do something at that time. And then they were supposedly trying it out to see if it would work among the whole fifth grade. They are very good friends outside of school, so I think they were just talking and just did it. They didn't realize that it had hurt me. When I told them how much it did, we talked about it and debriefed everything. We understood each other's point of view and went on.

With an explanation and an apology, Kathy was willing to accept that the action had not been done maliciously, and as a result she was able to let her hurt feelings go and move on.

In a trusting school environment, there was also more willingness to give students the benefit of doubt. There was greater recognition that the students were, after all, just children and could be expected to make some mistakes in judgment. There seemed to be more of a tendency to be lenient with students, at least on the first or second offense, and to give them the opportunity to rebuild the trust that had been lost. Further, at Brookside teachers had more positive contacts with parents. These were opportunities to build trust with the parents, creating relational resources that could be "spent" in addressing the inevitable problems that arose. The high level of trust throughout the school community created the context in which breaches of trust would be resolved and greater trust restored.

When I left my first teaching post after two years, there was an end-of-the-year breakfast where the departing staff were thanked and given the opportunity to say a few words. There was a considerable amount of infighting and interdepartmental conflict at the school, and with the audacity of youth, I spontaneously decided to share some advice with the staff on my way out the door. I first expressed that I was privileged to have worked with a gifted and dedicated staff and had learned a great deal from my peers as a new classroom teacher. Then I shared that I was troubled by the negativity that I saw, where many individuals didn't appreciate the variety of skills and gifts in their peers that I could see as a fresh observer. I noted that when I found myself in a situation of conflict, I would try to begin with the assumption that my "opponent" was working from the best of intentions even though those might not align with my own personal preferences. Through that lens I've found that a mutually acceptable outcome is more likely to be possible. Four months later, I happened to be back at the school when I was approached by the head of the English department—a man who was definitely one of the most proficient warriors. To my immense surprise, he thanked me for my words. He said that while at first irritated by my presumption, he couldn't get my suggestion out of his head so he resolved to give it a try. He told me how the change had improved the quality of his interactions as well as his personal happiness.

—CHRIS, HIGH SCHOOL TEACHER

WHOLE-SCHOOL CONVERSATIONS ABOUT TRUST

When distrust has spread beyond the interpersonal dynamics between a few individuals to a culture of distrust that pervades an entire school, a larger set of conversations about trust may be both appropriate and necessary for trust to be restored. Keeping those conversations constructive, however, takes great care and a sound structural framework. Appreciative inquiry (AI) provides just such a solid, research-based design for conducting such conversations (Watkins, Mohr, & Kelly, 2011). AI is a process for fostering whole-system change by focusing on strengths and what is going well rather than on problems, gaps, or discrepancies between the aspirations of people and the current reality of their relationships. This counterintuitive approach has been found to be surprisingly effective, especially when dealing with an issue as distressing as distrust in a workplace setting. There are many ways to organize an AI process. One of the approaches that I and my colleagues at the Center for School Transformation (www .schooltransformation.com) have used successfully when working to enhance trust in schools follows a "four-I" cycle: Initiate, Inquire, Imagine, Innovate.

The first phase of the cycle, to initiate, involves selecting the focus and method of inquiry. This phase has already been accomplished once the focus of inquiry has been determined to be building trust and the approach of appreciative inquiry has been selected. The second phase, to inquire, begins with conducting interviews in pairs, with each partner sharing and exploring the experiences he or she has had of high-trust relationships. Such storytelling and recalling of experiences can provoke profound learning. To maximize the diversity in groupings, participants are invited to find an interview partner on the principle of "max mix," meaning that they are to find a person whom they may not know well or with whom they typically have little ongoing communication. Then they ask each other some version of the following questions:

1. Tell me about one of your best experiences of working or playing on a team where trust was high. Pick a time when you felt most engaged and supported by the trust of others. Who was involved? What goals were you working on? What challenges did you face? What contributed to the high level of trust? Describe the event in detail.

2. Let's talk for a moment about some things that you value deeply, specifically, the things you value about your work in this school.
   a. When you are at your best, what do you value most about the contributions you make through your work here?
   b. Describe the ways the people, policies, or resources here help you to be your best.

3. Imagine that you could transform the quality of working relationships in this school in any way you wanted. What would that transformation look and feel like? How might this change heighten the vitality and health of this organization? If you had three wishes for bringing your vision into being, what would they be?

When each pair has had sufficient time to tell and explore their stories as well as to appreciate their values and wishes, they then find one or two other pairs that have also finished their interviews to form a small group of four to six people. In the context of those small groups, each person briefly retells his or her original partner's story, values, and wishes to the whole group. As the sharing unfolds, group members listen for and identify three to five themes in regard to what brings energy and life to the members of the group, capturing them on chart paper, sentence strips, or electronically. These themes are then shared with the large group after all the small groups have finished. An "energy check" of the various themes is then conducted, with each person being given three colored dots or other mechanisms to indicate the themes that most resonate with their current energy and imagination.

The next phase in the process, to imagine, involves developing a vivid image of what the school would look and feel like if the themes were fully honored and if the quality of relationships were just as people would most desire. Participants either remain with the same groups or form new ones based on particular themes for which there is a lot of energy. The intention of the work is to develop a creative presentation of an image each group holds for what the school would look, feel, and be like if it were to build on current strengths in the realm of trusting relationships and establish a set of norms and practices that would foster the quality of work captured by the theme. The images may be conveyed through drawings, collages, music, skits, or some combination of these or other modalities. Only after the group develops a holistic image of the future, creatively conveyed, do group members try to capture that desired reality in a statement that claims that new reality, as if it were already present and fully expressed in the organization.

In the final phase, to innovate, the small groups formed during the Imagine phase convene to plan action steps for moving the school closer to the beautiful, vivid images developed in the previous step.

Moving through these steps can take place across a number of shorter meetings or in a daylong "summit" devoted to this process. Either way, the AI process provides a constructive way for groups to engage in productive conversations about how they want to move their school forward, to higher levels of trust, even if the current reality is one of a great deal of distress, distrust, and pain. Appreciative inquiry creates the space needed to dream into being a new, present-tense vision of the future.

The superintendent across the table from me was worried. Diane, the principal he had assigned two years earlier to turn around an underperforming school, was in trouble with her faculty. Members of the faculty had been to the school board and even to the local newspaper seeking to have her removed. He was concerned that the teachers were feeling so distressed, but on the other hand, test scores were up dramatically and the school was poised to make AYP (annual yearly progress) for the first time. So he wanted to find a way to rebuild relationships if he could. The previous principal in the building had been very lax. So when Diane began enforcing district policy forbidding teachers from wearing flip-flops to work, the teachers protested by all wearing flip-flops on a particular day. And to show that they didn't appreciate her professional attire in their mostly rural surroundings, they organized a day to mock her by emulating her style of dress. Trust was certainly frayed on both sides of the divide. Diane was feeling hurt, frustrated, and angry.

We designed and conducted an intervention that included an appreciative inquiry process and six months of leadership coaching. The process began with a faculty meeting in early June, before school let out for the summer. The superintendent communicated to teachers that he was genuinely concerned about the distress they were feeling and that he invited their participation in the appreciative inquiry process as a means to create a school environment more to their liking without losing ground on the impressive gains they had made. The faculty and staff engaged in paired interviews, and met in small groups to discern the themes that emerged from these conversations. These themes served as the basis for a full-day AI summit when they returned to school in August. The mood of the group on that day shifted palpably from apprehensive to enthusiastic and hopeful as teachers, administrators, and staff together envisioned the school as they hoped it might be. Design teams were formed to develop plans for bringing various dimensions of the dream into being. Time was reserved at faculty meetings throughout the fall for the teams to check in on their progress and to continue their work. At the end of the first faculty meeting in the fall, one of the teachers who had been one of the most outspoken critics of Diane, and a leader of "the opposition," stood to say that she was feeling better about the school than she had in a long, long time and that she once again felt proud and happy to come to work each morning. When Diane met with this teacher privately afterward to thank her for her words, Diane acknowledged, "You didn't have to do that." "Oh yes, yes I did," the teacher replied.

—MEGAN, PROFESSOR, AUTHOR, AND COACH

 PUTTING IT INTO ACTION

Trust is a critical resource for schools; indeed, it is a key, distinguishing mark of leadership and relationships in successful schools. Accomplishing the mission of your school without trust is unlikely—perhaps even impossible. When trust has been disrupted, and when conflicts have resulted in feelings of betrayal, it is important that mechanisms be in place to help members of the school community restore their broken relationships. School leaders therefore have a special responsibility to make sure that these mechanisms are not only in place but also used so that the distrust resulting from unresolved disputes does not impair the ability of a school community to fulfill its mission and goals. Because of the arduous and uncertain nature of trust repair, however, schools and school leaders are far better off avoiding broken trust in the first place.

Conflict is an inevitable part of the organizational change process. Even where there is agreement on the goals of that process, there are usually differences of opinion about how to achieve them. Change

(continued)

disrupts the power dynamics within a school, advantaging some and disadvantaging others. Change also involves loss. It disrupts the way people make meaning of their lives at work. As people in your school cope with the loss inherent in change, it is important for you to recognize their reactions as normal grief responses and not to take them personally, as evidence that the change is the wrong direction to go, or as a sign that the people who are resisting the change are somehow "bad people" if they are initially less than enthusiastic at the prospect of doing things differently. Listening skillfully to people as they react to change can be a powerful way to foster trust in the midst of change.

Although conversations to restore damaged trust are by no means easy or comfortable, it is essential for school leaders to develop the skills needed to manage these conversations. The health of a school community is dependent on a leader who can mediate the conflicts inherent in the vital and complex work of schools. It is also important for leaders to assist teachers and students in learning constructive conflict management strategies. Finding ways to overcome broken trust and to rebuild damaged relationships will pay strong dividends in supporting the positive outcomes a school can achieve.

KEY POINTS ABOUT RESTORING BROKEN TRUST

- To restore trust, each side must believe that doing so is worth the effort when weighed against finding other ways of having his or her needs met.
- The violator and the victim have different roles and responsibilities in the reestablishment of trust.
- The principal can be a powerful role model in showing how to restore trust. It is important for school leaders not to be "above the fray"; instead, they should engage actively in repairing trust when it has been broken.
- The four A's of absolution are Admit it, Apologize, Ask for forgiveness, and Amend your ways.

- It is important to articulate and respect boundaries in any relational context, whether personal or organizational. The four progressive stages of setting and managing boundaries are inform, request, insist, and then, if necessary, leave.
- Trust repair is bolstered by unconditionally adopting constructive attitudes and actions, establishing clear boundaries, communicating promises and credible threats, and using constructive conflict resolution strategies.
- Enhancing the overall quality of trust in a school is best achieved by taking a strengths-based approach, such as appreciative inquiry, rather than by airing grievances publicly in a way that leads to finger-pointing and blame.

QUESTIONS FOR REFLECTION AND DISCUSSION

1. What has been your best experience of restoring a relationship after a breach of trust? What helped create the conditions for that trust repair? How did the process of rebuilding trust reflect the four A's of absolution?
2. Consider an incident that led you to forgive but not forget a betrayal. What contributed to the restoration of the relationship? How was the relationship different afterward?
3. Think of a time when you had an understanding as to the nature or cause of a conflict or feud that was totally different from that of another person involved. What did those differences generate, and how did things end up? How might you have used the approaches in this chapter to facilitate a different, more positive outcome?
4. How have you set clear boundaries with the members of your school community? Did you inform and request before you reached a point of insisting? Under what circumstances do you feel you would want or need to leave?

5. What could you, as a school leader, do to intervene in a long-standing conflict between two teachers or groups of teachers in your school to help them rebuild trust with one another? How might that reconciliation serve the good of the school?

6. How might structuring strengths-based conversations facilitate positive change in your school, especially in the area of repairing broken trust? What might you do to make that happen? What would your school gain from repairing trust in this way?

CHAPTER 10

BECOMING
A TRUSTWORTHY
LEADER

To be trusted is a greater compliment than to be loved.
—GEORGE MACDONALD

Throughout this book we have considered the five facets of trust—benevolence, honesty, openness, reliability, and competence—as they relate to the five different constituencies of schools (administrators, teachers, students, parents, and the general public). These considerations have demonstrated the importance of trust to building productive schools. If trust breaks down among any constituency, distrust can spread like a cancer, undermining academic performance and, ultimately, the tenure of instructional leaders. In this day and age, no leader can long survive the demise of trust.

This book has described and documented the importance of trust to cultivating productive schools; it has also investigated how the absence of trust impedes effectiveness and progress. School leaders need to build trust with teachers and other constituencies because governance structures that include collaborative decision making can make use of helpful, new insights from the very people

251

closest to the action concerning the core mission of the school, bringing these insights to bear on solving the complex problems schools face. These collaborative governance structures depend on trust (Hoy & Tarter, 2008; Smylie & Hart, 1999). Without trust, communication becomes constrained and distorted, making problems more difficult to resolve (M. Tschannen-Moran, 2009). A proliferation of rules, often stemming from a lack of trust, causes resentment and alienation among teachers and students alike (Fox, 1974; Govier, 1992). Even when school leaders work hard to build a common vision and to foster the acceptance of group goals, their constituencies will not be inspired to go beyond minimum requirements without trust (M. Tschannen-Moran, 2003).

Teachers need trust from their leaders and with their colleagues to cope with the stress of changing expectations and the demands that the accountability movement places on them. As teachers are asked to change their fundamental beliefs and instructional techniques, they need to build new professional communities anchored in trust and teamwork (R. T. Putnam & Borko, 1997; Seashore & Kruse, 1995). Even within the classroom, relationships are shifting to forms that require greater trust. Cooperative and project-based learning create higher levels of interdependence, which demand higher levels of trust.

Students need trust to engage productively with the learning environment at school and to access the opportunities made available to them. Without trust, students' energy is diverted toward self-protection and away from the learning process. Learning to trust the people at school can be a transformative experience for students whose lives outside of school have not provided them with trustworthy adults whom they can rely on. These experiences in school give students opportunities to see and experience the world in new ways.

The trust of parents and of the wider school community is also important for school success. To be active partners in the educational process, parents must have trusting relationships with teachers, administrators, and other school personnel. The trust of school personnel in parents is also important. Including parents in the educational process, especially school governance, requires administrators, teachers, and other school personnel to trust that parents are motivated to work for the common good and not just for their own narrow interests. Garnering additional resources from the community through partnerships and entrepreneurial efforts also requires trust, because the community must trust that the school is making the most of the resources it already has and will make the most of any additional resources provided. In short, a school leader needs to foster trust within each of the constituencies of his or her school.

At the same time that schools face a greater need for trust, they encounter many obstacles to fostering trust. The difficulties of achieving new and higher societal expectations for equity in schools have led to suspicion of schools and school personnel. Higher standards and greater accountability have contributed to conditions of distrust and blame. Moreover, schools have to accommodate greater diversity and transience. A multicultural society with diverse values and shifting populations makes the cultivation of trust a significant challenge. Adding to this formidable task is the tendency for distrust, once established, to be self-perpetuating. There is a propensity for news of broken trust to spread faster and further than news of intact or restored trust. What is more, the way media outlets pounce on bad news aggravates the spiral of distrust once it gets started.

In sum, for schools to realize the kind of positive transformation envisioned by school improvement and reform efforts, attention must be paid to issues of trust. Finding ways to overcome the breakdown of trust is essential if we want schools to reach our aspirations for them. Meeting this challenge is one of the most important tasks facing school leaders.

TRUSTWORTHY SCHOOL LEADERSHIP

A principal sets the tone for his or her school (M. Tschannen-Moran, 2014). The principal's values, attitudes, and behaviors have a significant influence on the culture of the school. If a school is to reap the rewards of a trusting work environment, it is the principal's responsibility to build and sustain trusting relationships (Whitener, Brodt, Korsgaard, & Werner, 1998). To understand how this works, in practical terms, it is useful to consider the five facets of trust in relation not only to the five constituencies of schools but also to the five functions of instructional leaders: visioning, modeling, coaching, managing, and mediating.

Visioning

If anyone is responsible for lifting up a vision of the school as a trustworthy environment for all constituencies, it is the person charged with leading the school. The explorations of the meaning of trust in this book have given school leaders a framework from which to speak of trust in dynamic and proactive ways. I have not only documented the importance of trust to productive schools but also provided language that allows for conversations designed to consider and promote trust before it goes sour. Had Gloria, Fred, and Brenda made use of this framework, it could have made their job easier and their leadership more effective.

When Gloria arrived at Lincoln, she took over a school in need of change. The students were not being educated well enough to meet even minimum accountability standards, and she suspected that members of the faculty were not doing their best for Lincoln students. Her vision of turning the school around was admirable, but her methods were not. By failing to first establish a benevolent relationship with the people she was charged with leading, her zeal for change came across as judgmental and impatient. It damaged trust with the teachers before trust had time to take root.

Even when a principal has assumed leadership of a school in which he or she feels that the teachers do not deserve to be trusted, such as in a truly dysfunctional school with negative, cynical attitudes and low expectations for student achievement, it does not relieve the principal of the obligation to be trustworthy. There are schools where some teachers actively try to sow discord and distrust toward the school leader, and yet the principal must not retaliate or respond in ways that undermine trust. In fact, as we have seen, it is only through trustworthy leadership that such situations can be turned around.

Gloria had a vision for improved student learning at Lincoln. In failing to be open and forthcoming with information and plans, however, Gloria was not seen as trustworthy. Instead of honoring her vision for change, teachers suspected her of harboring hidden agendas. Instead of getting on board with a common goal, the teachers spent energy monitoring her behavior and maneuvering to protect their own interests. A better understanding of the relationship between trustworthy leadership and the dynamics of the change process would have enabled Gloria to be more successful in lifting up the vision of constructive change at Lincoln (Fullan, 2001).

Through trustworthy leadership and a participative, strengths-based visioning process, Gloria could have engaged the faculty in developing a collective vision to which all were committed. In this way, she could have better focused their attention and released their energy on improving the educational environment at Lincoln. She could have structured a process whereby teachers could have participated actively in wrestling with the data and developing a plan for building on the areas of strength. These activities would have laid the foundation for Gloria to be directly engaged with teacher improvement without being disrespectful of their current struggles and situation. She would have been better positioned to assist her teachers with making the needed changes.

Modeling

Effective school leaders not only talk the talk of trust but also walk the walk. Being a positive role model is never more necessary than when it comes to cultivating a culture of trust. Discontinuity between word and deed will quickly erode a principal's ability to lead. Setting a positive example is not a task to be flaunted by principals, however; it is more a matter of leading *quietly* to earn the trust and cooperation of faculty. Principals who lead quietly are soft on people and hard on projects. They combine personal humility—exercising restraint and modesty—with tenacity and determination to see that the requisite professional tasks of educating students are accomplished and accomplished well (Collins, 2002).

Fred failed to earn the trust of his faculty because his actions did not reflect his talk of high expectations and stern consequences. In wanting to be liked by one and all, and in fearing and avoiding conflict, Fred failed to provide the teachers and students at Fremont with trustworthy leadership. Although Fred genuinely cared about the students and teachers in his school, his lack of leadership around the professional tasks of education left his students and teachers vulnerable to the mounting problems at the school.

Developing the will and ability to deal with problems successfully is where having a framework of trust can help school leaders to both monitor their own behavior and communicate in a straightforward manner. Part of the art of trustworthy leadership is the ability to speak hard truths in a way that communicates caring as well as valuing the other person and the relationship. This takes courage, but it is more likely to produce constructive change than laissez-faire leadership. Trustworthy leaders model norms of conduct that promote the well-being of all members of a school community and explicitly invite others to abide by those norms as well. They defend those norms in ways that make clear that disrespect is not an option, even in their own approach to the person whose disrespect they are challenging.

We see this approach modeled in Brenda's more trustworthy leadership. When Brenda arrived at Brookside, she had many innovative ideas for what she would like to see happening at the school. But Brenda wisely understood that these changes would require extra effort and risk taking on the part of her teachers. She knew she couldn't get there alone and that she would need the teachers to be on board, so she was patient and gradually developed the necessary relationships. A strategy of pursuing small, early wins on some key tasks can help build trust in both the principal's and the school's competence. As the sense of collective efficacy among teachers grows, motivation to invest energy and ideas in the collective effort builds momentum toward making the school more productive.

To consistently serve as models of trustworthy leadership, educational leaders should reflect regularly on their words and actions. In the pressure cooker of a school system, this is a particularly challenging task. It is difficult for school leaders to find the time to follow the recommendation that they STOP—Step back, Think, and Organize their thoughts before they Proceed (Gallwey, 2000). Trustworthy leaders nevertheless make that time, making reflection a regular part of their daily and weekly routines. Brenda made sure that she arrived early at school, before everyone else, giving her a chance to collect herself at the start of the day. Others engage in regular reflective writing. Longer school breaks, both midyear and in the summer, may provide leaders with another opportunity to consider the broader view. The key is to find and to follow a system of reflection that works for them and that incorporates the reflections of others in the process.

Our principal attended a workshop where she encountered the concept of temporarily setting aside topics that you'll want to

come back to later as putting them in a "parking lot." Well,
she misunderstood the intent and took the term
literally. She came back and announced a ban
on all talking in the school parking lot!

—PATRICK, ELEMENTARY SCHOOL ASSISTANT PRINCIPAL

Coaching

Beyond lifting up the vision of a high trust school community
and modeling the behavior of trustworthy leadership, principals
can also build or damage trust by how they engage in conversation around the instructional matters of the school. Applying
too much or too little pressure, being too pushy or not involved
enough, serves to undermine trust and makes their leadership of
the instructional program less and less effective over time. The
concept of coaching leadership is one way to frame the approach
that effective school leaders take in fostering a culture of trust.
Coaches in any arena assist people in reaching their goals through
conversation, strategy, practice, and their way of being with people. Effective coaches know when to push and when to back off,
based on the needs of the situation. They show genuine concern
both for the task at hand and for the welfare of those who have
to accomplish that task. Great coaches epitomize all five facets of
trust in their dealings with people.

A growing body of research and literature summarizes core
coaching competencies and professional ethics. These competencies include establishing a personal presence, active listening, powerful questioning, creating awareness, communicating
directly, designing actions, aligning environments, planning and
goal setting, as well as managing progress and accountability
(International Association of Coaching, 2003, 2009; International
Coach Federation, 2008a, 2008b). My husband, Bob, and I have
built these professional standards into a person-centered, no-
fault, strengths-based coaching model specifically designed for

use by school leaders, which we have called evocative coaching (B. Tschannen-Moran & Tschannen-Moran, 2010). Mastering the core competencies of effective coaching is important for instructional leaders who seek to generate professional growth, support self-efficacy, and fuel enthusiasm among teachers.

> What makes the biggest difference is to have a principal who really listens. When you talk to our principal, he is not really paying attention. You can talk to him later about the same topic, and he has no memory of the conversation.
>
> —ERIKA, ART TEACHER

Coaching mastery is predicated on the establishment of trust. As principals issue the challenge to their teachers to find new ways to meet the diverse needs of all students—including high-achieving students, students with special needs, as well as more typical students—those who have earned the trust of their teachers will be more successful at motivating them to expend the extra effort required. When a culture of trust pervades a school, teachers will be more willing to take risks in trying new instructional strategies. In cultivating a professional learning community committed to professional inquiry and data-based decision making, as well as helping teachers learn to adapt to new technologies and methods of instruction, a trustworthy principal can move his or her school to higher levels of productivity and effectiveness.

Evaluation is one aspect of the principal's role as an instructional leader where the establishment of trust is especially important. Not surprisingly, trust has been found to play a significant role in determining how employees react to supervision. In a study of perceptions of the fairness of performance evaluations by supervisors, the level of trust in the supervisor was more important in regard to perceived fairness than any other characteristics of the evaluation process (Fulk, Brief, & Barr, 1985). The traditional norms of schools have afforded teachers a great deal of autonomy and have offered them very little useful supervision. Teachers have enjoyed the trust, or at least the neglect, of their supervisors. In the age of accountability, however, this state of affairs has changed. New systems of teacher evaluation require greater inspection of teachers' classroom practice. Greater scrutiny may be perceived by both teachers and administrators as a lessening of trust and may in fact lead to less trust. When supervisors master the art of coaching leadership, however, teachers may perceive the greater attention paid as increased care, and a collaborative approach to problem solving and professional development may result (B. Tschannen-Moran & Tschannen-Moran, 2011). In this way, principals have an opportunity to demonstrate their competence and expertise as instructional partners rather than as bosses who tell teachers what to do. Trustworthy leadership is, in many respects, coaching leadership because it positions supervisors as active and constructive partners who contribute to improved instruction and, therefore, improved results in the school.

I was a struggling new teacher at a school for students with emotional disturbances. I soon learned that if I approached my principal with concerns about a classroom management problem, I would read my own words repeated back to me in my next teacher evaluation. I sought other avenues of support after that.

—BUD, SPECIAL EDUCATION TEACHER

One of the greatest dilemmas faced by school leaders occurs when they don't trust the competence and motivation of their teachers. It is the responsibility of the principal as coach to create the circumstances that foster a greater sense of purpose and competence among these educators. The trustworthy principal understands that teachers function within the culture of a school, which influences their behavior. If they have worked within a culture that tolerated or even encouraged a slackening of effort, the principal's responses need to take into consideration these environmental factors that have contributed to poor performance. The principal also needs to shift that culture to one in which there is a common press for improved results without a fear of failure or retribution. Coaching leadership can help make that happen.

Because school cultures emerge as groups of people solve problems together, a principal who wants to change the culture of a school needs to unleash creativity as teachers and administrators alike find new solutions to old problems (Schein, 2010). When a faculty member fails to meet expectations, the principal as coach addresses the issues directly but discretely and in a way that preserves that person's dignity. This approach enables teachers to modify their behavior and conform to expectations without compromising their standing or identity in the school community. This coaching approach to instructional leadership both stems from and results in a culture of disciplined professional inquiry (Collins, 2002; Fullan, 2001). It lies at the heart of effective professional development.

Managing

In addition to a principal's role as instructional leader and coach, he or she is also responsible for management and administration. Here, too, the understanding and implementation of the five facets of trust are important to a principal's effectiveness and success. In their capacity as managers, trusting and trustworthy principals will earn critical efficiencies in what is at times an overwhelming set of job responsibilities. Principals willing to delegate control will find that they are not so bound by the need to do everything themselves. Trustworthy principals who have been successful in cultivating a high-trust school culture will find that they need fewer rules and rigid procedures to ensure that teachers are doing what they are supposed to. Greater organizational citizenship will offer lubrication for the smooth functioning of an organization. And principals who have fostered a strong sense of trust with parents and the local community will find that they spend less time explaining their actions and engaging in investigations of the actions of others.

Trustworthy school leaders cultivate a school-wide culture of discipline in which the norms and expectations support people's productive engagement in the necessary tasks, so that each person contributes constructively to school improvement (Collins, 2002; Fullan, 2001). Here too, in how they handle the rules, principals need to strike a balance between how much and how little they control. Gloria pushed too hard, adopting a manipulative and overly rigid approach to the enforcement of rules. She tried to pressure her teachers by using the teaching contract against them, but this did not make for a productive school environment. Fred didn't push hard enough. He was not trustworthy because, in his attempts to support and empower teachers, he did not confront and take the necessary action to correct bad behavior. Fred lost the trust of his faculty through the lax enforcement of rules and by avoiding conflict. Trustworthy principals find the right balance in their handling of policies, rules, and procedures. They do not abuse their power through manipulation or an overreliance on a strict interpretation of rules, nor do they abdicate their responsibility for leadership. Trustworthy principals demonstrate flexibility by focusing more on the generation of possibilities for success and of solutions to problems than on control. They see rules as means to an end rather than as ends in themselves.

We had a problem of stealing. Things were missing—people's lunches from the refrigerator, money from sales would be missing here and there, small items would disappear from your classroom. After we complained to our principal about what was going on, there was an investigation. Then it was announced that a certain staff person would be

> taking a leave of absence, and she never came back.
> After that, the problems stopped. We were glad the
> situation was dealt with but also that it was handled
> discretely so as not to embarrass anyone.
>
> —JODI, MIDDLE SCHOOL TEACHER

Mediating

Even the most trustworthy of school leaders will have to deal with times of conflict and betrayal in the school environment. Trustworthy principals know how to deal with conflict and how to repair trust through a process of mediation. For one thing, they lift up the vision that such repair is possible. In a fractured society characterized by increasingly discordant public discourse and diminishing civility, trustworthy school leaders stand for something different. They let all their constituencies know that conflict and distrust are not necessarily the last word. They hold out the confidence as well as the hope that there will be reconciliation and the repair of trust.

It is not enough to just lift up the vision, however; a trustworthy leader must play the role of mediator when trust breaks down. It is important for members of the school community, whether students, teachers, or parents, to have trusted resources to turn to when they find themselves in the midst of conflict, and one of those resources should be the school leader. Trustworthy school leaders not only are skillful themselves in the use of conflict management strategies but also create the structures and provide the training for others to improve their skills in this realm as well. Cultivating more productive ways of dealing with conflict is an important part of building a culture of trust in schools. It not only helps to restore trust that has been broken but also helps to prevent future breaches of trust when disputants are supported by norms and processes that allow them to negotiate solutions that meet the needs of all parties.

The five functions of leadership, namely, visioning, modeling, coaching, managing, and mediating, have been shown to matter when it comes to the impact of school leaders on the schools they lead. So, too, do these functions have a bearing on leaders' intention and ability to foster trust. In a study of principals with a reputation for building and sustaining the capacity for change in their school, Cosner (2009) found that principals who emerged as most effective in a statewide sample identified fostering trust as an explicit goal in their leadership strategies. These principals reported that, to foster greater trust, they articulated and defended stronger norms within their school, devoted more time to and created new structures for teacher collaboration and shared decision making, and introduced opportunities for teachers to enhance their skills to manage the inevitable conflicts that collective work entails. These strategies were seen by these school leaders as essential to building capacity for constructive change. Taken together, these findings make clear that the ability to foster trust is an essential competency of leadership.

PRODUCTIVE SCHOOLS

Trustworthy leaders form the heart of productive schools. Trustworthy leadership gets everyone on the same team, pulling in the same direction. At Brookside, Brenda's trustworthy leadership was contagious; it resulted in more trusting relationships throughout the school community. The faculty clearly came to care for one another. This caring was not limited to small groups of friends within cliques, but rather extended to every person on the faculty. On a professional level, faculty members looked out for one another, and especially for new teachers. Teachers freely shared ideas and resources. On a personal level, people were also willing to share about their lives outside of school with the expectation that they would receive a caring response. Teachers respected one another's expertise and enjoyed a strong sense of shared commitment to the mission of the school. There was no sense of competition to outdo one another or to prove who was the best teacher. There was no sense of defensiveness among teachers about their own classroom performance. Teachers welcomed one another into their respective classrooms, whether informally, for visits or to borrow something, or more formally, for peer observations. Teachers were not worried about being judged harshly or unfairly. They respected each other's integrity and could count on one another to be reliable in their commitments.

When we trusted teachers to have more say over their time, whether they wanted to teach on the block or not, whether to team, and how they arranged their time within the block, to take breaks when it made sense to them within their lessons, we noticed that it trickled down and that they began to trust their students more too.

—DAN, HIGH SCHOOL PRINCIPAL

Trust was no less important among students and parents. In making trust judgments about children, the teachers in this study looked for respect—respect for teachers and other adults, respect for other children, and self-respect. Judgments of all of the other facets of trust—honesty, openness, reliability, and competence—seemed to follow from this baseline assessment of respect. Further, teachers wanted to feel that the parents of their students were at least as concerned about the children's well-being as they themselves were. They also wanted the parents to believe that teachers had every child's best interests at heart and that they were willing to work together to solve any problems as partners in a shared project. Teachers also trusted parents who avoided placing blame but were willing to take responsibility for their own actions. They respected parents who encouraged their children to do the same.

Across the various actors in schools, whether principals, teachers, or students, the same five facets were important to the cultivation of trust. At a more basic level, trustworthiness had to do with
concern for relationships combined with concern for the task.
At the administrative level, this balance was evident in the high-
support, high-challenge principal. Among teachers, it was expressed
in the high-commitment, high-competence teacher. Among students, it was seen in the high-respect, high-motivation student.
No matter the role within the school community, earning trust
had to do with the dual concerns of care for the shared task and
care for relationships. Trustworthy leaders show the way through
example and by providing the norms, structures, and resources
to encourage others to be trustworthy as well. Trustworthy leaders
create a culture of trust within their building; this trust is at the
crux of successful schools.

 PUTTING IT INTO ACTION

You can make use of the ideas presented in this book to foster greater
trust in your school and reap the benefits of greater efficiency, adaptability, and quality. By integrating the five facets of trust with the five
functions of leadership as you relate to the various constituencies of
your school, you will gain new insight and direction as to what needs
to be done. Through increased awareness of how trust works and of
its importance to productive schools, you will be more successful in
leading your school to fulfill its vital mission. If, on the one hand,
there is a high level of trust in the interpersonal relationships within
your school, you and your teachers can celebrate that fact and take
action to strengthen the cycle, fostering even greater levels of trust. If,
on the other hand, the level of trust is not what you would hope for in
your school, the five-facet model presented in this book can increase
your awareness of the importance of and strategies for addressing the
relevant issues.

Awareness brings with it the responsibility to take constructive
action for change. It is the duty of the person with greater power in a
hierarchy to accept greater responsibility for the cultivation of trust.

Even if you feel wronged and misunderstood, you have the responsibility as well as the opportunity to work toward renewed trust by being meticulously trustworthy yourself, by announcing your intentions to others, and by creating effective communication structures for conflict resolution within the organization. Restoring lost trust is possible, but it is not easy. The effort requires courage, persistence, and forgiveness. The rewards, however, are worth the effort for schools mired in the dysfunctional consequences of a distrustful culture. The model of trust presented in this book can generate new ideas and possibilities, enabling you and your constituents to interrupt the spiral of distrust and begin the journey back to restored trust.

There are no quick fixes. Only in conversations with teachers and other constituents can a new vision and new strategies emerge. And with a strengths-based orientation to these conversations, you will be in a position to engage in a positive strategy of change. Appreciative inquiry, described in chapter 9, is a powerful means of structuring needed conversations about how to improve the quality of trusting relationships within your school through the development of a shared vision of the desired future. Design teams can then be formed to develop action plans for making that vision a reality. One-on-one coaching can help individuals stay with, develop, and follow through on those plans over time.

Trust is a significant factor in productive schools. Schools that enjoy a culture of trust are likely to benefit from having members of the school community who willingly work together and go beyond the minimum requirements of their respective positions. Communication flows more freely without the encumbrance of a proliferation of rules. A high level of trust helps make a school a wonderful place to learn and grow, characterized by a positive, open, and healthy climate. The costs of broken trust are great. When distrust pervades a school, constrained communication, poor organizational citizenship, and an abundance of dysfunctional rules are often the result. Trust hits schools' bottom line by making a difference in student achievement. It is related to the collective sense teachers have that they can make a difference in the lives of their students and that they can deal constructively with conflict. Although the building of trust in schools requires time, effort, and leadership, the investment will bring lasting returns. Trust pays big dividends in helping each school succeed at fulfilling its mission to be a productive, professional learning community.

KEY POINTS ABOUT BECOMING
A TRUSTWORTHY LEADER

- Trustworthy leaders apply the five facets of trust to the five functions of leadership. They construct a shared vision, model trustworthy behavior, provide coaching, manage the environment, and mediate breakdowns of trust.

- The five-facet model articulated in this book can assist educational leaders in proactively fostering a culture of trust in their school. It can also help them diagnose and correct problems of trust before these get so large that they seem insurmountable.

- Trustworthy leaders put the culture of trust ahead of their own ego needs. Skillful principals often earn the trust of their faculty by leading *quietly:* they are soft on people and hard on projects. They combine personal humility—exercising restraint and modesty—with tenacity and the professional will to see that the complex work of educating a diverse group of students is accomplished at a high level of quality.

- Trustworthy principals foster the development of trust in their school by demonstrating flexibility, adopting a problem-solving stance, refusing to play the blame game, and involving teachers in making important decisions.

- Trustworthy leaders strike the right balance between taking too much responsibility and taking too little, between pushing too hard and pushing too little.

- Taking a strengths-based approach to school-wide conversations about rebuilding trust is likely to be more constructive than rehashing old conflicts and betrayals in a public forum.

- Trustworthy leadership is at the heart of productive schools.

QUESTIONS FOR REFLECTION
AND DISCUSSION

1. What are the best experiences you have had of high-trust relationships in schools? What made those relationships so positive and productive? How were you supported by the trust of others in such instances? How did the high level of trust contribute to your engagement and commitment to the work? Who was involved? What goals were you working on? What challenges did you face? What contributed to the high level of trust?

2. What does the concept of trustworthy leadership mean to you? How would you contrast that form of leadership with other forms of leadership? How does this concept align with your core values?

3. When you are at your best, what do you value most about the contribution you make through your work at your school?

4. Who has helped you to become a more trustworthy leader? Whom have you helped to become a more trustworthy leader? What concepts or processes have proved to be most effective in this regard?

5. What are some of the costly structures, systems, and practices at your school that could be reduced or eliminated if there were more trust between parents and the school? Between teachers and administrators? Between teachers and students?

6. Imagine that you could transform the quality of the working relationships in your school in any way you wanted. What would this change look like? How might the transformation heighten the vitality and health of this organization? If you could make any three wishes come true for bringing your vision into being, what would they be?

MEASURES OF TRUST IN SCHOOLS

Three trust surveys are included in this appendix—surveys to assess students' trust in faculty, parents' trust in the school, and faculty members' trust in students and parents. These measures are the result of many years of research. It is my hope that including them will facilitate productive conversations about trust in schools.

It is critical that ethical standards be adhered to in administering the surveys. They should be administered anonymously so that there is no way for the results to be traced to the individual who completed the survey. Participants should be told that their participation is voluntary and that they will suffer no penalty for refusing to complete the survey. They should also be told that they may skip any items they are uncomfortable answering.

Scoring directions are provided for each of these three surveys, as well as evidence concerning the reliability and validity of the scales. Directions for calculating a standardized score are included so that schools can compare their results with those of other schools. The standardized score is presented on a scale with a mean of 500 and a standard deviation of 100, much like an SAT or GRE score. For example, a school's score of 600 on faculty members' trust in students and parents (or "clients") is one standard deviation above the average score on that measure for all schools in the sample. That means that the school has higher trust in students and parents among the faculty than 84 percent of the schools in the sample, according to the range of the standardized scores presented here:

- If the score is 200, it is lower than that of 99 percent of the schools.
- If the score is 300, it is lower than that of 97 percent of the schools.
- If the score is 400, it is lower than that of 84 percent of the schools.
- If the score is 500, it is average.
- If the score is 600, it is higher than that of 84 percent of the schools.
- If the score is 700, it is higher than that of 97 percent of the schools.
- If the score is 800, it is higher than that of 99 percent of the schools.

Ready-to-print versions of these surveys are available as PDF files in the Research Tools section on my website (www.MeganTM .com) for both educators and scholars interested in studying trust in schools.

SURVEY OF STUDENTS' TRUST IN TEACHERS

The Student Trust in Teachers Scale (C. M. Adams & Forsyth, 2009) measures the level of trust students have for their teachers (see exhibit A.1). It is based on the five-facet model of trust described in this book. C. M. Adams and Forsyth developed this measure to "capture student perceptions and recollections of

Exhibit A.1 Student Trust in Teachers Scale

Student Survey

Directions: **Please tell us how much you agree or disagree with each of the statements about your school by filling in the bubbles on the right, choosing from (1) Strongly Disagree, (2) Disagree, (3) Neutral, (4) Agree, or (5) Strongly Agree.**

	Strongly Disagree				Strongly Agree
1. Teachers are always ready to help.	①	②	③	④	⑤
2. Teachers are easy to talk to at this school.	①	②	③	④	⑤
3. Students learn a lot from teachers in this school.	①	②	③	④	⑤
4. Students at this school can depend on teachers for help.	①	②	③	④	⑤
5. Teachers at this school do a terrific job.	①	②	③	④	⑤
6. Teachers at this school really listen to students.	①	②	③	④	⑤
7. Teachers always do what they are supposed to do.	①	②	③	④	⑤
8. Students are well cared for at this school.	①	②	③	④	⑤
9. Teachers at this school are good at teaching.	①	②	③	④	⑤
10. Teachers at this school are always honest with me.	①	②	③	④	⑤

teacher behavior, which allow for judgments to be made about their relative openness, benevolence, reliability, competence, and honesty" (p. 264).

Scoring Directions for the Student Survey

Step 1: Calculate the Average Score for Each Survey Participant

Complete this step by calculating the mean of all ten survey items for each participant.

Step 2: Calculate the Grand Mean Score for Your School

Complete this step by taking an average of all of the participants' individual scores.

Step 3: Compute the Standardized Score for Students' Trust in Teachers

In this step you will convert your school's score to a standardized score with a mean of 500 and a standard deviation of 100, making comparison with other schools possible. First compute the difference between your school's score on students' trust in teachers, STT, and the mean for the normative sample. For a high school, this would mean $STT - 3.059$. Then multiply the difference by 100: $100(STT - 3.059)$. Next divide the product by the standard deviation of the normative sample, which here is 0.728. Then add 500 to the result. You have computed a standardized score: **Standard Score for Students' Trust in Teachers**. Note that the student survey has a five-point response scale, whereas the parent and teacher surveys have a six-point response scale.

For high schools, calculate standardized trust scores using the following formula:

Standard Score for Students' Trust in Teachers $= 100(STT - 3.059)/0.728 + 500$

For middle schools, calculate standardized trust scores using the following formula:

Standard Score for Students' Trust in Teachers $= 100(STT - 3.142)/0.861 + 500$

For elementary schools, calculate standardized trust scores using the following formula:

Standard Score for Students' Trust in Teachers $= 100(STT - 4.107)/0.781 + 500$

Reliability and Validity of the Student Survey

To establish the content validity of the Student Trust in Teachers Scale, C. M. Adams and Forsyth (2009) submitted the items to a panel of eight professional educators, who were asked to assess the clarity of items; to examine the relevance of items to teacher-student interactions; and to identify the conceptual indicator (that is, facet) measured by each item. Next, a field test was conducted in which exploratory factor analysis demonstrated construct validity because all of the items loaded on a single factor with factor coefficients that ranged from 0.62 to 0.85. In addition, scores on the survey were strongly associated with affective conditions that underlie student behavior, such as students' perceptions of academic press and their identification with school (C. M. Adams & Forsyth, 2009; M. Tschannen-Moran, Bankole, Mitchell, & Moore, 2013). Reliability, which was assessed using Cronbach's alpha coefficient of internal consistency, ranged from 0.90 to 0.93 in previous studies (C. M. Adams & Forsyth, 2009; M. Tschannen-Moran et al., 2013). These tests indicated that the Student Trust in Teacher Scale appears to be a reasonably valid and reliable measure of the concept.

The norms for the Student Trust in Teachers Scale are based on the responses of 7,982 students in grades 3 through 12 sampled from forty-nine schools in an urban district. These included thirty-five elementary schools, nine middle schools, and five high schools. Specifically, the student responses included 4,702 from elementary school students in grades 3 through 5; 1,978 from middle school students in grades 6 through 8; and 1,301 from high school students in grades 9 through 12. Comparisons to students' trust in teachers in other contexts should be made with caution.

SURVEY OF PARENTS' TRUST IN THE SCHOOL

The Parent Trust in School Scale is a fifteen-item measure that assesses parents' perceptions of the benevolence, honesty, openness, reliability, and competence of school personnel (see exhibit A.2). Items that make up this scale were adapted from a ten-item measure of parents' trust in the school and a ten-item measure of parents' trust in the principal developed by Forsyth and Adams (Forsyth, Adams, & Hoy, 2011), with some alternate items included to capture additional aspects of parents' perceptions of the school and school personnel (M. Tschannen-Moran et al., 2013).

Scoring Directions for the Parent Survey

Step 1: Calculate the Average Score for Each Survey Participant

Complete this step by calculating the mean of all fifteen items for each participant.

Step 2: Calculate the Grand Mean Score for Your School

Complete this step by taking an average of all of the participants' individual scores.

Step 3: Compute the Standardized Score for Parents' Trust in the School

In this step you will convert your school's score to a standardized score with a mean of 500 and a standard deviation of 100, making comparison with other schools possible. First compute the difference between your school's score on parents' trust in the school, *PaTS*, and the mean for the normative sample. For example, for an elementary school, that would be $PaTS - 5.171$. Then multiply the difference by 100: $100(PaTS - 5.171)$. Next divide the product by the standard deviation of the normative sample, which here is 0.831. Then add 500 to the result. You have computed a standardized score: **Standard Score for Parents' Trust in the School**.

For high schools, calculate standardized trust scores using the following formula:

Standard Score for Parents' Trust in the School $= 100(PaTS - 4.680)/0.941 + 500$

For middle schools, calculate standardized trust scores using the following formula:

Standard Score for Parents' Trust in the School $= 100(PaTS - 4.687)/0.988 + 500$

For elementary schools, calculate standardized trust scores using the following formula:

Standard Score for Parents' Trust in the School $= 100(PaTS - 5.171)/0.831 + 500$

Reliability and Validity of the Parent Survey

In testing the construct validity of the Parent Trust in School Scale, a factor analysis of this measure among forty-nine urban schools found that all fifteen items formed a single factor (Pennycuff,

Exhibit A.2 Parent Trust in School Scale

Parent Survey

Directions: **This questionnaire is designed to help us gain a better understanding of your perceptions of your child's school. Your answers are anonymous, and you may skip any item you are uncomfortable answering.**

Please indicate the extent to which you agree or disagree with each of the statements about your child's school, marking in the columns on the right, ranging from (1) Strongly Disagree to (6) Strongly Agree.

	Strongly Disagree					Strongly Agree
1. Teachers at my child's school are good at teaching.	①	②	③	④	⑤	⑥
2. Students can depend on teachers for help.	①	②	③	④	⑤	⑥
3. This school keeps me well informed.	①	②	③	④	⑤	⑥
4. Teachers are willing to go the extra mile to help my child.	①	②	③	④	⑤	⑥
5. Teachers at this school are trustworthy.	①	②	③	④	⑤	⑥
6. Teachers at my child's school are helpful.	①	②	③	④	⑤	⑥
7. I trust that school personnel are looking out for my child's best interests.	①	②	③	④	⑤	⑥
8. School personnel listen to me if I have a concern.	①	②	③	④	⑤	⑥

9. People at the school care about my child.	①	②	③	④	⑤	⑥
10. Teachers at my child's school are fair.	①	②	③	④	⑤	⑥
11. My child has access to extra help at school if needed.	①	②	③	④	⑤	⑥
12. Teachers at my child's school do a terrific job.	①	②	③	④	⑤	⑥
13. I am kept informed of my child's progress.	①	②	③	④	⑤	⑥
14. I can get help for my child from the school if needed.	①	②	③	④	⑤	⑥
15. I can reach my child's teachers easily.	①	②	③	④	⑤	⑥

2009). Reliability, which was established using Cronbach's alpha coefficient of internal consistency, was 0.96.

The norms for the Parent Trust in School Scale are based on the responses of 2,959 parents (1,867 urban and 1,092 suburban). These were nested within sixty-four schools (forty-nine urban and fifteen suburban). Comparisons to parents' perceptions of schools in other contexts should be made with caution.

SURVEY OF FACULTY MEMBERS' TRUST IN STUDENTS AND PARENTS

The Faculty Trust in Clients Scale includes nine items (see exhibit A.3). It can be used at the elementary school, middle school, or high school level. It is interesting to note that when teachers in schools in a variety of contexts have been asked separately about their trust in students and their trust in parents, the results have been so closely aligned that they were statistically indistinguishable and had to be combined for analysis.

Scoring Directions for the Faculty Survey

Step 1: Calculate the Average Score for Each Survey Participant

Complete this step by taking the mean of all nine items for each participant.

Step 2: Calculate the Grand Mean Score for Your School

Complete this step by taking an average of all of the participants' individual scores.

Step 3: Compute the Standardized Score for Faculty Members' Trust in Students and Parents

In this step you will convert your school's score to a standardized score with a mean of 500 and a standard deviation of 100, making

Exhibit A.3 Faculty Trust in Clients Scale

Faculty Survey

Directions: Please indicate the extent of your agreement with each of the statements by marking in the columns on the right side, ranging from (1) Strongly Disagree to (6) Strongly Agree.

This questionnaire is designed to help us gain a better understanding of the kinds of relationships in schools. Your answers are confidential.

	Strongly Disagree					Strongly Agree
1. Teachers in this school trust their students.	①	②	③	④	⑤	⑥
2. Students in this school are caring.	①	②	③	④	⑤	⑥
3. Students in this school can be counted on to do their work.	①	②	③	④	⑤	⑥
4. Teachers here believe that students are competent learners.	①	②	③	④	⑤	⑥
5. Teachers in this school trust the parents.	①	②	③	④	⑤	⑥
6. Teachers in this school can count on parental support.	①	②	③	④	⑤	⑥
7. Parents in this school are reliable in their commitments.	①	②	③	④	⑤	⑥
8. Teachers think most of the parents do a good job.	①	②	③	④	⑤	⑥
9. Teachers in this school can believe what parents tell them.	①	②	③	④	⑤	⑥

© 1999 Hoy & Tschannen-Moran.

comparison with other schools possible. First, compute the difference between your school's score on faculty members' trust in students and parents, *FTSP,* and the mean for the normative sample. For a middle school, this would mean $FTSP - 3.420$. Then multiply the difference by 100: $100(FTSP - 3.420)$. Next divide the product by the standard deviation of the normative sample, which here is 0.466. Then add 500 to the result. You have computed a standardized score: **Standard Score for Faculty Members' Trust in Students and Parents**.

For high schools, calculate standardized trust scores using the following formula:

Standard Score for Faculty Members' Trust in Students and Parents $= 100(FTSP - 3.685)/0.349 + 500$

For middle schools, calculate standardized trust scores using the following formula:

Standard Score for Faculty Members' Trust in Students and Parents $= 100(FTSP - 3.420)/0.466 + 500$

For elementary schools, calculate standardized trust scores using the following formula:

Standard Score for Faculty Members' Trust in Students and Parents $= 100(FTSP - 3.966)/0.584 + 500$

Reliability and Validity of the Faculty Survey

Factor analytic studies of the Faculty Trust in Clients Scale support the construct validity of the measure. The reliability of this scale, calculated using Cronbach's alpha coefficient of internal consistency has typically ranged from 0.90 to 0.98. For more information on the reliability and validity of the faculty survey, see "The Conceptualization and Measurement of Faculty Trust in Schools: The Omnibus T-Scale" (Hoy & Tschannen-Moran, 2003).

The norms for the Faculty Trust in Clients Scale are based on a sample of 97 high schools in Ohio, 66 middle schools in Virginia, and 146 elementary schools in Ohio from diverse contexts throughout each state. Comparisons to faculty members' trust in students and parents in other contexts should be made with caution.

GUIDELINES FOR PRESENTING THE RESULTS OF THE TRUST SURVEYS TO YOUR FACULTY

The study of trust has been likened to the study of the roots of a delicate plant. Without great care, the examination can damage or even destroy the very thing about which greater understanding is sought. Consequently, I urge caution in the use of these trust scales. Although they can be powerful tools in helping to reveal the underlying dynamics of trust in the reciprocal relationship teachers have with students and parents in your school, they can do more harm than good if the information is not handled with sensitivity and care. If these data reveal that there are problems in the patterns of trust within your building, there is no better time to begin to exercise trustworthy behavior than in the presentation of these results.

Although these tools hold the possibility of contributing to improved productivity and effectiveness in your school by identifying areas in need of enhanced trust, the revelation of distrust or even trust that is less than optimal can be hard to take and can feel like a personal attack. But you must not lash out in reaction to this perceived insult. Instead, it is important to seek to understand the perceptions and feelings that are revealed through the surveys; try to appreciate the opportunity to get a window into others' thinking that might not otherwise be available to you. If you don't want to know the truth, don't administer the surveys in the first place. Moreover, suppressing negative results will only lead to greater distrust, so do not administer the surveys if you do not intend to share the results with those who offered their opinions.

In presenting the results of the surveys to the faculty or other stakeholders, it is important to avoid blaming or looking for scapegoats. This is the time for openness, vulnerability, and authenticity. It is the time for open-minded curiosity about how things got to be the way they are, followed by a conversation about how participants would like things to be and about how to make that happen. Compelling evidence on the importance of trust to high-performing schools has been presented in this book. If your scores indicate that there is a problem with trust in your building, you have the opportunity to make it a priority to address these concerns.

APPENDIX B

ADDITIONAL
RESOURCES

ATTACHMENT THEORY

Freiberg, H. J., Huzinec, C. A., & Templeton, S. M. (2009). Classroom management—a pathway to student achievement: A study of fourteen inner-city elementary schools. *The Elementary School Journal, 110,* 1–18.

Freiberg, H. J., & Lamb, S. M. (2009). Dimensions of person-centered classroom
management. *Theory into Practice, 48,* 99–105.

Pianta, R. C. (1999). *Enhancing relationships between children and teachers.* Washington,
DC: American Psychological Association.

Pianta, R. C. (2006). Classroom management and relationships between chil-
dren and teachers: Implications for research and practice. In C. M. Evertson &
C. S. Weinstein (Eds.), *Handbook of classroom management* (pp. 685–709).
Hillsdale, NJ: Lawrence Erlbaum Associates.

Streight, D. (2013). *Breaking into the heart of character: Self-determined moral action
and academic motivation.* Portland, OR: Center for Spiritual and Ethical
Education.

Tough, P. (2012). *How children succeed: Grit, curiosity, and the hidden power of character.* New York, NY: Houghton Mifflin Harcourt. The beginning chapter
presents a compelling case for the role of attachment in children's healthy
development with clear implications for classroom practice.

Watson, M. (2003). *Learning to trust: Transforming difficult elementary classrooms
through developmental discipline.* San Francisco, CA: Jossey-Bass.

Watson, M. S. (2006). Long term effects of moral/character education in elementary school: In pursuit of mechanisms. *Journal of Research in Character*

Education, 4, 1–12. This article reports on a follow-up study describing several of the students from *Learning to Trust* (see previous reference) at the end of their sophomore year in high school.

Watson, M. S., & Battistich, V. (2006). Building and sustaining caring communities. In C. M. Evertson & C. S. Weinstein (Eds.), *Handbook of classroom management* (pp. 253–279). Mahwah, NJ: Lawrence Erlbaum Associates.

APPRECIATIVE INQUIRY

Bushe, G. R. (2008). AI at Metropolitan School District. In D. L. Cooperrider, D. Whitney, & J. M. Stavros (Eds.), *AI handbook for leaders of change* (2nd ed., pp. 314–317). Brunswick, OH: Crown Custom.

Cooperrider, D. L., Whitney, D., & Stavros, J. M. (2008). *AI handbook for leaders of change* (2nd ed.). Brunswick, OH: Crown Custom.

Daly, A. J., & Chrispeels, J. (2005). From problem to possibility: Leadership for implementing and deepening the processes of effective schools. *Journal for Effective Schools, 4*(1), 7–25.

Daly, A. J., Millhollen, B., & DiGuilio, L. (2007). Soaring toward excellence: The case of the Esperanza School District. *AI Practitioner, 5*(3), 27–39.

Tschannen-Moran, M., & Tschannen-Moran, B. (2011). Taking a strengths-based focus improves school climate. *Journal of School Leadership, 21,* 422–448.

Watkins, J. M., Mohr, B. J., & Kelly, R. (2011). *Appreciative inquiry: Change at the speed of imagination* (2nd ed.). San Francisco, CA: Jossey-Bass.

Whitney, D., Trosten-Bloom, A., & Cooperrider, D. (2010). *The power of appreciative inquiry: A practical guide to positive change* (2nd ed.). San Francisco, CA: Berrett-Koehler.

Willoughby, G., & Tosey, P. (2007). Imagine Meadfield: AI as a process for leading school improvement. *Educational Management, Administration, & Leadership, 35,* 499–520.

Websites with Resources for Appreciative Inquiry

Appreciative Inquiry Commons: http://appreciativeinquiry.case.edu

AI Practitioner Online Journal: http://www.aipractitioner.com

The Center for School Transformation: http://www.schooltransformation.com

NONVIOLENT COMMUNICATION IN EDUCATION

Hart, S., & Hodson, V. K. (2004). *The compassionate classroom: Relationship-based teaching and learning*. Encinitas, CA: PuddleDancer Press.

Hart, S., & Hodson, V. K. (2006). *Respectful parents, respectful kids: 7 keys to turn family conflict into cooperation*. Encinitas, CA: PuddleDancer Press.

Hart, S., & Hodson, V. K. (2008). *The no-fault classroom: Tools to resolve conflict and foster relationship intelligence*. Encinitas, CA: PuddleDancer Press.

Leu, L. (2003). *Nonviolent communication: Companion workbook*. Encinitas, CA: PuddleDancer Press.

Rosenberg, M. (2003). *Life-enriching education: Nonviolent communication helps schools improve performance, reduce conflict, and enhance relationships*. Encinitas, CA: PuddleDancer Press.

Rosenberg, M. (2005). *Nonviolent communication: A language of life* (2nd ed.). Encinitas, CA: PuddleDancer Press.

Rosenberg, M. (2005). *Teaching children compassionately: How students and teachers can succeed with mutual understanding*. Encinitas, CA: PuddleDancer Press.

Rosenberg, M. (2006). *The nonviolent communication training course* [Audiobook]. Louisville, CO: Sounds True.

Websites with Resources for Nonviolent Communication in Education

The Center for Nonviolent Communication: http://www.cnvc.org/

The No-Fault Zone: http://www.thenofaultzone.com

REFERENCES

Abdul-Adil, J. K., & Farmer, A. D. (2006). Inner-city African American parental involvement in elementary schools: Getting beyond urban legends of apathy. *School Psychology Quarterly, 21*, 1–12.

Adams, C. (2010). Social determinants of student trust in high-poverty elementary schools. In W. K. Hoy & M. F. DiPaola (Eds.), *Analyzing school contexts* (pp. 255–280). Charlotte, NC: Information Age.

Adams, C. M., & Forsyth, P. B. (2009). Conceptualizing and validating a measure of student trust. In W. K. Hoy & M. DiPaola (Eds.), *Studies in school improvement* (pp. 263–279). Charlotte, NC: Information Age.

Adams, C. M., & Forsyth, P. B. (2013). Revisiting the trust effect in urban elementary schools. *The Elementary School Journal, 114*, 1–21.

Adams, C. M., Forsyth, P. B., & Mitchell, R. M. (2009). The formation of parent-school trust: A multilevel analysis. *Educational Administration Quarterly, 45*, 4–33. doi:10.1177/0013161X08327550

Adams, K. S., & Christenson, S. L. (1998). Differences in parent and teacher trust levels. *Special Services in the Schools, 14*, 1–22. doi:10.1300/J008v14n01_01

Adams, K. S., & Christenson, S. L. (2000). Trust and the family-school relationship: Examination of parent-teacher differences in elementary and secondary grades. *Journal of School Psychology, 38*, 477–497.

Adler, P. S., & Borys, B. (1996). Two types of bureaucracy: Enabling and coercive. *Administrative Quarterly, 41*, 61–89.

Ainsworth, M.D.S., Blehar, M. C., Waters, E., & Wall, S. (1978). *Patterns of attachment.* Hillsdale, NJ: Lawrence Erlbaum.

Allinder, R. M. (1994). The relationship between efficacy and the instructional practices of special education teachers and consultants. *Teacher Education and Special Education, 17*(2), 86–95.

Allison, S. T., & Messick, D. M. (1985). The group attribution error. *Journal of Experimental Social Psychology, 21,* 563–579.

Anderson, R. N., Greene, M. L., & Loewen, P. S. (1988). Relationships among teachers' and students' thinking skills, sense of efficacy, and student achievement. *Alberta Journal of Educational Research, 34,* 148–165.

Armor, D., Conry-Oseguera, P., Cox, M., King, M., McDonnell, L., Pascal, A., ... & Zellmann, G. (1976). Analysis of the school preferred reading program in selected Los Angeles minority schools. Santa Monica, CA: Rand Corporation.

Ashton, P. T., & Webb, R. B. (1986). Teachers' sense of efficacy, classroom behavior, and student achievement. In P. T. Ashton & R. B. Webb (Eds.), *Teachers' sense of efficacy and student achievement* (pp. 125–144). New York, NY: Longman.

Baier, A. C. (1994). *Moral prejudices.* Cambridge, MA: Harvard University Press.

Bandura, A. (1993). Perceived self-efficacy in cognitive development and functioning. *Educational Psychologist, 28,* 117–148.

Bandura, A. (1997). *Self-efficacy: The exercise of control.* New York, NY: Freeman.

Barber, B. (1983). *The logic and limits of trust.* New Brunswick, NJ: Rutgers University Press.

Barney, J. B., & Hansen, M. H. (1994). Trustworthiness as a source of competitive advantage. *Strategic Management Journal, 15,* 175–190.

Barnyak, N., & McNelly, T. A. (2009). An urban school district's parent involvement: A study of teachers' and administrators' beliefs and practices. *School Community Journal, 19*(1), 33–58.

Baron, R.A. (1997). Positive effects of conflict: Insights from social cognition. In C.K.W. De Dreu & E. Van de Vliert (Eds.), *Using conflict in organizations* (pp. 101–115). Thousand Oaks, CA: Sage.

Barth, R. (1981). The principal as staff developer. *Journal of Education, 163*(2), 144–162.

Berg, J., Dickhaut, J., & McCabe, K. (1995). *Trust, reciprocity, and social history.* Unpublished working paper, University of Minnesota, Minneapolis.

Berliner, D. C., & Biddle, B. J. (1995). *The manufactured crisis: Myths, fraud, and the attack on America's public schools.* Reading, MA: Addison-Wesley.

Bies, R. J., & Tripp, T. M. (1996). Beyond distrust: "Getting even" and the need for revenge. In R. M. Kramer & T. R. Tyler (Eds.), *Trust in organizations* (pp. 246–260). Thousand Oaks, CA: Sage.

Bigley, G. A., & Pearce, J. L. (1998). Straining for shared meaning in organization science: Problems of trust and distrust. *Academy of Management Review, 23,* 405–421.

Blake, M., & MacNeil, A. J. (1998). Trust: The quality required for successful management. In Y. Cano, F. H. Wood, & J. C. Simmons (Eds.), *Creating high functioning schools: Practice and research* (pp. 29–37). Springfield, IL: Charles C. Thomas.

Bowlby, J. (1988). *A secure base: Parent-child attachment and healthy human development.* London, UK: Routledge.

Brewer, M. B. (1995). In-group favoritism: The subtle side of intergroup discrimination. In D. M. Messick & A. Tenbrunsel (Eds.), *Behavioral research and business ethics* (pp. 101–117). New York, NY: Russell Sage Foundation.

Bryk, A. S., & Schneider, B. (1996). *Social trust: A moral resource for school improvement.* Chicago, IL: Consortium on Chicago School Research.

Bryk, A. S., & Schneider, B. (2002). *Trust in schools: A core resource for school improvement.* New York, NY: Russell Sage Foundation.

Burt, R. S., & Knez, M. (1996). Trust and third-party gossip. In R. M. Kramer & T. R. Tyler (Eds.), *Trust in organizations* (pp. 68–89). Thousand Oaks, CA: Sage.

Butler, J. K., & Cantrell, R. S. (1984). A behavioral decision theory approach to modeling dyadic trust in superiors and subordinates. *Psychological Reports, 55,* 81–105.

Cloke, K., & Goldsmith, J. (2002). *The end of management and the rise of organizational democracy.* San Francisco, CA: Jossey-Bass.

Coach U. (2003). *Personal foundation—level 2.* Steamboat Springs, CO: Author.

Coleman, J. S. (1990). *Foundations of social theory.* Cambridge, MA: Belknap Press of Harvard University Press.

Collins, J. (2002). *Good to great: Why some companies make the leap . . . and others don't.* New York, NY: HarperBusiness.

Conway, K., & Houtenville, A. (2008). Parental effort, school resources, and student achievement. *The Journal of Human Resources, 43,* 437–453.

Cosner, S. (2009). Building organizational capacity through trust. *Educational Administration Quarterly, 45,* 248–291.

Creed, W.E.D., & Miles, R. E. (1996). Trust in organizations: A conceptual framework linking organizational forms, managerial philosophies, and the opportunity costs of controls. In R. M. Kramer & T. R. Tyler (Eds.), *Trust in organizations* (pp. 16–38). Thousand Oaks, CA: Sage.

Cummings, L. L., & Bromily, P. (1996). The Organizational Trust Inventory (OTI): Development and validation. In R. M. Kramer & T. R. Tyler (Eds.), *Trust in organizations* (pp. 302–330). Thousand Oaks, CA: Sage.

Daly, A. (2009). Rigid response in an age of accountability: The potential of leadership and trust. *Educational Administration Quarterly, 45,* 168–216.

Daly, A. J. (2010). Mapping the terrain. In A. J. Daly (Ed.), *Social network theory and educational change* (pp. 1–16). Cambridge, MA: Harvard Education Press.

Dasgupta, P. (1988). Trust as a commodity. In D. Gambetta (Ed.), *Trust: Making and breaking cooperative relations* (pp. 213–238). Cambridge, MA: Basil Blackwell.

Deluga, R. J. (1994). Supervisor trust building, leader-member exchange and organizational citizenship behavior. *Journal of Occupational and Organizational Psychology, 67,* 315.

Deutsch, M. (1960). The effect of motivational orientation upon trust and suspicion. *Human Relations, 13,* 123–139.

Deutsch, M. (2000). Cooperation and competition. In M. Deutsch & P. T.
Coleman (Eds.), *The handbook of conflict resolution: Theory and practice* (pp.
21–40). San Francisco, CA: Jossey-Bass.

Dirks, K. T., & Ferric, D. I. (2001). The role of trust in organizational settings.
Organizational Science, 12, 450–467.

Elangovan, A. R., & Shapiro, D. L. (1998). Betrayal of trust in organizations.
Academy of Management Review, 23, 547–566.

Elmore, R. F., Peterson, P. L., & McCarthey, S. J. (1996). *Restructuring the classroom: Teaching, learning, and school organization.* San Francisco, CA: Jossey-Bass.

Epstein, J. L. (1988). Effects on student achievement of teachers' practices for
parent involvement. In S. Silvern (Ed.), *Literacy through family, community, and
school interaction.* Greenwich, CT: JAI Press.

Finders, M., & Lewis, C. (1994). Why some parents don't come to school.
Educational Leadership, 51(8), 50–55.

Fisher, R., & Brown, S. (1988). *Getting together.* Boston, MA: Houghton Mifflin.

Forsyth, P. B., Adams, C. M., & Hoy, W. K. (2011). *Collective trust: Why school can't
improve without it.* New York, NY: Teachers College Press.

Fox, A. (1974). *Beyond contract: Work, power and trust relations.* London, UK:
Farber & Farber.

Fulk, J., Brief, A. P., & Barr, S. H. (1985). Trust in the supervisor and perceived
fairness and accuracy of performance evaluations. *Journal of Business Research,
13,* 301–313.

Fullan, M. (2001). *Leading in a culture of change.* San Francisco, CA: Jossey-Bass.

Fullan, M. (2003). *The moral imperative of school leadership.* Thousand Oaks, CA:
Corwin.

Gallwey, W. T. (2000). *The inner game of work.* New York, NY: Random House.

Gibson, S., & Dembo, M. H. (1984). Teacher efficacy: A construct validation.
Journal of Educational Psychology, 76, 569–582.

Goddard, R. D. (2001). Collective efficacy: A neglected construct in the study
of schools and student achievement. *Journal of Educational Psychology, 93,*
467–476.

Goddard, R. D., Hoy, W. K., & Woolfolk Hoy, A. (2000). Collective teacher efficacy: Its meaning, measure and effect on student achievement. *American
Educational Research Journal, 37,* 479–507.

Goddard, R. D., Salloum, S. J., & Berebitsky, D. (2009). Trust as a mediator of
the relationships between poverty, racial composition, and academic achievement: Evidence from Michigan's public elementary schools. *Educational
Administration Quarterly, 45,* 292–311.

Goddard, R. D., Tschannen-Moran, M., & Hoy, W. K. (2001). A multilevel examination of the distribution and effects of teacher trust in students and parents
in urban elementary schools. *The Elementary School Journal, 102,* 3–17.

Goldring, E. B., & Rallis, S. F. (1993). *Principals of dynamic schools: Taking charge of change*. Thousand Oaks, CA: Corwin.

Goodlad, J. I. (1984). *A place called school: Prospects for the future*. New York, NY: McGraw-Hill.

Govier, T. (1992). Distrust as a practical problem. *Journal of Social Philosophy, 23*, 52–63.

Greenberg, J. (1993). The social side of fairness: Interpersonal and informational classes of organizational justice. In R. Cropanzano (Ed.), *Justice in the workplace* (pp. 79–103). Hillsdale, NJ: Erlbaum.

Gregory, A., & Ripski, M. B. (2008). Adolescent trust in teachers: Implications for behavior in the high school classroom. *School Psychology Review, 37*, 337–353.

Gulati, R. (1995). Does familiarity breed trust? The implications of repeated ties for contractual choice in alliances. *Academy of Management Journal, 38*, 85–112.

Handford, V., & Leithwood, K. (2013). Why teachers trust school leaders. *Journal of Educational Administration, 51*, 194–212.

Hardin, R. (2006). The street-level epistemology of trust. In R. M. Kramer (Ed.), *Organizational trust: A reader* (pp. 21–47). Oxford, UK: Oxford University Press.

Harris, G. G. (1994). *Trust and betrayal in the workplace.* (Unpublished doctoral dissertation). University of Utah, Salt Lake City.

Hattie, J. (2012). *Visible learning for teachers: Maximizing impact on learning.* New York, NY: Routledge.

Henderson, A. T., & Mapp, K. L. (2002). *A new wave of evidence: The impact of school, family and community connections on student achievement.* Austin, TX: Southwest Educational Development Lab. Retrieved from http://www.sedl.org/connections/resources/evidence.pdf

Henderson, J. E., & Hoy, W. K. (1982). Principal authenticity, school climate, and pupil-control orientation. *Alberta Journal of Educational Research, 2*, 123–130.

Hill, N. B., & Tyson, D. F. (2009). Parental involvement in middle school: A meta-analytic assessment of the strategies that promote achievement. *Developmental Psychology, 45*, 740–763. doi:10.1037/a0015362

Hirschhorn, L. (1997). *Reworking authority: Leading and following in a post-modern organization.* Cambridge, MA: MIT Press.

Hocker, J. L., & Wilmot, W. W. (1985). *Interpersonal conflict* (2nd ed.). Dubuque, IA: William C. Brown.

Howes, C., & Ritchie, S. (2002). *A matter of trust.* New York, NY: Teachers College Press.

Hoy, W. K. (2002). Faculty trust: A key to student achievement. *Journal of School Public Relations, 23*(2), 88–193.

Hoy, W. K., Hannum, J., & Tschannen-Moran, M. (1998). Organizational climate and student achievement: A parsimonious and longitudinal view. *Journal of School Leadership, 8*, 336–359.

Hoy, W. K., & Kupersmith, W. J. (1985). The meaning and measure of faculty trust. *Educational and Psychological Research, 5*(1), 1–10.

Hoy, W. K., & Miskel, C. G. (2008). *Educational administration: Theory, research, practice.* Boston, MA: McGraw-Hill.

Hoy, W. K., & Sweetland, S. R. (2001). Designing better schools: The meaning and nature of enabling school structure. *Educational Administration Quarterly, 37,* 296–321.

Hoy, W. K., & Tarter, C. J. (2008). *Administrators solving the problems of practice: Decision-making, concepts, cases, and consequences* (3rd ed.). Boston, MA: Allyn & Bacon.

Hoy, W. K., Tarter, C. J., & Hoy, A. W. (2006). Academic optimism of schools: A force for student achievement. *American Educational Research Journal, 43,* 425–446.

Hoy, W. K., & Tschannen-Moran, M. (1999). Five faces of trust: An empirical confirmation in urban elementary schools. *Journal of School Leadership, 9,* 184–208.

Hoy, W. K., & Tschannen-Moran, M. (2003). The conceptualization and measurement of faculty trust in schools: The omnibus T-Scale. In W. K. Hoy & C. G. Miskel (Eds.), *Studies in leading and organizing schools* (pp. 181–208). Greenwich, CT: Information Age.

Hurley, R. F. (2012). *The decision to trust: How leaders create high-trust organizations.* San Francisco, CA: Jossey-Bass.

International Association of Coaching. (2003). IAC ethical principles. Retrieved from http://www.certifiedcoach.org/ethics/IACethics.pdf

International Association of Coaching. (2009). IAC coaching masteries overview. Retrieved from http://www.certifiedcoach.org/learningguide/PDFs/IAC_Masteries_Public.pdf

International Coach Federation. (2008a). ICF code of ethics. Retrieved from http://www.coachfederation.org/includes/media/docs/Ethics-2009.pdf

International Coach Federation. (2008b). ICF professional coaching core competencies. Retrieved from http://www.coachfederation.org/includes/media/docs/CoreCompEnglish.pdf

ISQ Briefings. (2007). Managing challenging behaviour: How do we help young people with emotional, behavioural and social difficulties? *ISQ Briefings, 11*(6), 1–3.

Janis, I. L. (1982). *Groupthink: Psychological studies of policy decisions and fiascos.* Boston, MA: Houghton Mifflin.

Jeynes, W. (2005). A meta-analysis of the relationship of parental involvement to urban elementary school student academic achievement. *Urban Education, 40,* 237–269.

Johnson, J. F., Perez, L. G., & Uline, C. L. (2013). *Teaching practices from America's best urban schools: A guide for school and classroom leaders.* Larchmont, NY: Eye on Education.

Johnson-George, C. E., & Swap, W. C. (1982). Measurement of specific interpersonal trust: Construction and validation of a scale to assess trust in a specific other. *Journal of Personality and Social Psychology, 43,* 1306–1317.

Jones, G. R., & George, J. M. (1998). The experience and evolution of trust: Implications for cooperation and teamwork. *Academy of Management Review, 23,* 531–546.

Jones, W., & Burdette, M. P. (1994). Betrayal in relationships. In A. Weber & J. Harvey (Eds.), *Perspectives on close relationships* (pp. 243–262). Boston, MA: Allyn & Bacon.

Karakus, M., & Savas, A. C. (2012). The effects of parental involvement, trust in parents, trust in students and pupil control ideology on conflict management strategies of early childhood teachers. *Educational Sciences: Theory & Practice, 123,* 2977–2985.

Kauffman, T. R. (2013). *Middle school students' lived experiences of teacher relationship impact.* (Unpublished doctoral dissertation). Walden University, Minneapolis, MN.

Kipnis, D. (1996). Trust and technology. In R. M. Kramer & T. R. Tyler (Eds.), *Trust in organizations* (pp. 39–50). Thousand Oaks, CA: Sage.

Kirby, M., & DiPaola, M. F. (2011). Academic optimism and community engagement in urban schools. *Journal of Educational Administration, 49,* 542–562.

Klassen, R. M., Tze, V.M.C., Betts, S. M., & Gordon, K. A. (2011). Teacher efficacy research 1998–2009: Signs of progress or unfulfilled promise? *Educational Psychology Review, 23,* 21–43.

Klayman, J., & Ha, Y. W. (1997). Confirmation, disconfirmation, and information in hypothesis testing. In W. M. Goldstein & R. M. Hogarth (Eds.), *Research on judgment and decision making: Currents, connections, and controversies* (pp. 205–243). Cambridge, UK: Cambridge University Press.

Konovsky, M. A., & Pugh, S. D. (1994). Citizenship behavior and social exchange. *Academy of Management Review, 37,* 656–669.

Kramer, R. M. (1996). Divergent realities and convergent disappointments in the hierarchic relation: Trust and the intuitive auditor at work. In R. M. Kramer & T. R. Tyler (Eds.), *Trust in organizations* (pp. 216–245). Thousand Oaks, CA: Sage.

Kramer, R. M., Brewer, M. B., & Hanna, B. A. (1996). Collective trust and collective action: The decision to trust as a social decision. In R. M. Kramer & T. R. Tyler (Eds.), *Trust in organizations* (pp. 357–389). Thousand Oaks, CA: Sage.

Kramer, R. M., & Cook, K. S. (2004). *Trust and distrust in organizations: Dilemmas and approaches.* New York, NY: Russell Sage Foundation.

Kratzer, C. C. (1997, March). *A community of respect, caring, and trust: One school's story.* Paper presented at the annual meeting of the American Educational Research Association, Chicago, IL.

Lareau, A. (1987). Social class differences in family-school relationships: The importance of cultural capital. *Sociology of Education, 60,* 73–85.

Lareau, A., & Horvat, E. M. (1999). Moments of social inclusion and exclusion: Race, class, and cultural capital in family-school relationships. *Sociology of Education, 72,* 37–53.

Lawrence-Lightfoot, S. (2003). *The essential conversation: What parents and teachers can learn from each other.* New York, NY: Ballantine Books.

Lee, S.-J. (2007). The relations between the student-teacher trust relationship and school success in the case of Korean middle schools. *Educational Studies, 33,* 209–216.

Lee, V. E., & Bryk, A. S. (1989). A multilevel model of the social distribution of high school achievement. *Sociology of Education, 62,* 172–192.

Lee, V. E., & Smith, J. B. (1999). Social support and achievement for young adolescents in Chicago: The role of school academic press. *American Educational Research Journal, 36,* 907–945.

Leonard, P. E. (1999, November). *Do teachers value collaboration? The impact of trust.* Paper presented at the annual meeting of the University Council for Educational Administration, Minneapolis, MN.

Lewicki, R. J., & Bunker, B. B. (1996). Developing and maintaining trust in work relationships. In R. M. Kramer & T. R. Tyler (Eds.), *Trust in organizations* (pp. 114–139). Thousand Oaks, CA: Sage.

Lewicki, R. J., McAllister, D. J., & Bies, R. J. (1998). Trust and distrust: New relationships and realities. *Academy of Management Review, 23,* 438–458.

Lewis, J. D., & Weigert, A. (1985). Trust as a social reality. *Social Forces, 63,* 967–985.

Limerick, D., & Cunnington, B. (1993). *Managing the new organization.* San Francisco, CA: Jossey-Bass.

Lindskold, S., & Bennett, R. (1973). Attributing trust and conciliatory intent from coercive power capability. *Journal of Personality and Social Psychology, 28,* 180–186.

Linse, C. T. (2010). Creating taxonomies to improve school-home connections with families of culturally and linguistically diverse learners. *Education & Urban Society, 43,* 651–670. doi:10.1177/0013124510380908

Louis, K. S., Kruse, S., & Associates. (1995). *Professionalism and community: Perspectives on reforming urban schools.* Thousand Oaks, CA: Corwin.

Louis, K. S., Kruse, S., & Marks, H. M. (1996). School-wide professional community: Teachers' work, intellectual quality, and commitment. In F. W. Newman & Associates (Eds.), *Authentic achievement: Restructuring schools for intellectual quality* (pp. 179–203). San Francisco, CA: Jossey-Bass.

Malen, B., Ogawa, R. T., & Kranz, J. (1990). Evidence says site-based management hindered by many factors. *School Administrator, 47*(2), 30–32, 53–56, 59.

Mapp, K. (2004). Family engagement. In F. P. Schargel & J. Smink (Eds.), *Helping students graduate: A strategic approach to dropout prevention* (pp. 99–113). Larchmont, NY: Eye on Education.

Marks, H. M., & Louis, K. S. (1997). Does teacher empowerment affect the classroom? The implications of teacher empowerment for instructional practice and student academic performance. *Educational Evaluation and Policy Analysis, 19*, 245–275.

Martin, R. (2002). *The responsibility virus.* New York, NY: Basic Books.

McAllister, D. J. (1995). Affect- and cognition-based trust as foundations for interpersonal cooperation in organizations. *Academy of Management Journal, 38*, 24–59.

McGuigan, L., & Hoy, W. K. (2006). Principal leadership: Creating a culture of academic optimism to improve achievement for all students. *Leadership and Policy in Schools, 5*, 203–229.

McKnight, D. H., Cummings, L. L., & Chervany, N. L. (1998). Initial trust formation in new organizational relationships. *Academy of Management Review, 23*, 473–490.

Miller, G. J. (2004). Monitoring, rules, and the control paradox: Can the good soldier Svejk be trusted? In R. M. Kramer & K. S. Cook (Eds.), *Trust and distrust in organizations* (pp. 99–126). New York, NY: Russell Sage Foundation.

Mishra, A. K. (1996). Organizational responses to crisis: The centrality of trust. In R. M. Kramer & T. R. Tyler (Eds.), *Trust in organizations* (pp. 261–287). Thousand Oaks, CA: Sage.

Mitchell R., Forsyth, P., & Robinson, U. (2008). Parent trust, student trust, and identification with school. *Journal of Research in Education, 18*(1), 116–123.

Mitchell, R. M., Kensler, L., & Tschannen-Moran, M. (2010, November). *The role of trust and school safety in fostering identification with school.* Paper presented at the annual meeting of the University Council for Educational Administration, New Orleans, LA.

Moolenaar, N. M., Karsten, S., Sleegers, P.J.C., & Zijlstra, B.J.H. (2010). Linking social networks and trust: A social capital perspective on professional learning communities. In. N. M. Moolenaar (Ed.), *Ties with potential: Nature, antecedents, and consequences of social networks in school teams* (pp. 135–160), Amsterdam, Netherlands: Netherlands Organisation for Scientific Research.

Moolenaar, N. M., & Sleegers, P.J.C. (2010). Social networks, trust, and innovation: The role of relationships in supporting an innovative climate in Dutch schools. In A. J. Daly (Ed.), *Social network theory and educational change* (pp. 97–114). Cambridge, MA: Harvard University Press.

Moore, D. M. (2010). *Student and faculty perceptions of trust and their relationships to school success measures in an urban school district.* (Unpublished doctoral dissertation). College of William & Mary, Williamsburg, VA.

Moye, M. J., Henkin, A. B., & Egley, R. J. (2005). Teacher-principal relationships: Exploring linkages between empowerment and interpersonal trust. *Journal of Educational Administration, 43*, 260–277.

National Policy Forum for Family, School, and Community Engagement. (2010). Retrieved from http://www.nationalpirc.org/engagement_forum/

Noddings, N. (2005). *The challenge to care in schools: An alternative approach to education.* New York, NY: Teachers College Press.

Organ, D. W. (1988). *Organizational citizenship behavior: The good soldier syndrome.* Lexington, MA: Lexington Books.

Owens, M. A., & Johnson, B. L. (2009). From calculation through courtship to contribution: Cultivating trust among urban youth in an academic intervention program. *Educational Administration Quarterly, 45,* 312–347.

Payne, C. M., & Kaba, M. (2001). So much reform, so little change: Building-level obstacles to urban school reform. In L. B. Joseph (Ed.), *Education policy for the 21st century: Challenges and opportunities in standards-based reform,* Chicago, IL: University of Chicago Press.

Peña, D. C. (2000). Parent involvement: Influencing factors and implications. *The Journal of Educational Research, 94*(1), 42–54.

Pennycuff, L. L. (2009, April). *An analysis of the impact of the academic component of response to intervention on collective efficacy, parents' trust in schools, and referrals for special education, and student achievement.* (Unpublished doctoral dissertation). College of William & Mary, Williamsburg, VA.

Peterson, C., & Peterson, J. (1990). Fight or flight: Factors influencing children's and adults' decisions to avoid or confront conflict. *Journal of Genetic Psychology, 151,* 461–471.

Pianta, R. C., & Stuhlman, M. W. (2004). Teacher-child relationships and children's success in the first years of school. *School Psychology Review, 33,* 444–458.

Podsakoff, P. M., MacKenzie, S. B., Moorman, R. H., & Fetter, R. (1990). Transformational leader behaviors and their effects on followers' trust in leader, satisfaction, and organizational citizenship behaviors. *The Leadership Quarterly, 1,* 107–142.

Pounder, D. G. (1998). *Restructuring schools for collaboration: Promises and pitfalls.* Albany: State University of New York Press.

Purkey, S., & Smith, M. (1983). Effective schools: A review. *The Elementary School Journal, 83,* 427–452.

Putnam, R. D. (1993). The prosperous community: Social capital and public life. *The American Prospect, 13,* 35–42.

Putnam, R. D. (2000). *Bowling alone: The collapse and revival of American community.* New York, NY: Simon & Schuster.

Putnam, R. T., & Borko, H. (1997). Teacher learning: Implications of new views of cognition. In B. J. Biddle, T. L. Good, & I. F. Goodson (Eds.), *The international handbook of teachers and teaching* (pp. 1223–1296). Dordrecht, Netherlands: Kluwer.

Rachman, S. (2010). Betrayal: A psychological analysis. *Behaviour Research and Therapy, 48,* 304–311.

Reina, D., & Reina, M. (2005). *Trust and betrayal in the workplace* (2nd ed.). San Francisco, CA: Berrett-Koehler.

Riley, P. (2010). *Attachment theory and the teacher-student relationship: A practical guide for teachers, teacher educators and school leaders.* London, UK: Routledge.

Roberts, K. H., & O'Reilly, C. O. (1974). Failure in upward communication in organizations: Three possible culprits. *Academy of Management Review, 17,* 205–215.

Robinson, S. L. (1996). Trust and breach of the psychological contract. *Administrative Science Quarterly, 41,* 574–599.

Robinson, S. L., Dirks, K. T., & Ozcelik, H. (2004). Untangling the knot of trust and betrayal. In R. M. Kramer & K. S. Cook (Eds.), *Trust and distrust in organizations: Dilemmas and approaches* (pp. 327–341). New York, NY: Russell Sage Foundation.

Rosen, B., & Jerdee, T. H. (1977). Influence of subordinate characteristics on trust and use of participative decision strategies in a management simulation. *Journal of Applied Psychology, 62,* 628–631.

Rosenberg, M. B. (2005). *Nonviolent communication: A language of life.* Encinitas, CA: PuddleDancer Press.

Ross, J. A. (1992). Teacher efficacy and the effects of coaching on student achievement. *Canadian Journal of Education, 17*(1), 51–65.

Rotter, J. B. (1967). A new scale for the measurement of interpersonal trust. *Journal of Personality, 35,* 651–665.

Rotter, J. B. (1980). Interpersonal trust, trustworthiness, and gullibility. *American Psychologist, 35,* 1–7.

Rousseau, D., Sitkin, S. B., Burt, R., & Camerer, C. (1998). Not so different after all: A cross-discipline view of trust. *Academy of Management Review, 23,* 393–404.

Rubin, J. Z., Pruit, D. G., & Kim, T. (1994). *Social conflict: Escalation, stalemate, and settlement.* New York, NY: McGraw-Hill.

Ryan, R. M., & Stiller, J. D. (1994). Representations of relationships to teachers, parents, and friends as predictors of academic motivation and self-esteem. *Journal of Early Adolescence, 14,* 226–250.

San Antonio, D. M., & Gamage, D. T. (2007). Building trust among educational stakeholders through participatory school administration, leadership and management. *Management in Education, 21*(1), 15–22. doi:10.1177/0892020607073406

Sapienza, H. J., & Korsgaard, M. A. (1996). Managing investor relations: The impact of procedural justice in establishing and sustaining investor support. *Academy of Management Journal, 39,* 544–574.

Schein, E. H. (2010). *Organizational culture and leadership* (4th ed.). San Francisco, CA: Jossey-Bass.

Schlenker, B. R., Helm, B., & Tedeschi, J. T. (1973). The effects of personality and situational variables on behavioral trust. *Journal of Personality and Social Psychology, 25,* 419–427.

Seashore, K., & Kruse, S. D. (1995). *Professionalism and community: Perspectives on reforming urban schools.* Branchville, NJ: Broad Street Books.

Shapiro, D. L., Sheppard, B. H., & Cheraskin, L. (1992). Business on a handshake. *Negotiation Journal, 8,* 365–378.

Shapiro, S. P. (1987). The social control of impersonal trust. *American Journal of Sociology, 93*, 623–658.

Shaw, R. B. (1997). *Trust in the balance: Building successful organizations on results, integrity, and concern.* San Francisco, CA: Jossey-Bass.

Short, P. M., & Greer, J. T. (1997). *Leadership in empowered schools: Themes from innovative efforts.* Columbus, OH: Merrill.

Simons, T. L. (1999). Behavioral integrity as a critical ingredient for transformational leadership. *Journal of Organizational Change Management, 12*, 89–104.

Sitkin, S. B. (1995). On the positive effect of legalization on trust. In R. J. Bies, R. J. Lewicki, & B. H. Sheppard (Eds.), *Research in negotiations in organizations* (Vol. 5, pp. 185–217). Greenwich, CT: JAI Press.

Sitkin, S. B., & Roth, N. L. (1993). Explaining the limited effectiveness of legalistic "remedies" for trust/distrust. *Organizational Science, 4*, 367–392.

Sitkin, S. B., & Stickel, D. (1996). The road to hell: The dynamics of distrust in an era of quality. In R. M. Kramer & T. R. Tyler (Eds.), *Trust in organizations* (pp. 196–215). Thousand Oaks, CA: Sage.

Smith, P. A., Hoy, W. K., & Sweetland, S. R. (2001). Organizational health of high schools and dimensions of faculty trust. *Journal of School Leadership, 12*, 135–150.

Smylie, M. A., & Hart, A. W. (1999). School leadership for teacher learning and change: A human and social capital perspective. In J. Murphy & K. S. Louis (Eds.), *Handbook of research on educational administration* (pp. 421–441). San Francisco, CA: Jossey-Bass.

Solomon, R. C., & Flores, F. (2001). *Building trust in business, politics, relationships, and life.* New York, NY: Oxford University Press.

Spuck, D. W., & MacNeil, A. J. (1999, November). *Understanding trust relationships between principals and teachers.* Paper presented at the annual meeting of the University Council for Educational Administration, Minneapolis, MN.

Staw, B. M., Sandelands, L. E., & Dutton, J. E. (1981). Threat-rigidity effects in organizational behavior: A multilevel analysis. *Administrative Science Quarterly, 26*, 501–524.

Strike, K. A. (1999). Trust, traditions, and pluralism. In D. Carr & J. Steutel (Eds.), *Virtue, ethics and moral education* (pp. 224–237). London, UK: Routledge.

Tarter, C. J., Bliss, J. R., & Hoy, W. K. (1989). School characteristics and faculty trust in secondary schools. *Educational Administration Quarterly, 25*, 294–308.

Tarter, C. J., Sabo, D., & Hoy, W. K. (1995). Middle school climate, faculty trust and effectiveness: A path analysis. *Journal of Research and Development in Education, 29*, 41–49.

Thomas, K. (1976). Conflict and conflict management. In M. D. Dunnette (Ed.), *Handbook of industrial and organizational psychology* (pp. 889–936). Chicago, IL: Rand McNally.

Tjosvold, D. (1997). Conflict within interdependence: Its value for productivity and individuality. In C.K.W. De Dreu & E. Van de Vliert (Eds.), *Using conflict in organizations* (pp. 23–37). Thousand Oaks, CA: Sage.

Tschannen-Moran, B., & Tschannen-Moran, M. (2010). *Evocative coaching: Transforming schools one conversation at a time.* San Francisco, CA: Jossey-Bass.

Tschannen-Moran, B., & Tschannen-Moran, M. (2011). The coach and the evaluator. *Educational Leadership, 69*(2), 10–16.

Tschannen-Moran, M. (2001). Collaboration and the need for trust. *Journal of Educational Administration, 39,* 308–331.

Tschannen-Moran, M. (2003). Fostering organizational citizenship: Transformational leadership and trust. In W. K. Hoy & C. G. Miskel (Eds.), *Studies in leading and organizing schools* (pp. 157–179). Greenwich, CT: Information Age.

Tschannen-Moran, M. (2004, November). *What's trust got to do with it? The role of faculty and principal trust in fostering student achievement.* Paper presented at the annual meeting of the University Council for Educational Administration, Kansas City, MO.

Tschannen-Moran, M. (2009). Fostering teacher professionalism: The role of professional orientation and trust. *Educational Administration Quarterly, 45,* 217–247.

Tschannen-Moran, M. (2014). The interconnectivity of trust in schools, In D. Van Maele, P. B. Forsyth, & M. Van Houtte (Eds.), *Trust relationships and school life: The influence of trust on learning, teaching, leading, and bridging.* Dordrecht, Netherlands: Springer. DOI 10.1007/978-94-017-8014-8_3

Tschannen-Moran, M., Bankole, R., Mitchell, R., & Moore, D. (2013). Student academic optimism: A confirmatory factor analysis. *Journal of Educational Administration, 50,* 150–175.

Tschannen-Moran, M., & Barr, M. (2004). Fostering student achievement: The relationship between collective teacher efficacy and student achievement. *Leadership and Policy in Schools, 2,* 187–207.

Tschannen-Moran, M., & Chen, J. (2014). Attention to beliefs about capability and knowledge in teachers' professional development. In L. E. Martin, S. Kragler, D. J. Quatroche, & K. L. Bauserman (Eds.), *Handbook of professional development in preK–12: Successful models and practices* (pp. 246–264). Oxford, UK: Guilford Press.

Tschannen-Moran, M., & Goddard, R. D. (2001, April). *Collective efficacy and trust: A multilevel analysis.* Paper presented at the annual meeting of the American Educational Research Association, Seattle, WA.

Tschannen-Moran, M., & Hoy, W. K. (1998). A conceptual and empirical analysis of trust in schools. *Journal of Educational Administration, 36,* 334–352.

Tschannen-Moran, M., & Hoy, W. K. (2000). A multidisciplinary analysis of the nature, meaning, and measurement of trust. *Review of Educational Research, 71,* 547–593.

Tschannen-Moran, M., Salloum, S. J., & Goddard, R. D. (in press). Context matters: The influence of collective beliefs and norms. In H. Fives & M. G. Gill (Eds.), *International handbook of research on teachers' beliefs.*

Tschannen-Moran, M., Woolfolk Hoy, A., & Hoy, W. K. (1998). Teacher efficacy: Its meaning and measure. *Review of Educational Research, 68,* 202–248.

Tyler, T. R., & Degoey, P. (1996). Trust in organizational authorities: The influence of motive attributions on willingness to accept decisions. In R. M. Kramer & T. R. Tyler (Eds.), *Trust in organizations* (pp. 331–356). Thousand Oaks, CA: Sage.

Tyler, T. R., & Kramer, R. M. (1996). Whither trust? In R. M. Kramer & T. R. Tyler (Eds.), *Trust in organizations* (pp. 1–15). Thousand Oaks, CA: Sage.

Uline, C., Tschannen-Moran, M., & Perez, L. (2003). Constructive conflict: How controversy can contribute to school improvement. *Teachers College Record, 105,* 782–815.

Van Maele, D., Forsyth, P. B., & Van Houtte, M. (Eds.). (2014). *Trust relationships and school life: The influence of trust on learning, teaching, leading, and bridging.* Dordrecht, Netherlands: Springer. DOI 10.1007/978-94-017-8014-8

Van Maele, D., & Van Houtte, M. (2009). Faculty trust and organizational school characteristics: An exploration across secondary schools in Flanders. *Educational Administration Quarterly, 45,* 556–589.

Van Maele, D., & Van Houtte, M. (2011). The quality of school life: Teacher-student trust relationships and the organizational school context. *Social Indicators Research, 100,* 85–100. doi:10.1007/s11205-010-9605-8

Wahlstrom, K. L., & Louis, K. S. (2008). How teachers experience principal leadership: The roles of professional community, trust, efficacy, and shared responsibility. *Educational Administration Quarterly, 44,* 458–495.

Watkins, J. M., Mohr, B. J., & Kelly, R. (2011). *Appreciative inquiry: Change at the speed of imagination* (2nd ed.). San Francisco, CA: Jossey-Bass/Pfeiffer.

Watson, M. (2003). *Learning to trust: Transforming difficult elementary classrooms through developmental discipline.* San Francisco, CA: Jossey-Bass.

Westat and Policy Studies Associates. (2001). *The longitudinal evaluation of school change and performance in Title I schools.* Washington, DC: US Department of Education, Office of the Deputy Secretary, Planning and Evaluation Service.

Whitener, E. M., Brodt, S. E., Korsgaard, M. A., & Werner, J. M. (1998). Managers as initiators of trust: An exchange relationship framework for understanding managerial trustworthy behavior. *Academy of Management Review, 23,* 513–530.

Wicks, A. C., Berman, S. L., & Jones, T. M. (1999). The structure of optimal trust: Moral and strategic implications. *Academy of Management Review, 24,* 99–116.

Wrightsman, L. S. (1966). Personality and attitudinal correlates of trusting and trustworthy behaviors in a two-person game. *Journal of Personality and Social Psychology, 4,* 328–332.

Zand, D. E. (1997). *The leadership triad: Knowledge, trust, and power.* New York, NY: Oxford University Press.

Zucker, L. G. (1986). The production of trust: Institutional sources of economic structure, 1840–1920. In B. M. Staw & L. L. Cummings (Eds.), *Research in organizational behavior* (Vol. 8, pp. 55–111). Greenwich, CT: JAI Press.

ABOUT THE AUTHOR

Megan Tschannen-Moran is a professor at the College of William & Mary in Williamsburg, Virginia. In this capacity, she prepares prospective principals to be trustworthy school leaders. She uses a combination of case studies, problem-based learning simulations, role playing, coaching, and direct instruction to hone her students' leadership skills.

Megan's research interests center on how the quality of interpersonal relationships affects the outcomes a school can achieve. Trust is central to these relationships. Another of her lines of inquiry focuses on the self-efficacy beliefs of teachers and principals as well as the collective efficacy beliefs within a school. In the course of her work, she has developed a number of measures to capture important aspects of school functioning and of the beliefs and perceptions of organizational participants. Her scholarly work has appeared in journals such as *Review of Educational Research, Teachers College Record, Educational Administration Quarterly, Journal of Educational Administration,* and *Teaching and Teacher Education.*

In conjunction with her husband, Bob Tschannen-Moran, a professional performance and life coach, Megan has developed a coaching model to guide school leaders and coaches to host energizing and productive conversations with teachers about their instructional practices. This coaching model, which is grounded in her work on trust and teacher self-efficacy as well as in the concepts of appreciative inquiry, nonviolent communication, and design thinking, is presented in their book, *Evocative Coaching: Transforming Schools One Conversation at a Time* (Jossey-Bass, 2010).

INDEX

Page numbers in italics refer to figures and tables.